£2·40

THE HAMLYN BOOK OF
WILD FLOWERS

Contents

Evolution of Plants

It is believed that life evolved on Earth in the Precambrian Era about three thousand million years ago. Primitive plants – bacteria and algae – were already present in the early Palaeozoic. At that time our planet was largely covered by seas. Fossil records of the first land plants are from the Silurian, when mountains were raised and a continuous land mass began to be formed in the northern hemisphere. The ensuing geological periods saw the appearance of non-seed-bearing plants and ancient kinds of seed-bearing plants. Non-seed-bearing plants, all of which reproduce by means of spores, include the thallophytes (fungi, algae and lichens), bryophytes and pteridophytes.

Lichens are dual plants composed of fungal hyphae and the cells of algae, with no differentiation into root, stem and leaf.

Bryophytes are plants usually differentiated into a stem with leaves and a setum with capsule.

Pteridophytes include club-mosses, horsetails and ferns. Their 'golden age' was in the Carboniferous when the climate was generally warm and moist and the land masses were covered with lush swamp forests of tree-like horsetails, club-mosses and ferns. Over the ages the decaying substance of these tree-like plants formed layers of hard black coal which to this day yield fossil records of the flora of bygone ages.

The late Palaeozoic saw the appearance of the first primitive gymnosperms, e.g. cycads and cordaita and related species of the Maidenhair tree *(Ginkgo)*. Gymnosperms are seed plants having the ovules borne on open scales as is the case with the commonest gymnosperms of the present day, namely the conifers, in which the ovules are borne on scales arranged in cones from which they fall when ripe.

The earliest periods of the Mesozoic, about 180 million years ago, saw the appearance of the first angiosperms. These are now the most widespread, largest and most diversified group of plants and include all the species described in this book.

Angiosperms are generally green multicellular plants characterized by having the seeds enclosed in an ovary. Angiosperms are generally differentiated into roots, stem and leaves and have a well-developed conducting system of tubes, known as vascular bundles. These vascular bundles convey water and food in the plant and are composed of tracheae and tracheids. A trachea is a continuous tube composed of a vertical row of long single-cell segments the end walls of which have been either partially or completely dissolved, while the side walls have become woody and variously thickened; the cytoplasm has entirely disappeared. Tracheids differ from tracheae in that they generally have slanting end walls; they are primitive tube-like cells and it is from these that the tracheae are derived.

Whereas gymnosperms are all woody plants, angiosperms include woody as well as herbaceous plants. Angiosperm leaves are relatively large, usually with flat blades. The reproductive organs are located in the flower; the carpels are united to form a pistil which contains the ovules. After pollination and fertilization the pistil, or rather the ovary, matures and develops into a fruit and the ovules develop into seeds.

Angiosperms are divided into two groups: dicotyledons and monocotyledons.

Dicotyledons (Magnoliidae) differ from monocotyledons (Liliidae) in several ways. The most striking difference is in the number of cotyledons, or seed leaves. With the exception

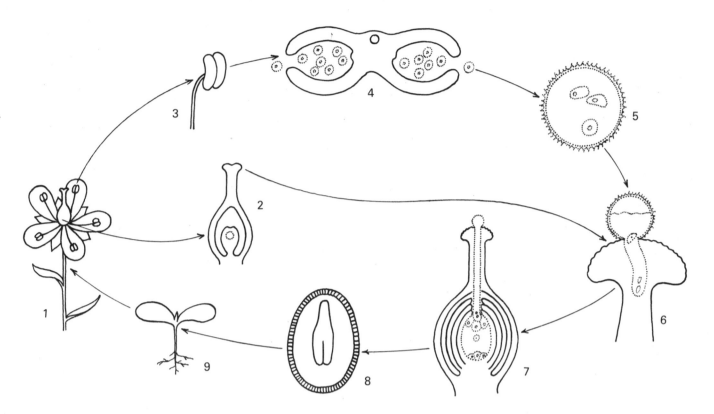

Life cycle of angiosperms — (from left to right and clockwise) 1 — flower 2 — longitudinal section of pistil 3 — stamen 4 — cross-section of anther 5 — pollen grain 6 — penetration of stigma by pollen tube 7 — fertilization 8 — longitudinal section of seed 9 — germinating embryo seedling

of the water-lily family, the dicotyledons have an embryo with two opposite seed leaves and a growing point in the middle. During the course of germination and growth the primary root, or radicle, changes into a main root with lateral roots. The leaves are net-veined. The floral parts are differentiated into a calyx and corolla and are often arranged in fives. The flowers are either borne singly or in inflorescences.

Monocotyledons have an embryo with one seed leaf and a growing point on one side at the base of the cotyledon. The radicle disappears soon after germination and is replaced by numerous adventitious roots. The leaves, usually alternate and often without a stalk, are generally simple with entire margins and prominent parallel veins. The floral parts are usually not differentiated into a calyx and corolla and the perianth is often one colour. The flowers are generally 3-merous (the floral parts are in threes, or in multiples of three) and often arranged in inflorescences.

Dicotyledons and monocotyledons also differ in the presence or absence of certain chemical substances such as tannins, essential oils, alkaloids, saponins, etc.

The origin and evolution of seed plants is shown in the following chart.

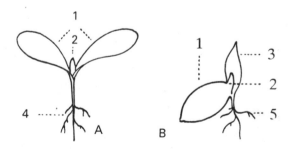

Germination — A: dicotyledon B: monocotyledon 1 — cotyledons 2 — growing point 3 — first leaf 4 — root 5 — adventitious roots

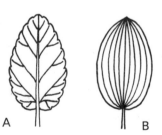

Leaf venation — A: dicotyledon B: monocotyledon

Some stages in the course of plant evolution

Geological period	Epoch	Approx. no. of years ago	Principal features
Quaternary	Holocene	15,000—13,000	present-day plants
	Pleistocene	1 million	ice age
Tertiary	Palaeocene	65—67 million	formation of areas of distribution of plant families
Mesozoic	Cretaceous	135 million	expansion of angiosperms
	Jurassic	181 million	appearance of first dicotyledons
Palaeozoic	Permian	280 million	expansion of seed plants
	Carboniferous	355 million	seed plants more abundant
	Devonian	405 million	first seed plants
	Silurian	425 million	first land plants
Precambrian		2,000—4,000 million	first evidence of life on Earth
Archaean		4,600—5,000 million	origin of the planet Earth

As we see from the chart the expansion of angiosperms begins in the Mesozoic, in the Cretaceous period. They already include a surprisingly large number of types, even ones that are highly advanced, and are the dominant group of land plants.

In the Tertiary there are already marked distinctions between the climatic zones but the differences between them are not as great as they are today. The temperate zones extend far into the arctic regions and the tropical zone is very wide, extending far into Europe. From this it is evident that even central Europe was a region where tropical plants flourished. In the late Tertiary, however, the climate cooled and the tropical plants of central Europe were replaced by subtropical plants similar to those now growing in the Mediterranean region. As the climate continued to cool the areas of tropical vegetation moved towards the equator. The climate in the north was very cold at this time and the vegetation there consisted of coniferous and deciduous broad-leaved forests and herbaceous plants. Central Europe saw the appearance of mountain flora in the young Alpine-Carpathian ranges which were formed in the Tertiary, eastern Europe saw the appearance of heat- and draught-resistant vegetation which spread there from central Asia. The reason for this was the gradual change in climate and the fact that steppe vegetation was well-adapted to a short growing season and dry, warm conditions.

The Quaternary was marked by further cooling of the climate which caused the formation of a huge continental ice sheet that began to spread southward. At the same time the mountains of central Europe were covered with separate small, individual glaciers, this being most marked in the Alps. The cooling of the climate was not uniform. There were four very cold glacial periods and three warmer interglacial periods.

When the ice sheet was at its peak it covered all of northern Europe from Scandinavia to the northern border of Czechoslovakia. The alpine glaciers likewise increased in size at this time, their tips extending far into Bavaria, Austria and even the south of France. Only the north-eastern part of Europe was not covered by ice.

When the climate cooled the various plant species became extinct in most cases, or else they were forced to retreat to places where conditions were not so harsh. Some species were forced to retreat as far as southern Europe where, in the warm climate of the Balkan Peninsula, they have survived to this day; not all returned to their original habitats. Two such central European plants that have survived to this day are Asarabacca (*Asarum europaeum*) and Common Baneberry (*Actaea spicata*).

The vegetation of the northernmost parts of Europe was pushed southward by the ice sheet and settled at its edge — in tundras (boggy areas with dwarf woody plants) and alpine grasslands (mountain areas with herbaceous vegetation but no woody plants). This is called arctic vegetation. High-mountain vegetation forced by growing alpine glaciers to retreat to lower elevations in central Europe is called alpine flora and includes such plants as Dwarf Primrose *(Primula minima)* and Milkweed Gentian *(Gentiana asclepiadea)*.

Species that came to central Europe during the Ice Age and still grow there as survivals from that period are called glacial relicts. Examples are Mountain Avens *(Dryas octopetala)*, Sudeten Lousewort *(Pedicularis sudetica)* and Cloudberry *(Rubus chamaemorus)*.

Later, when the ice sheet had retreated north again, the climate in central Europe was still rugged but draught-resistant vegetation began to appear there and tundras and alpine grasslands were replaced by steppe. Characteristic plants of steppe areas are the Spear-grasses *(Stipa)*.

Plants with a worldwide distribution are called cosmopolitan. Those that are restricted to a particular region and are found nowhere else are called endemic.

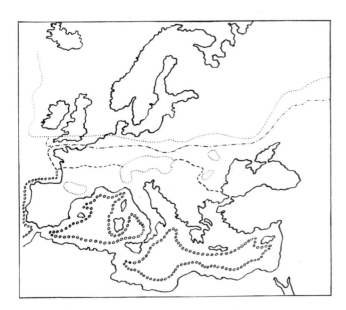

Ice sheet in central Europe during the period of greatest glaciation

ice sheet	....
tundra	— · — · — · —
steppe	— — — — —
forest	ooooooooo

Names of Plants

The scientific nomenclature of plants is governed by specific, internationally accepted rules according to which the names of plants are given in Latin. In addition to the scientific, Latin name plants also have common or vernacular names in different languages. Each valid Latin name must be properly published complete with an exact description of the given plant. If a plant is described more than once and is given a different name each time the law of priority states that, except in special instances, only the oldest name is to be used and the later ones are suppressed as synonyms. In some cases, however, the later name has become widely accepted and has therefore been retained as the valid, acknowledged name, with the older name appearing as the synonym.

Appearing after the name given to the systematic unit or taxon (the name of the species, genus, family, etc.), is the name or initial of the person who first described the taxon. However, in the interest of simplifying things these initials are often omitted in popular scientific literature.

Every plant may be classed together with many others in various systematic units or categories. The higher the category the greater the number of related plants included therein. The taxonomic categories in descending order from the highest and most inclusive to the lowest are: kingdom, subkingdom, phylum, subphylum, class, subclass, order, suborder, family, subfamily, genus, subgenus, species, subspecies, variety, subvariety and form or cultivar.

This book presents only angiosperms (class), dicotyledons and monocotyledons (subclasses); the text accompanying each illustrated plant gives the name of the family (a very important systematic unit in botany), genus, species and in some cases also the subspecies.

In some instances systematic botanists are not in agreement as to whether a given plant should be classed in a genus or subgenus; opinions differ. Sometimes distinctive but small microspecies differing only in minor details may be grouped together in one collective species. Several important characteristics differentiate this from another collective species which may likewise be divided into two or more microspecies. Other authors, however, may classify these same microspecies as subspecies, but every botanist has the prerogative of deciding which characteristics he considers more important and evaluating the plant accordingly. Such an evaluation of characteristics is called weighing of characteristics and the weight of the various traits may then be used in support of one or another evaluation.

System Used in This Book

As we have already said the family is an important systematic botanical unit. The multiformity and diversity of the plant realm is also reflected in the great number of families in which the plants are classed. The following list is a mere fraction of the whole and includes only those families which are represented in this book.

Class: angiosperms (Magnoliopsida)
Subclass: dicotyledons (Magnoliidae)

The **water-lily family** (Nymphaeaceae) includes aquatic herbaceous plants with stout rhizomes and floating leaves. Certain characteristics, especially the fact that the germinating embryo has one cotyledon, are reminiscent of monocotyledons with which they probably have common ancestors.

The **buttercup family** (Ranunculaceae) has hermaphroditic flowers that are radially or bilaterally symmetrical with perianth either undifferentiated or differentiated into a calyx and corolla. The fruits are follicles or achenes, very occasionally berries. The plants contain a number of poisonous substances, e.g. alkaloids.

The **poppy family** (Papaveraceae) has radially symmetrical flowers, the calyx falling early, and a large number of stamens; the fruits are many-seeded capsules.

The **fumitory family** (Fumariaceae) has hermaphroditic, bilaterally symmetrical flowers; the leaves are generally alternate, pinnate. The fruits are achenes or capsules.

Members of the **birthwort family** (Aristolochiaceae) are distinguished by having flowers in three parts.

Plants of the **crucifer** or **mustard family** (Cruciferae) have hermaphroditic, radially symmetrical flowers with four petals, six stamens of which four are longer than the others, and fruits of various kinds.

The **pink family** (Caryophyllaceae) embraces a great number of species. Characteristic features are more or less equal and opposite branching, flowers usually arranged in forking clusters and often having a corona.

The **violet family** (Violaceae) has bilaterally symmetrical flowers with the lower petal spurred. The fruits are generally capsules.

The **buckwheat family** (Polygonaceae) is characterized by having sheathing stipules which embrace the stem. The perianth is inconspicuous and the segments sometimes become enlarged and membranous in the fruit.

The **rock-rose family** (Cistaceae) has an ovary usually composed of three united carpels and a great many stamens. The fruit is a capsule.

Members of the **nettle family** (Urticaceae) are typical plants of waste places, coastal thickets and riverside woods. A characteristic feature is the presence of stinging hairs that cover the entire plant. The small flowers are arranged in inflorescences that are often quite rich. The fruits are generally achenes.

Carnivorous plants belong to the **sundew family** (Droseraceae). They grow in poor peaty soils, obtaining the nitrogenous substances absent in such soil from the bodies of the insects they trap in their specially modified leaves.

The **stonecrop family** (Crassulaceae) is characterized by fleshy leaves. The fruit is a follicle.

Plants of the **saxifrage family** (Saxifragaceae) generally grow in dry, rocky places, chiefly in mountains. The flowers are regular, in five parts, and the fruits are mostly capsules.

The **parnassus-grass family** (Parnassiaceae) has only a single representative in Europe − Grass of Parnassus (*Parnassia palustris*). The flowers are in five parts and the fruit is a capsule.

The **rose family** (Rosaceae) has regular, hermaphroditic flowers usually in five parts and with a prominent flower-tube. The fruits are follicles, achenes, drupes or pomes. This family embraces a great many genera containing a vast number of diverse species.

Typical of the **pea family** (Fabaceae, also known as Leguminosae) are butterfly-shaped flowers. Hence also the original name of the family: Papilionaceae. The fruit is generally a pod or legume.

The **geranium family** (Geraniaceae) has flowers in five parts and dry fruit that splits when ripe.

The **oxalis family** (Oxalidaceae) has long-stalked leaves divided into three leaflets and hermaphroditic flowers in five parts. The fruit is a capsule.

The **rue family** (Rutaceae) generally has hermaphroditic flowers in five parts, often with a prominent glandular disc beneath the ovary.

The hermaphroditic, bilaterally symmetrical flowers of the **milkwort family** (Polygalaceae) have a characteristic structure and are arranged in racemes.

Characteristic of the **spurge family** (Euphorbiaceae) are the simple flowers arranged in complex inflorescences. Often the plants have developed milk ducts which ooze a milky juice when bruised.

Members of the **wintergreen family** (Pyrolaceae) have simple evergreen leaves, in five parts, anthers that open by a terminal pore and pollen grains in groups of four.

Members of the **birdsnest family** (Monotropaceae) are parasitic plants without chlorophyll and with leaves reduced to scales.

The **heath family** (Ericaceae) includes plants with leaves that are often evergreen. The pollen grains are in groups of four.

Members of the **daphne family** (Thymelaeaceae) are either herbs or shrubs with entire, usually alternate leaves. The fragrant flowers have a flower-tube but no petals; the sepals are coloured as the corolla.

Plants of the **balsam family** (Balsaminaceae) have a fleshy stem and bilaterally symmetrical flowers. Characteristic are the fruits — capsules that split at the touch and eject the seeds when ripe.

A characteristic of the **mallow family** (Malvaceae) is the presence of an epicalyx. The stamens are united in a tube and the disc-like fruit is dry, splitting when ripe.

The tissues of plants of the **St. John's wort family** (Hypericaceae) contain a quantity of essential oils. The stamens are united in bundles.

The **loosestrife family** (Lythraceae) have angular stems and an elongated flower-tube. The fruit is a capsule.

The **willow-herb family** (Onagraceae) have flowers in four parts, and a flower-tube that becomes united to the ovary.

Members of the **water-chestnut family** (Trapaceae) are free-floating aquatic plants with long submerged stems, diamond-shaped leaves, flowers in five parts, and with a persistent woody calyx that gives the fruit its characteristic appearance.

The **ginseng family** (Araliaceae) includes climbing plants with holdfast roots. The flowers are in five parts and arranged in semi-globose umbels. The fruit is a berry.

The **parsley family** (Umbelliferae) takes its Latin name from the typical inflorescence, which is an umbel. All members have the same type of fruit — a double achene that splits into two separate achenes at maturity.

Members of the **primrose family** (Primulaceae) are herbaceous plants with a basal rosette of leaves. The flowers are in five parts, with a persistent calyx. The fruit is a capsule.

The **mistletoe family** (Loranthaceae) includes plants that are parasitic on trees and shrubs. Unlike Yellow-berried Mistletoe, Common Mistletoe (which is an important representative of the family) does not shed its leaves.

Plants of the **gentian family** (Gentianaceae) are characterized by opposite, undivided leaves and flowers in five parts.

Closely related to the preceding family are the plants of the **bogbean family** (Menyanthaceae), characterized by having leaves divided into three leaflets.

Also related are the plants of the **dogbane family** (Apocynaceae), which likewise have flowers in five parts and opposite simple leaves, usually without stipules.

The **bindweed family** (Convolvulaceae) includes plants that often have twining stems.

Plants of the **borage family** (Boraginaceae) are rough to bristly-hairy. The flowers are generally arranged in cymes, the fruits are nutlets.

Plants of the **mint family** (Labiatae) have a bilabiate corolla. The family is also known by the name of Lamiaceae. The fruit is a nutlet.

Members of the **nightshade family** (Solanaceae) are mostly poisonous plants because they contain numerous alkaloids. The fruit is usually a berry.

The **figwort family** (Scrophulariaceae) generally has bilaterally symmetrical flowers in five parts. The fruit is a capsule.

The **plantain family** (Plantaginaceae) has small flowers in four parts, arranged in spike-like inflorescences. The fruit is a capsule.

Plants of the **verbena family** (Verbenaceae) have leaves without stipules and flowers in four to five parts. The fruit is nearly always a nutlet.

The herbs of the **madder family** (Rubiaceae) have large stipules that resemble leaves, which is why Woodruff and Bedstraw appear to have whorled leaves. The fruit is a double achene.

The **valerian family** (Valerianaceae) has opposite leaves without stipules and flowers arranged in cymes.

The small flowers of the **teasel family** (Dipsacaceae) are arranged in dense terminal heads growing in the axil of an involucre with rigid scales on the receptacle.

The very name of the **bellflower family** (Campanulaceae) indicates that the flowers have a bell-shaped corolla. The fruit is a capsule.

The **composite** or **sunflower family** (Compositae, also known by the name Asteraceae) is considered the largest family of dicotyledonous plants, i.e. the one with the greatest number of genera. The individual flowers are arranged in compound inflorescences – in compact heads. There are two kinds of flowers: central tubular flowers and marginal strap-shaped flowers. The head may consist of both types together as in the daisy, of tubular flowers alone as in the thistle, or of strap-shaped flowers alone as in hawkweed. The fruit often carries a ring of fine hairs.

Subclass: monocotyledons (Liliidae)

The **flowering-rush family** (Butomaceae) is the oldest family of monocotyledons and has an undifferentiated perianth.

The **water-plantain family** (Alismataceae) has flowers with perianth differentiated into a calyx and corolla. The plants grow in water and have two kinds of leaves.

Members of the **pondweed family** (Potamogetonaceae) are also aquatic plants often with two kinds of leaves – submerged leaves and leaves floating on the water. The flowers, which are without a perianth, are arranged in spikes rising above the surface of the water.

Members of the **lily family** (Liliaceae) are plants that grow from a bulb, tuber or rhizome. The leaves are parallel-veined, sometimes net-veined, and are usually alternate. The flowers have a superior ovary and usually an undifferentiated perianth although it may sometimes be differentiated into a calyx and corolla. The fruit is often a capsule or berry.

The **iris family** (Iridaceae) has flowers with an undifferentiated perianth joined at the base in a tube which may be very long (e.g. Crocus).

The **amaryllis family** (Amaryllidaceae) greatly resembles the lily family, but unlike the latter has an inferior ovary.

Members of the **rush family** (Juncaceae) resemble grasses. The small flowers are generally arranged in an anthella; the fruit is a capsule.

The **sedge family** (Cyperaceae) also resembles the grasses. However, the stems are triangular, not hollow, and without joints. The perianth is rudimentary or modified into bristles.

Members of the **grass family** (Gramineae) are herbaceous plants with rounded stems that are hollow and jointed. The leaves are generally alternate and sheathed. The flowers are arranged in spikelets that form a compound inflorescence which may be a spike, a spike-like panicle or a panicle. Each spikelet grows in the axils of two bracts. The flower consists of two enclosing bracts (an outer or lower, one known as the lemma, which often carries a long bristle or 'awn', and an inner or upper one called the palea), three stamens with variable anthers and a pistil with two feathery stigmas. The inner ring of the perianth is reduced to two minute scales called lodicules. The fruit is a grain. The family is also known by the name Poaceae.

The **orchid family** (Orchidaceae) has underground tubers of diverse shape. The ovary is inferior and turns a full 180° prior to flowering. One of the petals is usually prolonged into a spur and the pollen grains group together in clusters. A characteristic of this family is that the plants are mostly mycorhizal – in other words they live in symbiotic association with the mycelium of a fungus.

The **arum family** (Araceae) has a striking inflorescence consisting of a dense spike of minute, usually unisexual flowers, enclosed by a large sheath-like bract or growing in its axil.

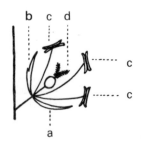

Flower of grasses:
a – lemma b – palea c – stamens d – pistil with two stigmas

Members of the **bur-reed family** (Sparganiaceae) are bog or aquatic plants. The unisexual flowers are crowded in separate globose heads — male heads above, female heads below. The perianth is composed of scales.

The **reedmace family** (Typhaceae) has flowers without a perianth or with perianth modified into hairs. The inflorescence is a dense, cylindrical spike (or 'poker') with male flowers above and female flowers below.

Members of the **duckweed family** (Lemnaceae) are tiny aquatic plants that generally float on the water. They have neither stems nor vascular bundles and often not even roots. Only rarely do they produce flowers.

Site Requirements

All plants have in common certain requirements as regards the site where they grow. Water is one of the things they need for good growth and development. Some plants need more and some less, and according to the abundance of water in their habitat they are designated as either moisture-loving or drought-resistant. The various species also differ in their requirements as regards temperature and are accordingly described as warmth-loving or cold-tolerant. Air and light are necessary for the respiration of plants and for photosynthesis. Carbon dioxide is absorbed by plants through microscopic openings called pores.

The type of soil is also important. Weathering of limestone, dolomite, impure chalk, basalt or marl gives rise to alkaline soil, whereas on silicic substrates the soil is acidic.

Because plants differ in their requirements as to habitat, the various types of soils naturally have their characteristic plant communities. For example, heat- and drought-resistant plants which grow in lime-rich soils form more or less similar communities in warm limestone regions throughout the continent. The branch of science that deals with these plant communities is called phytosociology, whereas the branch that is concerned particularly with the environment in which a plant lives is called geobotany.

The plants illustrated in this book are mostly typical of a specific environment, the general types being woods, meadows, fields, slopes, water, moors and rocks.

Forests, woods and glades

The term 'forest' includes several types of habitats that differ in many respects. It embraces coniferous forests (pine, spruce, fir), mixed forests (with conifers as well as broad-leaved trees) and broad-leaved forests (oakwoods, beechwoods, hornbeam-woods). Besides these common forests in some parts of Europe there are also surviving remnants of primeval forests such as the Boubín Forest (spruce-fir-beech in the Šumava region of Czechoslovakia and the Białowieża Forest on the Poland-USSR border.

Natural forests have in many places been replaced by cultivated forests which are generally composed of a single species of tree. Such woodlands are called forest monocultures.

The forest is a very complex plant community with a great diversity of species. Growing side by side there are fungi, lichens, mosses, pteridophytes (ferns etc.), gymnosperms and angiosperms. The forest is also divided vertically into levels or layers: a ground layer (composed for example of mosses and fungi) a herbaceous layer, a shrub layer, and a canopy or tree layer. Sometimes these layers consist of specific species characteristic of a given type of forest.

Thin stands of broad-leaved forests with a great diversity of herbaceous plants are called open woodlands.

Alongside large rivers, however, one will also frequently find prominent flood-plain forests with distinctive and diverse plants — examples of which are the Snowflake *(Leucojum vernum)*, Snowdrop *(Galanthus nivalis)*, Marsh Marigold *(Caltha palustris)*, Cabbage Thistle *(Cirsium oleraceum)*, Yellow Loosestrife *(Lysimachia vulgaris)*, and so on.

The forest plays an important role in determining the character of the environment. It freshens the atmosphere, is a natural reservoir of water and a source of wood. Places where trees are felled or destroyed by a natural calamity such as fire or a gale become glades, and an immediate change occurs in the composition of the plant species. Moisture-loving and shade-loving plants disappear and are replaced by ones that are fond of light, sun and dry conditions.

Meadows and pastureland

Meadows are habitats that have been created over the ages by man — by his felling trees and clearing land. The conditions they provide for the growth of plants are quite distinctive.

Natural meadows — treeless grassy tracts in the flood plains alongside large rivers — are practically nonexistent. The regulation of rivers has eliminated floods so that riverside meadows have generally been replaced by fields.

Meadow vegetation grows in relatively rich soil, in cultivated meadows in soil that may be further enriched with fertilizers. As a rule the plants have ample water. They are also exposed to the sun, for there are no shrubs or trees to shade them. Meadows are usually mown, and so the species that grow there are mostly perennial, the annuals only being represented by such plants as are able to reproduce by seeds before the first mowing. In pastureland the predominant species are those that tolerate cropping, trampling down and the application of fertilizer.

Meadow vegetation is usually short and grows in tufts. The underground parts are usually long branching rhizomes by means of which the plants spread and multiply.

A special case are the alpine meadows above the tree-line which have a specific microclimate of their own and characteristic vegetation.

Fields and fallow land

Fields are another man-made environment used to grow various crops and distinguished by specific conditions. Fields are ploughed, tilled, drained, irrigated, and harvested regularly. They are also enriched with fertilizer and the crops grown there are rotated. Besides cultivated plants, fields also contain wild plants the seeds of which make their way there together with the seeds of the sown crop or are deposited there by the wind or by animals. Such plants are called field weeds. They are adapted to the conditions of this environment and are usually annuals with a short growth period enabling them to produce seeds and thus ensure the propagation of the species within a short time. Most weeds can be classified into one of four groups. The first includes species that mature in spring, long before field crops are harvested, e.g. Wall Speedwell (*Veronica arvensis*). The second group includes weeds that mature at the same time as grain, their seeds falling to the ground when the crop is harvested, e.g. Corn Cockle (*Agrostemma githago*), Corn Crowfoot (*Ranunculus arvensis*).

The plants of the third group are perennial weeds that, even though they may be damaged during harvest, immediately grow again from their undamaged roots and flower a second time; e.g. Field Bindweed (*Convolvulus arvensis*). The fourth group includes species that do not mature until after the harvest, e.g. Wild Pansy (*Viola tricolor*).

Waste places

Waste places are formed where the natural environment has been suddenly altered by man, mostly in destructive ways — by processes such as throwing out rubbish, establishing rubbish-dumps, neglecting the vicinity of his dwelling places, building railways, highways, etc. These waste places have their own distinctive, so-called 'ruderal' vegetation.

Most of these plants thrive in soil in which there is a lack of nitrogenous substances — Stinging Nettle (*Urtica dioica*) and Silver Weed (*Potentilla anserina*) are examples — and in some cases, such as the Great Plantain (*Plantago major*), they will withstand continuous trampling and other disruptive influences on the part of man. These plants are often characterized by vegetative reproduction, by both underground and surface runners, as well as by an abundance of seeds.

Most ruderal species have spread and become established far from their native habitats. Examples of these species are Small-flowered Balsam (*Impatiens parviflora*) and Canadian Fleabane (*Erigeron canadense*) which are so vigorous and invasive that they often crowd out all other species and monopolize the entire plot themselves.

Sunny slopes, banks and hedgerows

The basic characteristics of this habitat are dry and warm conditions, sloping ground, plenty of rich soil and plenty of sun, and that is why heat-loving and drought-resistant species predominate. Like plants that grow on rocks, they are often covered with hairs which prevent excessive evaporation of water. The vegetation in such places is not affected much by man. Only occasionally are hedgerows still burned in spring and in autumn. This results in the extermination of some species as well as many animals, chiefly insects, but does not prevent the spread of weeds — on the contrary, it encourages them to spread.

Water and marshland

Water is essential to all living organisms, and seas, lakes, ponds and pools as well as rivers and streams contain many species of angiosperms. These species are aquatics adapted to life in this environment and they differ in many ways from land plants.

Some species are completely submerged, with roots anchored in the bottom; these are called submerged aquatics. Others are likewise rooted in the soil at the bottom but their leaves float on the surface and the flowers either float on the water or rise above it. These are called floating-leaved aquatics. Some species inhabit only the upper layers, their leaves and flowers floating on the surface and their roots freely suspended in the water. Others pass part of their life cycle rooted in the bottom but rise to the surface (either the entire plant or some of its parts) to bloom and bear fruit. Finally there are the plants that can grow both in water and on land when the water-level drops.

Plants are adapted to this aquatic environment in their shape and body structure, their method of nourishment, respiration and reproduction, the shape of the seeds and manner of seed dispersal, etc.

Water plants absorb carbon dioxide and oxygen, the gaseous elements required by all green plants for photosynthesis and respiration, through all parts of the body surface. Food is absorbed from the water in the same manner. That is why they have either rudimentary vascular bundles or none at all. Instead they have various bladders or air sacs that buoy up the leaves and help keep them afloat.

The stems and leaf stalks vary markedly in length, depending on factors such as the depth of the water, its currents, and so on. Submerged leaves usually do not have pores, the blades are thread-like and often arranged in whorls. This increases the surface area and also enables the plant to adapt more readily to changes in the aquatic environment. Leaves that float on the water, on the other hand, are often large and rounded. Pores are present only on the upper side, which furthermore is usually covered with a waxy membrane.

The flowers of water plants are generally minute. Unless they are self-pollinated (the process taking place inside the unopened flowers), the agents of pollination are either water currents or, in the case of flowers that rise above the water, insects or even certain aquatic molluscs.

Though many water plants multiply by vegetative means, in other words by means of various buds, pieces of rhizomes, tubers, etc., they also frequently multiply by means of seeds. The seeds or fruits have various means of staying afloat or else they may be covered with mucus so that they can adhere to the bodies of aquatic animals. Often they pass undamaged through the digestive tract of animals and can thus be transported great distances.

Between water and dry land there is another habitat, a combination of the two, which includes bogs, boggy shallows and swamps. They, too, have their typical plant communities. Such places not only have plenty of water but also a rich supply of nutrients provided by dead and decaying plants in the mud. Bog plants have thick, branching, creeping rhizomes. These not only anchor the plant in the ground but are also a means by which it spreads and multiplies. For this reason bog vegetation usually forms dense, spreading masses. The stems are firm and the leaves generally strap-shaped to longish-lanceolate and very flexible. This is very important, for it prevents the plant from being broken by the wind, which is always a hazard on account of its height, an adaptation necessitated by the fluctuating of the water-level.

Moors

Moors are formed on an impermeable, generally acidic substrate where water collects either from rainfall or from neighbouring springs or water courses. Besides sphagnum, the vegetation includes many typical angiosperms such as Cotton Grass (*Eriophorum*), Marsh Andromeda (*Andromeda polifolia*), Rannoch-rush (*Scheuchzeria palustris*), and others characteristically of low, mostly prostrate habit. The vegetation of moors, which are very poor in nutrients, also includes carnivorous plants such as Common Sundew (*Drosera rotundifolia*), which obtain the necessary nitrogenous substances from the bodies of trapped insects.

Being natural reservoirs of water moors play an important role in moisturizing the air around them, and in the context of land reclamation and various drainage projects it is always necessary to give serious thought to whether existing moors should be preserved or destroyed.

Moor is in general a term with wide scope, encompassing a number of habitats. One is the upland or high moor formed on acidic substrates in mountain and piedmont regions. This is a heather moor. Rainfall plays an important role in its water balance.

Another is the low-lying moor or fen, formed mostly on basic or neutral substrates generally in lowland or hill country. This is a moss moor or bog. Rainfall plays a negligible role in its water balance.

Peat meadows are very damp situations and are covered mostly with sedges. The vegetation includes such plants as Marsh Cinquefoil *(Potentilla palustris)*, Common Cottongrass *(Eriophorum angustifolium)* and Bogbean *(Menyanthes trifoliata)*.

Peat forests are a specific type of woodland community in very wet situations with a high water table. They are characterized by a herbaceous layer similar to that of peat meadows and high moors.

Most high moors were formed in the postglacial period when the climate gradually became warmer and the glaciers disappeared. The water supply increased as they melted, and various depressions were formed by the ensuing erosion, thus preparing the way for the formation of high moors.

Moors serve man as a source of peat. Dry peat is used as fuel, as fertilizer in agriculture, and in gardening.

For palaeontologists they are a source of information about the origin and evolution of plants, for preserved to this day in the various layers of peat are plant remnants and pollen grains that are thousands of years old.

Rocks and screes

Rocks in warm regions, where often we would not expect to find a plant of any kind, may in spring be covered with yellow cushions of Golden Alison *(Alyssum saxatile)*. Apart from this there are many other plants that inhabit these seemingly inhospitable places.

Such rock plants, however, must be adapted to the harsh conditions of their habitat. The soil is meagre and is continually washed away by rain and thus collects chiefly in crevices and hollows. The winds are very strong and the heat of the sun may be so great as to be practically intolerable at times, so that only markedly drought-resistant plants can survive. Shady spots, on the other hand, are occupied by moisture-loving species.

The body structure of rock plants is also adapted to the conditions of the given habitat. The roots are long and branched to enable them to reach the water deep in the rock crevices. The plants are usually of low, cushioned habit, which in the cold nights enables them to make the most of the heat absorbed by the rocks during the day. The leaves are often fleshy. In plants exposed to the sun they are covered with hairs which prevents excessive evaporation on sunny and windy days. The leaves of many plants curl up in hot weather, which likewise limits evaporation. Reproduction by vegetative means is a common characteristic. An important factor that governs the makeup of the plant community is the chemical composition of the rock substrate. This may be calcareous and hence basic, or silicic and hence acid, and the plants growing on the various rocks will include only species partial to the given acidity of the substrate.

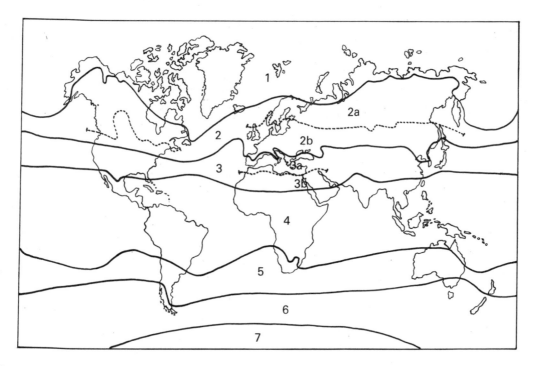

Vegetational zones:
1 − arctic zone 2 − north temperate zone 2a − boreal subzone 2b − submeridional subzone 3 − meridional zone 3a − north meridional subzone
3b − south meridional subzone 4 − tropical zone 5 − south tropical zone 6 − south temperate zone 7 − antarctic zone

Phytogeographic Distribution

The Earth's surface is phytogeographically divided into vegetational zones, altitudinal belts and floristic regions.

Vegetational zones

The various zones are determined first and foremost by the prevailing climate and hence also by the environment.

The **arctic zone** extends north of the forest limit (somewhat northwards of the Arctic Circle). It embraces the barren land and tundra of the arctic. In Europe it includes only the extreme northern parts of Scandinavia but is more extensive in North America and northern Asia.

The **north temperate zone** is a zone of coniferous and broad-leaved forests as well as deserts and semi-deserts. It is characterized by a mean annual temperature of O°−14° C. The north temperate zone embraces a vast territory and is therefore divided into two subzones − the northern, boreal subzone and the southern, submeridional subzone. There is no clear demarca-

tion between the two; in Europe the line separating them is between 55° and 45° latitude North. The boreal subzone is characterized by forests, mostly coniferous, and also moors. The submeridional subzone is characterized by broad-leaved forests where the climate is oceanic (i.e. rather moist) and by steppe to semi-desert where the climate is continental (i.e. rather dry).

The **meridional zone** extends to about 26° latitude North and includes evergreen forests, steppes and deserts. It is characterized by a high mean annual temperature ranging between 15° and 20° C. The southernmost parts of Europe extend only into its north subzone, which is characterized by evergreen forests and Mediterranean stands of low woody and herbaceous plants.

Further zones in the southward direction are the **tropical, south tropical, south temperate, and antarctic zone.**

Altitudinal belts

Altitudinal belts are determined according to the height above sea level.

The **lowland belt** includes sea coasts, river deltas and the lowest-lying land areas. It is

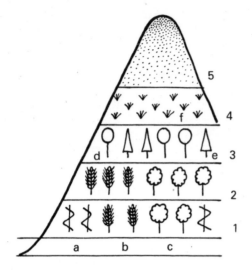

Altitudinal belts:
1 – lowland belt 2 – colline or hill belt 3 – mountain belt
4 – alpine belt 5 – nival belt; a – vineyards b – fields
c – meadows d – deciduous (broad-leaved) forests e – coniferous
forests f – mountain grasslands

characterized by meadow and pastureland vegetation, waterside thickets, cultivated crops such as fields and vineyards, and steppe vegetation.

The **hill** or **colline belt** is at a somewhat higher elevation and is characterized by undulating land.

The **mountain belt** extends to the forest limit and is generally characterized by the absence of cultivated stands.

The **high mountain** or **alpine belt** lies between the timber line and the snow belt and is characterized by shrubby thickets of dwarf pine, mountain grasslands and screes.

The last is the **nival belt** or **region of permanent snow** where conditions are not conducive to the growth of higher plants.

Floristic regions

The third form of phytogeographic division is based on the separate evolution of the continents and the gradual development of flora specific to them. The separate floristic regions therefore incorporate several altitudinal belts as well as different vegetational zones.

The **Holarctic region** includes the arctic, north temperate and north subtropical or meridional zone of the northern hemisphere.

The **Palaeotropical region** includes the tropical zone of the Old World.

The **Neotropical region** is confined to the tropics of Central and South America.

The **Capetown region** is distinguished by the draught-resistant vegetation of southernmost Africa.

The **Australian region** includes the flora of the whole of Australia except the parts that lie within the tropics.

The **Antarctic region** includes the flora of the whole of Antarctica.

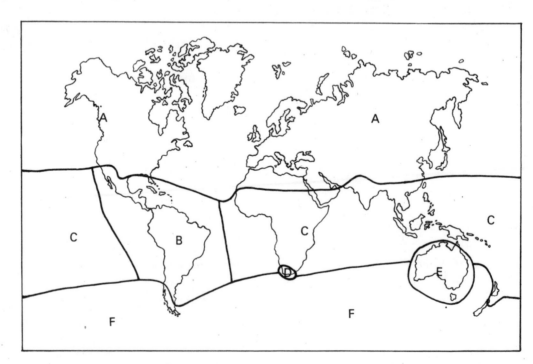

Floristic regions (from top to bottom):
A – Holarctic B – Palaeotropical C – Neotropical D – Capetown E – Australian F – Antarctic

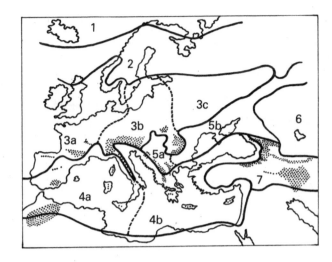

Floristic Elements of Europe

Floristic elements are plants that are typical of a given locality and this locality is the centre or focal point of their distribution. Europe may accordingly be divided from north to south into the following floristic provinces:

1/ **Arctic** – the northernmost, treeless part of Europe.

2/ **Boreal** – the part covered with coniferous forests and corresponding to the boreal subzone of the temperate zone.

3/ **Central European** – the part lying south of the boreal and covered with mixed forests. From west to east it is divided into three provinces: a) Atlantic – the sea coasts of western Europe; b) Central European proper – beechwoods and hornbeam stands of central Europe; c) East European – oakwoods of eastern Europe.

4/ **Mediterranean** – the part adjoining the Mediterranean Sea. It is divided into two subprovinces: a) the west Mediterranean and b) the east Mediterranean.

5/ **Pontic** – the steppe country extending from the middle Danube to the southern Urals. It is divided into two subprovinces: a) the Pannonian – the lowland region around the middle Danube, and b) the Pontic proper – extending from the Carpathian mountains to the southern Urals.

6/ **Aralocaspian** – extending only to the arid part of Russia by the Caspian Sea.

7/ **Eastern** – extending only to Transcaucasia.

8/ **Alpidic** – taking in the high mountains of Europe.

Botanical relationships in Europe are relatively complex and that is why so many floristic provinces are recognized. Each is characterized by specific floristic elements. For example, Bog Heather or Cross-leaved Heath *(Erica tetralix)* is an Atlantic element because it is characteristic of the Atlantic subprovince of the central European province (3a). Spiked Rampion *(Phyteuma spicatum)* is a central European element because the centre of its distribution is located in and corresponds to the central European subprovince (3b). Great Black Masterwort *(Astrantia major)* grows mostly in Europe's mountains, i.e. in the alpidic floristic province (8), and is hence an alpidic element.

Green Plants – Vital to Life on Earth

Apart from the regions of permanent snow, the ocean depths and the driest deserts, practically no place on Earth is without green plants. Their coverage is not uniform and depends on the local conditions in various zones or belts. In some places they occur in abundance, in several layers; elsewhere they are sparse but are present nevertheless. They are so much a part of our everyday lives we often forget how very important they are to life on our planet – without them there would be no life on Earth, for no other organism is able to transform mineral (inorganic) substances into organic substances. Only green plants can make food from raw minerals. The transformation of mineral substances into organic substances takes place in the presence of light in small bodies called chloroplasts, which contain the green colouring matter chlorophyll. This whole 'miracle' can be expressed by a relatively simple formula:

$$6\ CO_2 + 6\ H_2O \xrightarrow{\text{energy}} C_6H_{12}O_6 + 6\ O_2$$

In the presence of chlorophyll and sunlight, carbon dioxide and water (in other words inorganic substances) are transformed into sugars (i.e. organic substances), and oxygen is released into the atmosphere. This process is called photosynthesis.

Simple sugars, which are subsequently transformed into more complex substances − for example starch, the best-known reserve food of plants − are not the only important product of photosynthesis. The other, oxygen, which is released by every green cell in all green plant parts, continually replenishes the supply both in the atmosphere and in water, thereby making it possible for animals to breathe.

Plants, however, also breathe − that is they consume oxygen. At night, in the absence of light, the process that takes place within plant cells is roughly the reverse of that which takes place during the daytime: they absorb oxygen, break down part of the synthesized sugars and release carbon dioxide. As the sugars are broken down within the cell, energy (supplied in daytime in the form of sunlight) is released and this is used by the plant in the metabolism necessary for growth.

Since not all the synthesized sugars are needed by plants for their basic life functions they are stored as reserve food supplies in the roots, rhizomes, tubers, bulbs and cotyledons. However they are also used as food by man and many animals.

Not all plants are self-sufficient. Many are semi-parasites. They are usually green plants and thus carry on some photosynthesis, but obtain minerals from another plant, called the host.

Plants that are entirely dependent on a host plant for their food are called parasites. They are never coloured green and are unable to carry on photosynthesis.

Many plants live in symbiosis with a fungus, often microscopic, which carries out the absorb-

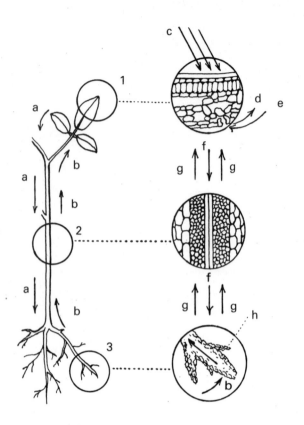

Diagram showing plant metabolism:
1 − leaf 2 − stem 3 − root a) products of photosynthesis b) water containing dissolved mineral substances c) sunlight d) oxygen e) carbon dioxide f) sieve tubes g) tracheae h) root hairs

tion of minerals. Such microscopic species are called mycorrhizal fungi and the process of plant nourishment is called mycorrhiza.

Structure of Plants

Roots

The root is the underground, unsegmented organ of the plant and unlike the stem does not have leaves, not even in the form of scales. The root anchors the plant in the soil and absorbs water and minerals. It also serves for the storage of food. The tip of the root is covered by a root cap that protects it during its progress through the soil. The walls of the cells on the outer surface of the cap are mucilaginous, thus facilitating the passage of the root tip between sharp soil particles. The root increases in length at the tip. Behind this region of elongation there is a covering of root hairs which are very fine, variously bent, and which adhere to the soil

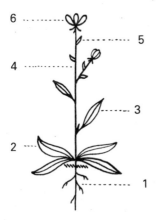

Diagram of an angiosperm:
1 – root 2 – basal leaves 3 – stem leaves 4 – stem 5 – upper leaves 6 – flower

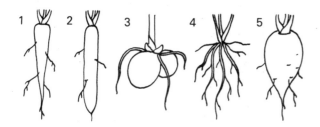

Root:
1 – spindle-like 2 – cylindrical 3 – tuberous 4 – adventitious roots 5 – turnip-like

particles. They are relatively short-lived and thus the root hair zone shifts downwards as the root grows longer and new root hairs are formed behind the growing point. The root surface is increased not only by the root hairs but also by branching of the root. These branch or secondary roots originate at some distance from the root tip.

Roots may also develop from the plant shoot. These are called adventitious roots. They may develop from underground stems, or rhizomes, or from the base of aerial stems. The ability of plants to form adventitious roots is utilized in methods of vegetative propagation (e.g. the propagation of begonias by leaf-cuttings).

Besides anchorage and the absorption of food adventitious roots may also participate in photosynthesis and in supplying air and water.

Stems and leaves

Above ground the root passes into aerial shoots which are generally differentiated into stems and leaves. Some plants have underground stems and of these the types known as rhizomes are of

particular importance. Stems are not restricted in their growth but this is affected by the conditions of the environment and the site. Aerial stems usually have green leaves, whereas on underground stems the leaves are in the form of scales without chlorophyll (and are not coloured green). The stems link the roots with the leaves and serve for the exchange of chemical substances between the two. The stems have tissues that enable them to position the leaves so they face the sun. The leaves are usually arranged in a definite pattern and may be alternate, opposite or whorled.

Aerial non-woody stems that die the same year are called herbaceous stems. A leafless stem terminated by a flower or inflorescence is called a scape (as in Primrose or Dandelion). The hollow, jointed stem of grasses, with nodes and internodes, is called a culm. Stems may be erect (as in Field Poppy); ascending – rising or curving upward from a trailing position (as in Clover (Trifolium hybridum); prostrate – growing on the ground; decumbent – growing on

Position of leaves:
A – alternate B – opposite C – whorled

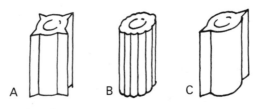

Cross-section of stem:
A – winged B – grooved C – two-edged

Attachment of leaves:
A – petiolate leaf with stipules B – sessile leaf C – amplexicaul (clasping) leaf D – sheathed leaf

21

the ground and rising slightly at the tip but not forming adventitious roots (Knotgrass); creeping — growing on the ground and rooting along the stem (Creeping Cinquefoil); twining — winding spirally around a support (Field Bindweed); or climbing — growing upward and adhering with tendrils (Pea) or holdfast adventitious roots (Ivy).

Plants with herbaceous stems are called herbs. These may be annual, biennial, plural-yearly, or perennial, according to how long they live. Annuals complete their life cycle from seed to seed within one growing season (Poppy). Biennials require two growing seasons with a rest period in between to complete their life cycle. The first year they germinate and usually produce a ground rosette of leaves, and in the second year they produce flowers, fruits and seeds and then die (Shepherd's Purse). Once-flowering, 'plural-yearly' herbs live several years without flowering, then flower, produce fruit and die (Angelica). Perennial herbs live more than two years, usually do not flower for one or more years but then produce flowers and seed regularly every year from the same root structure as this lives on when the top parts die down in winter (Coltsfoot, Celandine).

The top parts of some plants contain lactiferous ducts as evidenced by the 'milk', which may be coloured either white or orange, that oozes from the stems or leaves when bruised.

Lactiferous ducts may be unjointed, which is the case in those that have no transverse walls nor vestigial remains of such walls. They are already present in the embryo in the form of long tubular cells that lengthen as the plant grows, and branch and extend into all the plant

Pinnate leaves:
1 — pinnatilobate 2 — pinnatifid 3 — pinnatipartite 4 — pinnatisect

Palmate leaves:
1 — palmatilobate 2 — palmatifid 3 — palmatipartite
4 — palmatisect

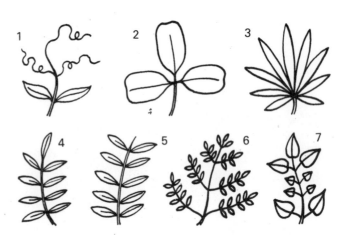

Compound leaves:
1 — leaf with one pair of leaflets, the remainder modified as tendrils 2 — trifoliolate 3 — digitate 4 — imparipinnate 5 — paripinnate 6 — bipinnate 7 — pinnate with interjected leaflets

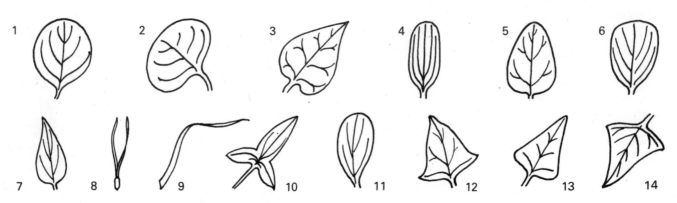

Simple leaves:
1 — orbicular 2 — reniform 3 — cordate 4 — oblong 5 — ovate 6 — obovate 7 — lanceolate 8 — acicular 9 — linear 10 — sagittate 11 — spatulate 12 — hastate 13 — deltoid (triangular) 14 — rhombic

organs. They may measure several metres in length. Their lateral branches are not interconnected. This type is found in members of the dogbane family and some spurges.

Jointed lactiferous ducts are formed by the union of a great many long cells, closely set one above the other, the end walls of which are absent except for negligible remnants. They differ from unjointed ducts in that they form a network in the body of the plant. Jointed lactiferous ducts are to be found in most members of the bellflower family, in the poppy family and in the composite family (Chicory, Dandelion, etc.).

The leaf is differentiated into a blade and petiole. The base of the leaf often forms a sheath and is furnished with stipules. The upper surface of the leaf may differ from the lower surface, or both may be the same. The margin of the blade may be entire, toothed, notched, lobed or divided by fissures of varying length. The blade may be all in one piece (simple leaf) and of diverse shape or composed of several separate leaflets (compound leaf). The latter may be palmately compound or pinnately compound.

Flower

The flower of angiosperms is a shoot or part of a shoot, usually of limited growth, with modified leaves that directly or indirectly take part in the process of sexual reproduction.

It is composed of a receptacle, floral envelopes (perianth), stamens and pistils. If the receptacle is hollowed to form a cup-like structure it is called a cupule (as in oak). If the lower parts of the floral envelopes and stamens are joined to form a cup it is called a hypanthium (as in cherry). The floral envelopes, which grow from the receptacle, may be undifferentiated (Anemone) or differentiated into a calyx and corolla, generally also differing in colour (Cyclamen). The calyx is typically green but it may also be brightly coloured like the corolla and take

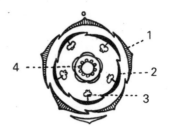

Diagram of the flower of a primrose *(Primula):*
1 — sepals (hatched lines) 2 — petals (black) 3 — stamens 4 — pistil. Where the perianth is not differentiated into a calyx and corolla it is designated with dots.

over the function of the corolla (Heather, Milkwort). The petals may be separate or joined together; if they are joined the corolla is bell-shaped, tubular, funnel-shaped etc. The Strawberry, Cinquefoil and members of the mallow family have an epicalyx beneath the calyx formed by the union of the stipules of two adjoining sepals.

According to the arrangement of the floral parts flowers may be radially symmetrical, (e.g. Lesser Celandine), bisymmetrical (Bleeding Heart), or bilaterally symmetrical (in other words they can be divided into two identical halves, e.g. Pea, Dead-nettle) or asymmetrical (Valerian).

The stamen consists of an anther and filament. The anther generally consists of two pollen sacs joined together by a slender connective. Each pollen sac is divided into two locules. If the pollen sacs are turned toward the centre of the flower the anthers are said to be introrse (Water-lily), if they face outward the anthers are extrorse (Crocus), and if they are located to the side the anthers are lateral (Poppy). The pollen sacs contain pollen grains differing in shape and surface structure according to the method of pollination of the respective species. In wind-pollinated plants the pollen grains are tiny and floury, thus being readily dispersed and carried by air currents. Such plants produce large amounts of pollen and the floral envelopes are

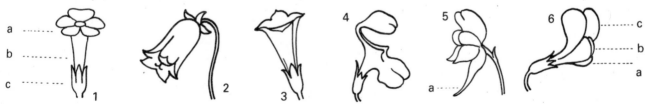

Corolla: 1 — **hypocrateriform corolla** with lobes (a) and tube (b) surrounded by calyx (c) 2 — campanulate (bell-shaped) 3 — funnel-shaped 4 — bilabiate 5 — bilabiate corolla with spur (a) 6 — papilionate corolla of the pea family with keel (a), wings (b) and standard (c)

usually small or even absent. Insect-pollinated plants do not produce as much pollen but usually have conspicuous floral envelopes. The pollen grains are dispersed singly or stuck together in groups of four, as in the heath family, or in larger masses called pollinia, as in the orchid family. In plants of the orchid family each locule in the pollen sac contains a single pollinium with a sticky peduncle at the base which adheres to the head of the pollinating insect. This minute peduncle dries when exposed to the air thereby bringing the pollinium forward towards the insect's feeding tube; then when the insect visits another flower the pollinium rubs against the stigma located beneath the anther of that flower. Pollinia adhere to the feeding tube or head of the insect permanently, so that a single pollinium may pollinate a number of flowers.

A flower may have only a single carpel forming a simple pistil (pea family) or several carpels. In the latter case each carpel may form a separate pistil and then the flower has several simple pistils (Buttercup, Marsh Marigold, Strawberry) or the carpels may be united to form a single compound pistil (Primula). The pistil is ordinarily differentiated into three parts — the ovary, the style and the stigma. The stigma is usually warty, sticky and of diverse shape designed to trap the pollen grains. The style connects the stigma with the ovary. According to its position relative to the stamens the ovary is described as inferior, semi-inferior or superior. Members of the orchid family have a single stamen united with the style to form a stalk called the gynostemium.

In the orchid family the ovary turns 180° inside the bud before the flower opens, thereby inverting the whole flower. That is why the spurred lip (the distinctively shaped petal characteristic of orchids) which was originally at the top of the flower ends up at the bottom. After pollination and after the flower has faded the ovary returns to its original position, one that is more suitable for seed dispersal.

The flowers of angiosperms are either bisexual (hermaphroditic, i.e. with both stamens and pistil in the same flower) or unisexual (having either stamens or pistils in one flower). If the male and female flowers are on the same plant it is said to be monoecious (hazel, maize). If the male and female flowers are on separate plants the plants are said to be dioecious (Stinging Nettle).

Pollen grains may reach the stigma in

Flower symmetry:
1 — regular, actinomorphic flower
2 — irregular, zygomorphic flower

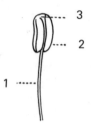

Stamen: 1 — filament 2 — anther 3 — connective

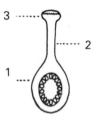

Pistil: 1 — ovary with ovules 2 — style 3 — stigma

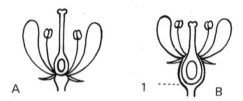

Ovary: A — superior ovary B — inferior ovary and hypanthium (1)

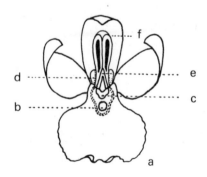

Diagram of a flower of the orchid family:
a — labium or lip b — mouth of spur c — stigma d — remnants of atrophied stamens e — beak-like elongation of style f — gynostemium

24

a number of ways. Either they are transferred there by the wind (grasses, sedges) or by insects that visit flowers to gather pollen or collect nectar (most members of the composite family). Some aquatic plants are pollinated by water currents (e.g. Pondweed). Other agents of pollination include birds (such as hummingbirds, chiefly in the case of tropical plants) and bats. Bog Arum is apparently pollinated by molluscs.

The pollen with which a flower is pollinated is usually from another flower on the same or a different plant. As a rule flowers are not self-pollinated, i.e. the pollen is not transferred from the anther to the stigma of the same flower. Nature has devised several methods of preventing this. The pistil may mature first and the stamens much later, as in some grasses and Plantain, or the pollen sacs may open first with the pistil maturing later, as in bellflowers. A similar condition encouraging cross-pollination is one in which flowers differ in the relative length of the stamens and pistils, such as Loosestrife, Primula. Some flowers even have hairs in the mouth of the corolla tube which prevent insects from leaving an unpollinated flower. Only after the pollen has been transferred to the stigma do the hairs droop to allow the insect to depart; the insect coated with pollen can then visit another flower (an example is the arum family). Self-pollination, of course, is also not uncommon (occurring for example in plants of the parsley and sundew families). Sometimes this takes place only if the plant was not or could not be cross-pollinated (Sweet Violet).

Inflorescences

Individual flowers may be arranged in clusters, or inflorescences. The two main types are racemose and cymose.

In the racemose inflorescence the lateral branches generally do not extend above the main axis. The individual flowers bloom in succession from the bottom upward or, if all are at the same level, from the margin inward towards the centre. The basic type of racemose inflorescence is the raceme (such as in Lily-of-the-valley). If the cluster is flat-topped with the outer flower peduncles long and those towards the centre progressively shorter so that all the flowers are at the same level it is a corymb (apple, pear). If the lateral branches are shorter than the main axis and the flowers are sessile, i.e. attached directly to the peduncle, the cluster is a spike (Plantain, Knotgrass). A spike with a weak, more-or-less drooping axis is called a catkin (hazel, willow). A dense spike with a thick fleshy axis is a spadix (Bog Arum). If the main axis is greatly shortened so that the flowers are crowded the cluster is called a head or capitulum (Clover). Another type of head is that of the composite family, called an anthodium, with main axis terminating in a flattened, disclike receptacle growing in the axil of an involucre — a ring of small bracts usually coloured green, so that the whole resembles a single flower. The umbel is an umbrella-shaped inflorescence in which the flower-peduncles branch from a central point at the top of the main axis and are of nearly equal length so that

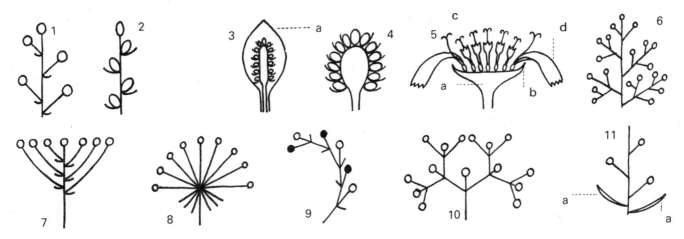

Types of inflorescences:
1 — raceme 2 — spike 3 — spadix and spathe (a) 4 — head, capitulum (of clover) 5 — anthodium — head of a composite plant: a — receptacle b — involucral bracts c — central tubular florets d — outer ligulate (strap-shaped) florets 6 — panicle 7 — corymb 8 — umbel 9 — monochasium (monochasial cyme) 10 — dichasium (dichasial cyme) 11 — three-flowered spikelet of grasses with glumes (a)

the flowers are more or less at the same height (Primula). The bracts at the base of the umbel form an envelope which is sometimes enlarged and resembles a corolla (Masterwort).

The cymose inflorescence is characterized by having a short main axis because its growth halts early while the lateral branches continue to grow and are thus longer. The uppermost flower blooms first followed by the lower ones, or if the cluster is flat the central flower blooms first followed by the outer ones. If there are several branches the cyme is multichasial (Woodrush, Club-rush). If there are two, usually opposite, branches it is a dichasial cyme or dichasium (Mistletoe, Catchfly, Campion). If there is only a single branch it is a monochasial cyme or monochasium.

In some plants simple inflorescences may be joined together to form a compound inflorescence. A panicle is a compound raceme composed of several simple racemes (Lilac); a spike is composed of spikelets (rye, wheat); a compound umbel is composed of simple umbels (caraway, carrot). Secondary bracts below each simple umbel of the compound inflorescence are called bracteoles.

Fruits

As the ovules develop into seeds the pistil develops into a fruit. When mature, fruits either open to release the seeds or else the seeds remain enclosed inside and are dispersed together with the fruit.

Dehiscent (splitting) fruits include various types as follows. The follicle is derived from a single carpel and generally dehisces along one suture — the seam where the edges of the carpels are joined (Marsh Marigold). The legume or pod is also derived from a single carpel but dehisces along two sutures (pea). The siliqua is derived from the union of two carpels (mustard); a short siliqua is called a silicula (Field Pennycress). The capsule is derived from the union of two or more carpels and may be unilocular or multilocular; it dehisces lengthwise either along the seam where the carpels are joined (St. John's Wort) or along the back of the carpels (Iris). It may also open by means of teeth (Primula, Catchfly, Campion), pores (Poppy, Bellflower), a lid (Pimpernel, Henbane), or fissures (Wood Sorrel).

Indehiscent fruits may be one-seeded or many-seeded, dry or fleshy. The nut is a one-seeded fruit with hard and woody shell, or pericarp, more or less separable from the seed itself (hazel). Achenes are dry, one-seeded fruits derived from a single carpel (Lesser Celandine); the achene of the composite family is also one-seeded but derived from two carpels and is called a cypsela. Grain is the fruit of grasses. Some dry indehiscent fruits also split at maturity into one-seeded mericarps — the double achene of caraway and the schizocarpic fruit of the mallow and geranium families are examples. Nutlets are fruits derived from four one-seeded locules of a two-carpel ovary as in the borage and mint families. The loment is a fruit that has evolutionary ties with the siliqua and pod, and separates transversely at its constrictions (Wild Radish). Fleshy, indehiscent fruits include the drupe with pericarp composed of three different

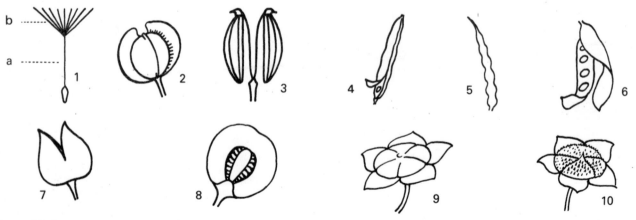

Types of fruits:
1 — cypsela with beak (a) and pappus (b) 2 — samara 3 — double achene 4 — siliqua 5 — loment 6 — pod 7 — capsule 8 — longitudinal section of berry 9 — schizocarpic fruit of the mallow family 10 — fruit of the mint and borage families composed of four nutlets

parts — a membranous epicarp, fleshy mesocarp and an inner stone or endocarp that contains the seed (cherry).

Another type is the berry — a fleshy fruit with seeds not enclosed by a hard stone but embedded in the flesh (currant).

Last of all there is the pome — a fleshy fruit divided into several membranous locules containing the seeds (apple).

Just as flowers may form an inflorescence so fruits at maturity may form a multiple, or collective, fruit derived from a number of ovaries from several flowers (e.g. Sunflower) or an aggregate fruit derived from a number of ovaries belonging to a single flower (strawberry, raspberry, blackberry).

Seeds and fruits are dispersed by various means. They may be adapted for distribution by the wind which often carries them far from the parent plant. Examples are the winged fruits of the maple, the cypselas of composite plants which bear a ring of fine hairs and the grains of the reed which also have hairs — all means that help keep them airborne.

The seeds and fruits of aquatic plants are distributed by water currents.

Many fruits and seeds have hooked or barbed projections that catch in the fur, feathers or on the bodies of animals. A typical example is Burdock in which the entire fruit clings to animals by means of hooked bristles and is thus transported.

Fleshy fruits with an indigestible seed coat are generally distributed by birds, the plants often being carried great distances with the birds' faeces. Some plants have seeds with various fleshy appendages and projections which serve as food for small animals. Examples are the seeds of Celandine and Violet which are distributed by ants.

Seeds may be distributed by means of explosive dehiscence, sometimes being ejected far from the parent plant (Touch-me-not, Wood Sorrel, and certain geraniums).

Aggregate fruit:
A — strawberry — fleshy receptacle with achenes
B — raspberry — cluster of drupelets

The Mysterious 2n

Essential to plant growth is an increase in the number of cells, brought about by division of the existing cells. Cells are composed not only of a cell wall and cell sap (cytoplasm) but also other parts such as plastids, which contain chlorophyll and food, and above all a cell nucleus. It is necessary for this nucleus to be divided as well. Nuclear division precedes cell division and is responsible for the formation of a new cell similar to the mother cell. Constriction of the cell nucleus gives rise to two nuclei, which are surrounded by cytoplasm encased by separate cell walls increasing in size until they reach the proportions of the original cell, thus giving rise to two new cells. This is direct nuclear division, which gives rise only to the type of cell that becomes differentiated into the plant tissues and organs — leaves, stems, roots and flowers. Plants not only grow in size but may also produce new plants by this means from leaves, stems and roots. Such reproduction is called asexual or vegetative reproduction.

Plants, however, also multiply by sexual means, by the fusion of the sperm nucleus in the pollen tube and the egg nucleus in the embryo sac. If, however, the content of the two were to be combined then the nucleus of the resulting cell would have double the content. This is prevented by reduction division, a process by which each nucleus of a sex or germ cell is reduced to a nucleus with precisely half the content. In some cases this process is visible under a microscope. Inside such a nucleus we will see the formation of rod-shaped bodies called chromosomes which at the end of the process number half as many as at the beginning. Thus a male germ cell with half the number of chromosomes unites with the nucleus of the female germ cell, likewise with half the number of chromosomes, to form a cell with the full number of chromosomes that develops into a new individual. The shape and number of chromosomes may vary greatly in different species. On the other hand whole groups of plants have the same number of chromosomes. In members of the same species the number is usually constant. However, it may sometimes fluctuate in species that are not fully uniform genetically. As we shall see such is often the case in those species that form subspecies or microspecies. All this explains the many diverse characteristics of plants. Chromosomes are important carriers of hereditary traits because they carry the genes by which all the aspects and properties of a plant are transmitted and determined. That is why knowing the number of chromosomes is so important. We have seen that somatic cells have a full (diploid) number of chromosomes and germ cells half that number. It is therefore necessary to distinguish the two, and so the diploid number is designated by the symbol 2n, n being the single chromosome number (haploid number). Of central European plants the small Adder's Tongue Fern *(Ophioglossum vulgatum)* has the highest somatic or diploid number (2n = circa 500) and Suncoth Hawksbeard *(Crepis capillaris)* the lowest (2n = 6).

The chromosome number of the other plants in this book is to be found in the text accompanying each illustration, after the designation 2n — which is not after all such a mysterious concept.

Plants and Man

This book contains illustrations of plants growing in the wild without any intervention on the part of man, some in places where we would never expect to find them. They are such a natural part of the world about us that sometimes we do not even take any notice of them.

They have been man's companions since time immemorial and man has always been dependent on them. In the beginning he gathered floury grains or roots, sweet fruits or leaves and other parts of plants for food and for treating his various ailments. The first time he sowed seeds intentionally marked a great step forward — marked the beginning of the cultivation of food plants. From there it was only a small step (even though this step again lasted several generations) to the grading of seeds, and to the selection of the best ones for sowing — in other words to the breeding of cultivated plants. Today, with man's knowledge of the basic rules of genetics, new levels of control have been reached with the hybridization of plants aimed at obtaining the most desirable and useful characteristics.

At the close of the 19th century there were relatively few (only several hundred) species of economically important plants, today there are several thousand species and varieties.

The principal crop plants are cereal grasses — wheat, barley, rye, oats, rice and maize. Rye, for instance, was a weed of the small wheat fields of Europe's first inhabitants. However, it withstood the rugged climate of the cold regions of central Europe better than wheat and barley — and that is how it came to be grown as a crop plant, although only in central Europe. Elsewhere rye is grown only for fodder.

Another important group of plants grown for food, particularly in the poorer parts of the world, are legumes (soya beans, peas, beans, lentils, etc.), which are the cheapest source of vegetable protein. Besides being rich in protein they also contain much oil, as do the olive, peanut, rape, sunflower, etc.

Sugar is another important vegetable food — cane sugar in the tropical regions all round the world, and in the temperate regions beet sugar and various fruits and vegetables, which besides containing readily digested sugars (glucose and fructose) and important vitamins are often also tasty foods that add pleasant variety to our daily fare.

Besides plants that provide man with the essential foods necessary to life and growth there are also plants whose products, though not vital to his well being, have become an inseparable part of his life. These include the tea plant, the leaves of which are dried and fermented to yield the popular beverage tea, and the coffee plant, cacao tree and tobacco plant.

In our list of cultivated plants we must not forget to include the fibre-producing plants, mainly cotton, flax and hemp, which were indispensable in the days before the introduction of man-made fibres and whose products are in great demand to this day.

Plants also serve man in other ways. For instance, trees are a source of timber, and forage plants used as food for livestock may be either cultivated by man for the purpose or growing naturally and cut and dried by man as fodder for the winter.

Not only cultivated plants but also wild plants can be used by man for various purposes. For example the leaves of Dandelion *(Taraxacum officinale)* are used as a salad, as are the young seedlings of various plants of the crucifer family; such a spring salad is rich in ascorbic acid, or Vitamin C. Salad is also made from the young leaves of Chicory *(Cichorium intybus)*, used like lettuce, as well as from the young leaves of the Common Nettle.

A large group of economically important plants, often growing naturally in the wild, are the medicinal herbs. Many plants contain substances that have been used to treat man's ailments since time immemorial, and today many not only continue to be collected in the wild but are also cultivated for use by the modern pharmaceutical industry. The collection and cultivation of these plants is very important because even today, when most substances can be produced artificially, natural products often remain unequalled. One example is the widely-used Chamomile, the essential oils of which contain highly effective terpenoid chamazulenes that have an anti-inflammatory and healing effect. The Opium Poppy and certain related species contain morphine alkaloids, which modern medicine could not do without.

Another group of substances important to man are the glycosides. Examples are the cyanogenic glycosides from 'bitter almonds', which readily split to yield the poisonous hydrocyanic acid, and the mustard glycosides (glucosinolates) characteristic of the crucifer family.

Many plant substances that aid man in modern medicine, however, are deleterious if used improperly or in excessive doses and some plants have hence been abused by man as poisons, abortifacients and the like. Examples are Deadly Nightshade *(Atropa bella-donna)*, Herb Paris and Tansy.

In conclusion let us consider those plants that are not of economic importance but merely beautiful, this being the reason they are grown and cultivated by man. Their beauty is different from that of the wild flowers of field and woodland; they decorate parks, gardens and rockeries and sometimes one marvels at their magnificent colour, perfect shape and fulness of bloom. Such plants are the objects of the loving care of keen amateur gardeners. Sometimes regrettably, this love and care is confined only to the space circumscribed by the limits of their own garden, where the enthusiastic flower-lover brings what catches his fancy in the wild, regardless of whether the plant is a rare species, often one protected by law, that may disappear and be irretrievably lost to the world.

There are many such plants in the meadows, fields and woodlands of Europe and irresponsible gardeners are not the only ones that threaten their existence. The greatest threat to these endangered species is man's unconsidered actions, by which he alters his environment thereby disrupting the balance of nature. Such actions include land reclamation, use of artificial fertilizers, filling-in of valleys, peat extraction, construction of large industrial plants, pollution of rivers with industrial wastes, and so on. Such actions destroy not only individual plants but entire biotopes, places where these rare species grow. It is therefore not enough to compile lists of endangered and protected plants. It is necessary to make important environmental alterations with care and forethought and also to protect certain select habitats where rare plants grow. The protection and preservation of plants for future generations is a problem that today is being dealt with by a spiecial branch of science — conservation.

Protected Areas in Europe

The progress of civilization, technology and exploitation of natural resources have brought with them the disruption and even devastation of nature. Today we see all around us evidence of the damaging effects of man's actions. Our environment has deteriorated to such an extent that it has become necessary to take defensive measures and solve these problems on a world-wide scale.

In the past two centuries the conservation movement has made efforts to save certain territories, and rare species of plants and animals that are declining in number, as well as other evidence of nature's evolution. This period has witnessed the establishment of a network of protected areas in all parts of the world. These include national parks, natural parks, nature preserves, protected landscape areas and other protected categories. The aim is to preserve tracts of land encompassing all of nature's diversity, the plant and animal communities found there, and testimony pertaining to the evolution of the Earth's crust and of life on the Earth. These protected areas are of inestimable importance to the preservation of their topography and their wealth of animal and plant life; they are important for the renewal of nature, for learning about nature, and for man's health.

In this and the preceding century many areas have been marked out for protection in Europe, and their number is continually growing. A complete list is beyond the scope of this book but we would like to draw attention to the following selection of the most important and interesting.

Great Britain has more than 100 protected areas including 22 nature preserves. The largest are in Scotland, e.g. Cairngorms (25,823 hectares), Inverpolly (10,865 hectares) and others on the Isle of Rhun (10,612 hectares). There are also 10 special protected areas — national parks — for recreational purposes, e.g. Snowdonia (218,855 hectares) in Wales and Phoenix (7,000 hectares) in Ireland.

Iceland had only one national park, the Thingvellir National Park (4,000 hectares) in the southwest but in 1967 another — the Skaftafjell National Park — was established in the southeast at the edge of Vatnajökull, the largest glacier in Europe.

In Scandinavia conservation has a tradition of long standing. Sweden was the first country in Europe to establish a national park in 1909 and to date has a total of 16. Besides these it has many nature preserves. The largest national parks are Padjelanta (204,000 hectares), Sarek (195,000 hectares), Stora Sjöfallet (150,000 hectares) and Muddus (49,200 hectares).

Norway has two national parks to date and 10 nature preserves; 14 more national parks are in the offing. The two are Rondane (57,000 hectares) in the south and Börgefjell (circa 100,000 hectares) in the north; the latter was proclaimed a protected territory by royal decree as far back as 1863.

Finland has a very well thought out network of protected areas, mainly in Lapland. Pallas-Ounastunturi (50,000 hectares) and Lemmenjoki (38,500 hectares) are two of the 9 existing national parks.

Denmark has several nature preserves consisting chiefly of swamps and moors.

The Netherlands has 14 nature preserves and 4 national parks. The two larger parks — Hoge Veluwe (5,700 hectares) and Veluwezoom (4,490 hectares) — are in the central part of the country, the third — Kennemerduinen (1,240 hectares) is near the city of Haarlem and the fourth — Weiden (2,500 hectares) — in the north.

Belgium has a greater number of nature preserves designed to protect the environment of the coast, moors, swamps and bird nesting sites.

France, too, has a similar system of natural parks used mainly for recreation. It also has three national parks (with others in the offing) and a large number of nature preserves. Of the national parks one is located near Toulon; the other two are the West Pyrenean (50,000 hectares) with a protective zone of 160,000 hectares, and the Vanoise in the Alps (52,800 hectares) with a protective zone of 143,000 hectares.

The German Federal Republic has a very large network of protected areas. Thanks to the 'Verein Naturschutzpark' this country has an extensive network of 59 natural parks with a total area of nearly 4.5 million hectares. It has a national park, the Bavarian Forest National Park, which covers an area of 37,400 hectares, and three natural parks in its border regions: the Deutsch-Luxemburgischer, Deutsch-Belgischer and Deutsch-Niederländischer Naturschutzpark. There are some 1,000 nature preserves which cover an area of approximately 300,000 hectares, e.g. Lünenburgerheide near Hamburg (20,000 hectares), Ammergebirge (20,500 hectares), Königssee (27,500 hectares), and Chiemgauer Alpen (15,000 hectares) and Karwendelgebirge (27,000 hectares) in Bavaria. Besides these protected areas, most important from the recreational viewpoint are the protected landscape areas, which number some six hundred.

The German Democratic Republic has more than five hundred nature preserves, 13 with an area of more than 1,000 hectares. The best known — Lewitz (7,137 hectares) and Müritzhof (6,250 hectares) — are in Mecklenburg.

Poland has a dense network of protected areas. To date it has established 13 national parks (with a total area of 103,614 hectares), some 700 nature preserves (in all more than 50,000 hectares) and almost one hundred protected landscape areas with an area of 1,600,000 hectares. The oldest of the national parks is the Białowieża National Park adjoining the Soviet nature preserve of the same name. The national park network extends from sea level to the high mountains — the Tatra National Park.

Czechoslovakia has the oldest natural primeval forest reservations, founded in 1838 and 1858 respectively. The present network of protected areas includes four national parks — the Krkonoše or Giant Mountains National Park, the High Tatra National Park, the Low Tatra National Park and the Pieniny National Park — 21 protected landscape areas, nearly 700 nature preserves and approximately 200 further categories of protected territory.

The Soviet Union has a great many protected areas including 76 large areas called 'zapoviedniky', which are approximately the equivalent of nature preserves. Most are not open to the public and are used mainly for scientific research. The aforementioned Białowieża zapoviednik (74,200 hectares) is located in the European USSR, another, the Pechoro-Ilichsky (730,000 hectares) in the western part of the north Ural foothills.

Hungary has 150 nature preserves and two national parks. The first, Tihany (1,100 hectares), is by Lake Balaton, the second — Hortobagy — is in the damp parts of the puszta.

Rumania has a nature preserve in the Danube delta where pelicans are the prime object of the conservation effort. Other than this there are more than 150 nature preserves. The largest national park is the Retezat National Park in the south Carpathian mountains, where the peak of the same name reaches a height of 2,484 metres above sea level. The oldest is the Bucegi National Park.

Bulgaria has four national parks. Three are in the mountains: Vitosha (22,800 hectares) near Sofia, Vichren (6,700 hectares) in the Pirin Mountains, and Steneto in the rugged Rhodope Mountains; one, Ropotamo, is by the Black Sea, in dunes and flooded land with a wealth of aquatic vegetation.

Two of Greece's three national parks were destroyed during the Second World War and so that country now has only one — Parnis near Athens.

Albania has four national parks: Dajty, Lura, and Tomori — each has an area of approximately 3,000 hectares of mountain territory — and

Divjakä (approximately 1,000 hectares), is in the coastal plain, with dunes and pine forests.

Yugoslavia to date has more than 30 nature preserves and 14 national parks, mostly in the mountains. Fruska Gora in Serbia covers an area of 22,000 hectares and takes in the forest stands on the right bank of the Danube. Best known and most frequently visited are Triglav National Park and Plitvice Lakes, the oldest national park. The former is in the Julian Alps and includes their highest peak, while the latter is in Croatia and is noted for its lovely lake scenery with countless waterfalls and distinctive shoreline vegetation.

Austria has some 300 nature preserves to date. Tauern Naturschutzpark (approximately 34,000 hectares) in Salzburg is noteworthy for its beautiful mountain scenery, glaciers and rare flora and fauna. Another noteworthy large nature preserve is Karwendel (72,000 hectares) in the Tyrol.

Switzerland has nearly 500 nature preserves with a total area of 55,400 hectares, and a national park, Engadin (16,887 hectares), which is noted for its remarkable scenery and rare vegetation as well as excellent organization; founded in 1909, it is one of the oldest national parks in Europe.

Italy has five national parks. Cirno (7,445 hectares) is located on the coast between Rome and Naples. Abruzzo (29,160 hectares) is in the mountains east of Rome. Two others are in the Alps: Gran Paradiso (62,000 hectares) in the Graian Alps adjoining France's Vanoise National Park, and Stelvio (57,772 hectares) in the Rhaetian Alps. And the last two, Adamell-Brenta (46,400 hectares) and Panaveggio — Pale di san Martino (15,800 hectares), are close together in the Dolomites.

Spain has three protected areas — the Covandorca o de Pena Santa National Park (16,900 hectares), the Valle de Ordersa o del Rio Ara National Park (2,046 hectares) and in the Pyrenees the nature preserve Marismas (7,000 hectares).

Glossary

achene — dry, indehiscent, one-seeded fruit developed from one or more carpels

actinomorphic — same as regular; radially symmetrical, with more than one plane of symmetry

adventitious root — root which develops in place of the extinct primary root; root which arises from an abnormal position

aggregate fruit — fruit derived from a number of ovaries belonging to a single flower and on a single receptacle

alpine grassland — usually an expanse of short-stemmed grasses on stony substrates above the tree line

alternate leaves — growing singly on opposite sides of the stem at different levels

amplexicaul leaf — sessile leaf growing directly from the stem and clasping or encircling the stem with its base

anthella — cymose inflorescence with erect, greatly prolonged lateral branches

anther — the part of the stamen which contains the pollen

anthodium — head of a composite plant; a simple, flattened inflorescence of sessile flowers attached to a common receptacle that is generally enlarged, sometimes subtended by an involucre

axil — angle between stem and leaf or stem and bract

base — the lowest or bottom part of an organ (e.g. the base of the blade is the lower part of the blade, in sessile leaves it is the part attached to the main stem, etc.)

beaked fruit — dry, schizocarpic fruit prolonged into a long, straight beak; it separates into several mericarps at maturity

berry — a rounded, fleshy fruit with one or many seeds freely embedded in the flesh

bifid — divided into two parts by a cleft

bilabiate calyx — calyx with two lips

bilabiate corolla — zygomorphic, gamopetalous corolla differentiated into an upper and lower lip, generally open

blade — the flat, expanded part of a leaf

bract — a modified leaf, small and leaf-like or scale-like, below the inflorescence or at the base of a flower-peduncle

bracteole — small or secondary bract on the flower-peduncle

bristly — having short, stiff, often prickly hairs — bristles

bud — a small swelling or projection on a plant, from which a shoot, cluster of leaves or flower develops

bulb — an underground bud-like structure consisting of a very short stem with fleshy base and fleshy scales

bulbil — small bud that falls off and develops into a new plant

caducous calyx — calyx falling off early, before the flower is fully open

calcifugous plant — plant that grows in lime-deficient soils

calyx — the outer, usually green whorl of sepals of a differentiated perianth

calcicolous plant — plant that grows in limy soils

capsule — a dry, dehiscent fruit of more than one carpel, which may be uniloculate or multiloculate (composed of one or more locules)

carpel — leaf-like structure of an angiosperm which bears the ovules and forms a simple pistil, or one of the segments of a compound pistil

ciliate — having long, stiff hairs that generally grow on the margin, on the veins or on the edges of various parts of the plant

claw — the bottom, narrowed part of the petals of a polypetalous corolla

closely subtended leaves — leaves spaced on the stem at intervals less than the length of the leaves themselves

columella — separate, central part of the capsule in the primrose family

compound inflorescence — inflorescence composed of several simple inflorescences

compound leaf — leaf composed of separate leaflets

connective — that part of a filament connecting the lobes (pollen sacs) of an anther

corolla — whole petal system or the inner floral leaves (usually other than green) of a flower with perianth differentiated into a corolla and calyx

corona — same as crown; membranous structures, separate or forming a ring or tube round the centre of the flower inside the corolla

corymb — a simple racemose inflorescence in which the lower pedicels are longer than the upper so that the flowers are more or less at the same height

corymbose panicle — a racemose inflorescence in which the lower lateral branches are longer so that it resembles a corymb

cotyledon — seed-leaf; the first single leaf or one of the first pair of leaves produced by the embryo of a flowering plant, often differing in shape from the later true leaves

crenate leaf — leaf with a scalloped edge, notched with rounded teeth

culm — the jointed stem of grasses, usually hollow, with sessile leaves

cymose inflorescence — inflorescence with a short main axis and longer lateral branches that rise above the terminal flower and branch further in the same manner

cypsela — the dry, indehiscent fruit of plants of the composite family derived from two carpels; analogous to the achene which is derived from one carpel

decurrent leaf — leaf with base extending down along the stem in the form of wings or ribs

decussate leaves — opposite leaves arranged in pairs growing at right angles to those above and below

deltoid leaf — leaf shaped like the Greek letter delta or an equilateral triangle

dentate leaf — leaf with a toothed margin

dichasium — dichasial cyme; simple cymose inflorescence with main axis terminated by a flower beneath which arise two opposite branches that are longer than the main axis and often branch further in the same manner

didynamous stamens — stamens of the mint and figwort families two of which have longer filaments than the other two

dioecious plants — plants with unisexual flowers, having the male and female flowers on separate plants

diploid chromosome number — the number of chromosomes (rod-like structures) occurring in the nucleus of somatic cells and usually characteristic and constant for each individual species. Besides the diploid number there is also a haploid number (designated by the letter 'n') — the number normally occurring in the mature germ cell (i.e. half the number of the usual somatic cell).

distant leaves — leaves spaced on the stem at intervals equal to at least twice their length

divided leaf — simple leaf with blade divided into lobes joined at the base; such leaves may be pinnately divided, palmately divided or pedately divided

double achene — dry, schizocarpic fruit derived from two carpels and splitting into two achenes at maturity

effuse — spread out loosely in all directions, without form

entire leaf — with an even margin, not toothed or divided, without notches or indentations

epicalyx — whorl of smaller leaflets closely adhering to the outside of the calyx

even-pinnate — see paripinnate

evergreen — having green leaves throughout the year; the leaves are not shed all at once but in succession

fertile — capable of producing seed; also, having normally developed viable pollen grains

filament — thread-like stalk of a stamen bearing the anther

floral envelopes — same as perianth; the outer, sterile parts of a flower (floral leaves) which are either similar in shape and colour (undifferentiated) or else differentiated into a calyx and corolla

flower — a specialized short shoot with modified leaves adapted for reproduction by sexual means — the seed-producing structure of an angiosperm

follicle — a fruit formed by one capsule developed from a single carpel which splits along one suture (the seed-bearing one) at maturity

fruit — structure containing the seeds; a ripened ovary, together with any other structures that ripen with it and form a unit with it

galea — a helmet-shaped part of a corolla, calyx or perianth

gamopetalous corolla — corolla having the petals united, at least toward the base, so as to form a tube

glabrescent — same as subglabrous; hairy at first, later nearly glabrous

glabrous — hairless, smooth

gland — an organ that produces and secretes some substance, either sticky or fragrant, also digestive substances serving to decompose the tissues of trapped insects

glume — either of the two empty sterile bracts at the base of a grass spikelet

grain — same as caryopsis; the one-seeded indehiscent fruit of grasses in which the ovary wall remains joined with the seed. It may be enclosed by a lemma and palea or naked (without a lemma and palea, as these fall off).

gynostemium — structure formed by the fusion of the style, stigma and stamen in members of the orchid family

hair — a thread-like, one-celled or many-celled outgrowth of the epidermis which may be simple or branched

hastate leaf — leaf with halberd-shaped blade, with two usually pointed, spreading or upturned lobes at the base forming an obtuse angle

head — same as capitulum; simple racemose inflorescence with a shortened main axis and sessile or nearly sessile flowers, as in clover

herbaceous stem (caulis) — stem that withers away to the ground after each season's growth

hermaphrodite flower — bisexual flower having stamens and pistils in the same flower

heterostyly — the condition in which flowers on different plants of the same species have styles of different lengths, thereby encouraging cross-pollination

hispid — covered with long stiff hairs

holdfast roots — adventitious roots that hold a liana to a support

host — living green plant from which another parasitic or semiparasitic plant obtains nourishment

hypanthium — a ring or cup around the ovary, usually formed by the union of the lower parts of the calyx, corolla and stamens

hypocrateriform corolla — regular gamopetalous corolla, with long tube spreading abruptly to form a wide flat rim, sometimes lobed

imparipinnate leaf — same as odd-pinnate; pinnate leaf with rachis terminated by a single odd leaflet

indumentum — the hairs or glands, collectively, that cover a plant

inferior ovary — an ovary with the other floral parts (calyx, corolla and stamens) attached to its summit

inflorescence — a cluster of flowers on a common axis arranged according to a certain pattern and usually growing in the axils of bracts

involucel — an involucre of the second order; tiny bracts beneath the involucre

involucre — any structure which surrounds the base of another structure; in angiosperms the set of bracts beneath an inflorescence

keel — the two lower petals of a papilionate corolla (corolla of the pea family) usually fused by their lower edges

keeled — with a sharp ridge resembling a keel; with a prominent midrib on the dorsal side

laciniate — deeply and irregularly divided into numerous linear or lanceolate segments; fringed

lanceolate leaf — narrow and tapering like a lance, about two to four times longer than it is wide and broadest in the lower third

leaflet — a leaf-like segment of a compound leaf

leaves — flat, thin, expanded organs, usually green, growing laterally from the stem of a plant in regular arrangement; they usually consist of a broad blade, a petiole or stalk and sometimes a sheath

lemma — the outer or lower of the two bracts or scales enclosing the flower of a grass

ligule — in grasses, a membranous outgrowth at the inner junction of the leaf sheath and blade

linear leaf — narrow, a number of times longer than wide, and of uniform width for practically the whole length

lip — modified, lip-like part of a labiate corolla or calyx formed by the fusion of several petals or sepals; also in the orchid family the lowest, enlarged perianth segment

lobe — broad, rounded division of a leaf; part or segment of a deeply divided structure, e.g. lobe of a corolla, calyx, perianth

locule — a seed cavity or chamber in an ovary or fruit containing ovules or seeds respectively; cavity in a pollen sac containing the pollen grains

loculisect capsule — capsule splitting open by valves, each valve being composed of the two halves of adjoining carpels (half of one and half of the other)

loment — a dry fruit, derived from two carpels, that separates at its constrictions into one-seeded segments when ripe

lyrate leaf — lyre-shaped; simple or compound leaf with terminal lobe or leaflet much larger than the lateral lobes or leaflets which are successively smaller towards the base

main root — usually the strongest, branched root growing as the underground continuation of the stem

membranous — like a membrane; colourless, thin and often translucent

mericarp — separate segment of a schizocarpic fruit

monochasium (cincinnus) — monochasial cyme; simple cymose inflorescence with main axis forming a spiral in youth. It has two rows of flowers on the upper side and usually bracts on the underside.

monoecious plants — plants with male and female unisexual flowers on the same plant

multiple fruit — same as collective fruit; derived from a number of ovaries from several flowers grown together into one mass

nectary — a gland which produces a sweet fluid (nectar) gathered by insects; nectaries differ in nature and may be inside or outside the flower

node — the joint on the culm of grasses; the point on a stem from which a leaf starts to grow

nut — dry, indehiscent fruit with hard shell (pericarp) more or less separable from the seed

nutlet — dry fruit of the mint and borage families — any of the segments of an ovary derived from two carpels which splits into four parts

ochrea — sheathing stipule; two joined stipules, usually membranous, forming a sheath that embraces the leaf stalk

odd-pinnate — see imparipinnate

opposite leaves — leaves growing in pairs on opposite sides of a stem and on the same level

orbicular leaf — leaf with blade circular in outline

ovary — the enlarged hollow part of the pistil containing the ovules

ovate — egg-shaped; having the shape of the longitudinal section of an egg with the broader end at the base

ovule — microscopic one-celled structure in the locule of an ovary developing into a seed after fertilization

palea — the inner or upper thin membranous bract enclosing the flower in grasses

palmately compound leaf — hand-shaped leaf with a number of separate leaflets, either sessile or short-stalked, radiating from a common centre

palmatifid leaf — simple leaf palmately divided about halfway to the base

palmatilobate leaf — simple leaf palmately divided about one-third to the base

palmatipartite leaf — simple leaf palmately divided about two-thirds to the base

palmatisect leaf — simple leaf palmately divided nearly to the base

panicle — racemose inflorescence with long main axis and shorter lateral branches

papilionate corolla — butterfly-shaped corolla of plants of the pea family with a large upper petal (standard), two lateral petals (wings) and two lower petals usually fused by their lower edges (keel)

pappus — the calyx or perianth modified to form a group or tuft of hairs, bristles or scales serving in the dispersal of fruit

parasitic plants — plants without chlorophyll that obtain food from a green host plant

paripinnate leaf — same as even-pinnate; having an equal number of leaflets on either side of the central stalk which may be terminated by a tendril (not a leaflet)

pedate leaf — leaf with two thicker veins branching off from the base of the primary vein, each furnished on the outer side with a further thick vein

peduncle — the stalk of a flower or fruit, the last section of the stem bearing the flower or fruit

peloric flower − seemingly terminal, regular flower in a plant with irregular (zygomorphic) flowers

pendent − drooping, nodding

perfoliate leaf − leaf completely encircling the stem so that the stem appears to pass through the middle

perianth − the floral leaves collectively, especially when the sepals and petals are not clearly differentiated from each other and are more or less similar in shape and colour

pericarp − the tissues forming the wall of the fruit, the modified wall of the ovary enclosing the seeds; it may consist of one layer (e.g. nut), two layers (e.g. berry) or three layers (e.g. drupe)

perigynium − the fruit of sedges consisting of an achene enclosed by a joined, membranous bracteole

petiole − leaf stalk

pinnate leaf − compound leaf with leaflets arranged in two rows on each side of a common axis like the barbs of a feather (see also paripinnate and imparipinnate)

pinnate leaf with interjected leaflets − leaf in which pairs of large leaflets alternate with pairs of small leaflets on the same stem

pinnatifid leaf − simple leaf pinnately divided about halfway to the midrib

pinnatipartite leaf − simple leaf pinnately divided about two-thirds of the way to the midrib

pinnatisect leaf − simple leaf pinnately divided about three-quarters or more of the way to the midrib

pistil − the female organ of the flower of angiosperms, consisting of one or several carpels joined together in a single unit and ordinarily differentiated into ovary, style and stigma (sometimes the style is absent)

pistillate flower − female flower having pistils but no stamens

pod − a dry fruit formed by one capsule developed from a single carpel; it is usually many-seeded and splits along two sutures

pollen grain − tiny male sex cell formed in the anther of the stamen in angiosperms

pollinium − a cluster of many pollen grains, transported as a unit during pollination

polymerous leaf − palmately compound leaf consisting of many leaflets

polypetalous corolla − corolla with the petals separate from each other

pyrene − the stone of an apple, pear, or other drupe that contains several seeds

racemose inflorescence − cluster of flowers growing on equally long pedicels or branches on a common axis and not extending above the axis

rachis − main axis of an inflorescence or a compound leaf

radiate flowers − marginal flowers of a more or less flattened inflorescence their petals gradually increasing in size from the centre of the inflorescence outward (those on the outside edge being the largest)

receptacle − the enlarged or convex, sometimes fleshy, upper end of the stalk to which the flower parts are attached

regular flower − same as actinomorphic flower

reniform leaf − kidney-shaped leaf with blade wider than it is long, broadly rounded at the tip and bluntly notched at the base

rhizome − underground stem of certain perennials persisting for more than one growing season

rhombic leaf − leaf shaped like a rhombus, diamond-shaped

root − underground, leafless organ of a plant that anchors the plant and absorbs water and nourishment from the soil

rosette − an arrangement of leaves crowded at the base of a stem, often lying in a circle on the ground

rotate corolla − gamopetalous corolla shaped like a wheel with very short tube and lobes spreading at the same level

ruderal − growing in waste places

runcinate leaf − simple leaf, either pinnatifid or palmatifid, with largest lobe at the tip and the others successively smaller

sagittate leaf − simple leaf shaped like an arrowhead with two pointed lobes at the base forming an acute angle

scale − any greatly reduced, usually dry and colourless scale-like leaf or bract

scape − leafless flower stalk growing directly from ground level, from the crown of the root

scarious − dry, thin, membranous, and not green, as some bracts

seed − reproductive structure of a flowering plant formed from a fertilized ovule

semi-inferior ovary − ovary united at the base with the other parts of the flower and free at the top

serrate leaf − leaf with margin toothed like a saw, with teeth pointing forwards

sessile leaf (flower) − having no pedicel or peduncle; attached directly to the main stem

sheath − a leaf base, usually expanded, enveloping a stem

silicula − a short siliqua, approximately equal in length and width

siliqua − dry, dehiscent fruit with two valves, derived from two carpels. It is many-seeded, divided by a thin membrane, and at least four times as long as it is wide.

simple leaf − leaf with a single blade that may be entire or divided but not composed of separate leaflets

spadix − a dense spike with a thickened or fleshy axis and sessile flowers

spathe − a large, sheath-like bract enclosing a flower cluster (especially a spadix)

spatulate leaf − leaf with blade about two to four times longer than it is wide, spoon-shaped in outline and attached at the narrow end

spike − simple racemose inflorescence with sessile flowers attached directly to the main axis

spikelet − a small spike; the spikelet of grasses usually consists of two glumes and one or more florets, each enclosed by a lemma and palea

spike-like inflorescence − cluster of flowers resembling a spike, e.g. a racemose inflorescence with shortened pedicels

spur − a hollow, narrow, conical or cylindrical projection from the calyx or corolla

stamen − the male organ of a flower usually consisting of a filament, anther and connective

staminate flower − male flower having stamens but no pistils

staminode − atrophied sterile stamen without an anther

standard − the upper, largest petal in a papilionate flower

stellate − spread out in various directions at the same level; shaped like a star (said of a hair)

stem (caulon) − the main upward-growing axis of a plant above the ground (without the leaves)

sterile − not capable of producing seed; a sterile flower does not have stamens and pistils,

a sterile spikelet is a spikelet without flowers

stigma − sticky tip of the pistil which receives the pollen

stinging hair − hair with point that breaks off readily and contains a substance that causes a sharp, sudden, smarting pain

stipules − small, paired, leaf-like structures at the base of a leaf-stalk or sessile leaf-blade

style − the usually slender part of a pistil between the stigma and the ovary; sometimes absent

subtend − (of leaves, bracts) to have arising from the axil branches, flowers, etc. (e.g. a bract subtends a flower)

subulate leaf − awl-shaped; small, short, with a sharp point

superior ovary − an ovary which is attached to the receptacle above the level of attachment of the other flower parts, with perianth round its base

taxon − a taxonomic unit or category, such as a species, genus, family, etc.

tendril − a thread-like twining structure, modified from a leaf or stem, serving to support a climbing plant by clinging to or coiling around an object

testa − seed coat; the usually dry, membranous outer covering of the seed

tetradynamous stamens − stamens of the crucifer family, four of which are longer than the other two

tomentose − covered with a dense layer of short, matted, woolly hairs

tripartite leaf − simple leaf divided about two-thirds of the way to the base into three segments

tooth − small pointed lobe

tube − lower fused part of a gamopetalous corolla, gamosepalous calyx, or perianth

tuber − swollen or fleshy underground part of a stem or root

two-edged stem − flattened stem with two sharp edges

umbel − a flower cluster in which the pedicels branch from a central point and reach the same height

unisexual flower − flower bearing only stamens or only pistils

urceolate corolla − flask-like; gamopetalous corolla shaped like a vase or urn, narrowed or constricted at the end, sometimes terminating in small recurved lobes

valve − any of the segments into which the pericarp of a dehiscent fruit (pod, capsule) separates when the fruit bursts open at maturity

veins − bundles of vascular tissue forming the framework of a leaf blade

venation − arrangement or system of veins as in a leaf, leaflet, perianth, calyx or corolla; such veins collectively

versatile anther − anther turning about freely on the filament to which it is attached; it is attached not at the base but in the middle by means of a movable joint

verticillaster − same as pseudowhorl; cymose inflorescence in the axils of decussate leaves − the flowers appear to be arranged in a whorl and have very short pedicels

whorl − a circular growth of three or more leaves, branches or flowers about the same point on a stem

wings − the two lateral petals of the papilionate corolla of the pea family; or two enlarged lateral sepals

zygomorphic flower − irregular; bilaterally symmetrical, i.e. symmetrical only in one plane (as opposed to regular or actinomorphic)

Further Reading

Clapham, A.R., Tutin, T.G., Warburg, E.F. **Flora of the British Isles** Cambridge 1962

Fitter, R., Fitter, A., Blamey, M. **The Wild Flowers of Britain and Northern Europe** London 1974

Keble Martin, W. **The Concise British Flora in Colour** London 1965

Polunin, O. **The Concise Flowers of Europe** Oxford 1972

Pursey, H. **Hamlyn Nature Guides: Wild Flowers** London 1978

Tutin, T.G. et al. **Flora Europaea** London 1964−1976

Větvička, V. **Hamlyn Colour Guides: Wildflowers of Field and Woodland** London 1980

White Water-lily

Nymphaea alba

This perennial aquatic, up to 2 metres 'long', grows in still waters, oxbow lakes and ponds. The leaves floating on the surface have long petioles attached to a stout rhizome rooted in the bottom. They are large, leathery and ovate with an entire margin and prominent lobes formed by a deep, wide basal cleft.

The flower consists of four sepals and numerous petals — sometimes more than forty. There are also many stamens with yellow anthers; the filaments of the inner stamens are linear, the outer ones are wide. The stamens cover practically the whole ovary which has a yellow stigma with more than twenty lobes. The related Pure White Water-lily (*Nymphaea candida*) has stamens covering only two-thirds of the ovary and filaments of the inner stamens wider than the anthers. The stigma is markedly convex, often reddish, with less than fourteen lobes.

Both species grow in fresh water throughout most of Europe. They are protected in many European countries but are declining in number because water courses and bodies of water are being polluted by wastes and runoffs from fields. Water-lilies are very sensitive to changes in the chemical composition of their aquatic habitat, and it is necessary to protect the cleanliness of the waters where they grow.

Type of plant
dicotyledon

Diploid no.
N. alba 2n — 84
N. candida 2n — 160

Flowering period
June — July

Fruit
capsule

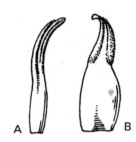

Stamens: A — inner stamens B— outer stamens

Yellow Water-lily

Nuphar lutea

The leaves of this perennial aquatic float on the surface of still or slow-flowing waterways, often forming spreading masses.

The plant, up to 2 metres long, grows from a creeping rhizome anchored by its roots in the bed of the waterway. The petioles are long and triangular, their length depending on the depth of the water. The blades are circular with an entire margin and wide basal cleft.

The flowers, which have an apple-like fragrance, are yellow and measure 4 to 6 cm in diameter. There are five yellow sepals and a great many petals and stamens; the petals are approximately one-third as long as the sepals. The ovary has a funnel-shaped, lobed stigma. The flowers are pollinated by insects. After pollination the flower-stalks contract pulling the flower below the surface, and the fruits, which are bottle-shaped follicles 3 to 4 cm long, mature under the water. Because it contains a large amount of air the fruit rises to the surface when it separates from the peduncle; there the thin cover bursts to release several crescent-shaped fleshy segments. These are dispersed by water currents and release hard, pointed, egg-shaped seeds that fall to the bottom where they develop into new plants.

This plant, like the preceding species, is also greatly endangered by the chemical changes in its habitat and is thus on the protected list in many countries.

fruit

seed

Type of plant
dicotyledon

Diploid no.
2n – 34

Flowering period
May – August

Fruit
follicle

Marsh Marigold

Caltha palustris

The Marsh Marigold, 10 to 30 cm high, grows in damp places near springs, in wet meadows, ditches and beside streams.

The ascending stems sometimes take root. The leaves are circular, heart- or kidney-shaped and are dark, glossy green, with a scalloped or even toothed margin. The basal leaves are long-stalked, the stem leaves have shorter stalks, and the uppermost leaves are sessile.

The flowers are a bright glossy yellow. They usually have five tepals, sometimes as many as 10, and a great many stamens varying in number. There are 5 to 10 pistils with superior ovaries. The young flower buds were at one time used as false 'capers'. After pollination and fertilization the pistils develop into follicles which are outspread and decurved, conspicuously crooked on the dorsal side and narrowed at the tip to form a 1.5 mm-long beak. The seeds, released when the fruit opens, are dispersed by rain or flood waters.

This plant occurs in several subspecies throughout Europe but is rare in the Mediterranean region. It is also found in Asia and North America.

The Marsh Marigold is slightly poisonous. Its ornamental double forms are often grown in the garden.

Type of plant
dicotyledon

Diploid no.
2n — 32(18—80)

Flowering period
March — June

Fruit
follicle

aggregate fruit

Globe Flower

Trollius europaeus

This perennial herb, which reaches a height of 30 to 60 cm, grows in damp and waterlogged meadows.

The stem is smooth, erect and unbranched. The dark green leaves are composed of three to five segments which are themselves divided into two or three parts. The bottom leaves have long petioles, whereas the top leaves are sessile or nearly so; they are also smaller and less divided.

The flowers, borne singly at the tips of the stems, are large, globular, up to 3 cm across, and coloured yellow. Occasionally one may come across specimens with several axillary flowers. The calyx is composed of golden-yellow segments arranged in a globe-like cluster. The corolla is composed of a variable number of yellow, linear segments shorter than the numerous yellow stamens. Pollination is carried out by insects, but sometimes the flowers are self-pollinated. The follicles are slightly crooked and about 12 mm long with a short beak at maturity. The seeds are ovoid and glossy black.

The Globe Flower is widespread throughout Europe but in the south is found only in the mountains and high ground. In some central European countries, it is a protected species.

It is noteworthy that Linné apparently described the plant according to specimens not from central Europe but from other parts. Globe Flowers growing in central Europe show a closer resemblance to the species described by Crantz as *Trollius altissimus*.

seed

follicle

aggregate fruit

Type of plant
dicotyledon

Diploid no.
2n — 16

Flowering period
May — June

Fruit
follicle

Common Baneberry

Actaea spicata

The Common Baneberry grows mostly in shady, broad-leaved woodlands, generally on limestone.

The erect stem is 30 to 60 cm high. The leaves are alternate, large and triple tripinnate.

The flowers, arranged in multiflowered racemes, are regular and hermaphroditic. The sepals, usually four or five, are white to yellowish. The petals, generally four, are white, linear and deciduous. The number of stamens is large and variable. Pollination is carried out both by insects and by the wind. The fruit is a glossy black berry about the size of a pea.

Common Baneberry is poisonous and has an unpleasant, foetid smell. It contains the saponin actein which, following the ingestion of berries from several plants, may cause hemolysis (destruction of the red corpuscles).

It is widespread in almost all Europe but in the south is found only in the mountains. *Actaea erythrocarpa* from northeastern Europe differs by having smaller berries that remain red even when ripe.

Some species from Japan, central Asia and North America are also grown as ornamental plants, chiefly as striking solitary specimens in parks and château gardens.

Type of plant
dicotyledon

Diploid no.
2n — 16

Flowering period
May — June

Fruit
berry

fruits

seed

45

Columbine

Aquilegia vulgaris

This striking and very decorative plant grows in open broad-leaved woods with humus-rich soil.

The erect, branching stem, up to 1 metre high, grows from a stout, short rhizome. The leaves at its base are long-stalked, bipinatipartite, with round or ovate leaflets. The stem leaves are short-stalked or sessile and are much smaller.

The stem bears three to ten terminal flowers. They are long-peduncled and drooping, and are up to 5 cm across. They range in colour from violet-blue to pink, and, sometimes, white. The sepals are broadly ovate, greenish at the tip and flared. The petals are prolonged into long, hooked spurs. The stamens are yellow and numerous; those in the centre are sterile. There are five pistils, each consisting of a single carpel. The fruits are follicles containing oval, glossy black seeds up to 2.5 mm long.

Columbine is a poisonous plant widespread throughout the whole of Europe, and is a protected species in many areas. It is sometimes grown for decoration in the garden. There are three other, differently coloured, species found chiefly in the Alps: *Aquilegia atrata* has brownish-purple flowers, *Aquilegia einseleana* has blue-violet flowers with nearly straight spurs, and *Aquilegia alpina* has dark-blue flowers up to 8 cm across.

seed

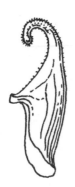

spurred petal of pendent flower

Type of plant
dicotyledon

Diploid no.
2n — 14

Flowering period
May — July

Fruit
follicle

Common Monkshood

Aconitum napellus

This perennial herb up to 150 cm high grows in woodlands and beside streams as well as in tall-grass meadows. It is found in mountains but is often washed down to lower elevations as well.

The stem is erect and smooth-skinned. The leaves are circular and are divided into from five to seven segments.

The inflorescence is branched, with four to six lateral racemes. The terminal raceme is long and dense. The calyx is dark blue-violet, smooth on the outside and ciliate on the lower edge. The upper two segments form a high-domed helmet (galea). Inside are long-stalked nectaries with a capitate spur (the nectaries are modified petals) and numerous stamens and pistils.

Monkshood is such a pretty and attractive plant that it is frequently grown in gardens and often becomes naturalized. For the same reason it is often picked and otherwise endangered by man in its natural habitat and therefore is on the list of protected species in many central European countries.

Identification of blue-flowered aconitums is extremely difficult because of their great variability. The individual characteristics are variously evaluated and so *Aconitum napellus* subspecies *hians* is sometimes designated as the species *Aconitum firmum* and at other times as *Aconitum callybotryon*. One way or the other, Monkshood is always a lovely decorative element of the mountains of central Europe.

Type of plant
dicotyledon

Diploid no.
2n — 32

Flowering period
July — August

Fruit
follicle

longitudinal section of flower

seed

Forking Larkspur

Delphinium consolida

Syn. *Consolida regalis*

This annual grows to a height of 60 cm to 1 metre, and is a weed of grain fields, chiefly in warmer regions. It also grows in meadows and pastureland.

The whole plant is glabrescent or only slightly hairy. The erect stem is branched in the upper half and covered with leaves composed of three bipartite or tripartite leaflets.

The flowers, with sepals coloured dark blue, but sometimes pink or even white, are arranged in small clusters. The upper sepal forms a spur; the petals are blue. After pollination and fertilization the flowers develop into smooth follicles.

Forking Larkspur is poisonous but was at one time used as a medicinal plant. It is found throughout most of Europe, extending north as far as southern Scandinavia, but is absent on most of the islands in the south and in the Balkans.

The related *Delphinium ajacis* is sometimes grown as an ornamental plant. It has thick, many-flowered clusters of blue flowers and follicles with a beak tapering to a point. Also cultivated as an ornamental plant is *Delphinium orientale,* coloured violet and having follicles with a short-pointed crooked beak. Cultivated varieties with red or white flowers are also grown.

fruit

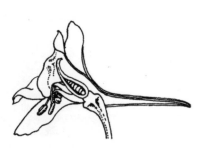

longitudinal section of flower

Type of plant
dicotyledon

Diploid no.
2n − 16

Flowering period
July − September

Fruit
follicle

Wood Anemone

Anemone nemorosa

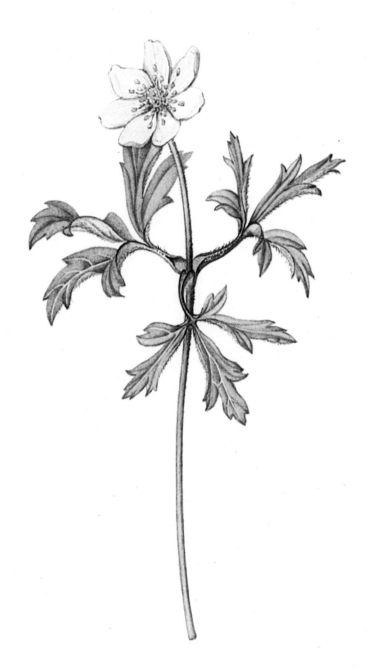

This perennial, with a herbaceous stem 10 to 25 cm high, grows in shady groves and woodlands as well as in lowland and mountain meadows.

The stem, which grows from a slender, creeping underground stem, has leaves resembling those at the plant's base. They are stalked and composed of three leaflets. The central leaflet is trilobate, the other two bilobate and short-stalked.

The flowers, 2 to 4 cm across, are long-peduncled and borne singly at the tip of the stem. The perianth is undifferentiated into a calyx and corolla and is composed of 6 to 8, but sometimes as many as 12, segments (sepals). These are glabrous and coloured white with a violet flush outside. There are a great many stamens with yellow anthers. The pistils, numbering 6 to 20, develop into hairy achenes.

This species is extremely variable and includes several described subspecies differing not only in ecology but also in the number of chromosomes, hence also the great variability in the diploid number.

The Wood Anemone is widespread throughout most of Europe but is rarely found in the Mediterranean region. It crossbreeds with the Yellow Wood Anemone *(Anemone ranunculoides)* but the hybrid offspring are sterile.

Type of plant
dicotyledon

Diploid no.
2n — 30, also 28—32, 37, 42, 45, 46

Flowering period
March — May

Fruit
achene

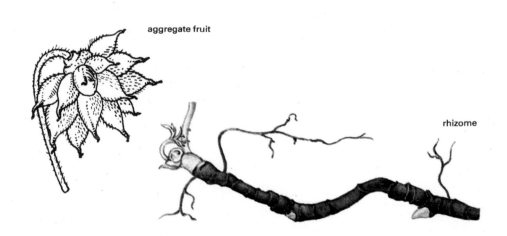

aggregate fruit

rhizome

Yellow Wood Anemone

Anemone ranunculoides

This anemone grows in broad-leaved woods as well as stands of fir, usually in masses. It is more partial to damp situations than the Wood Anemone.

The upright, hairy stem, 15 to 25 cm high, rises from a creeping, brown, scaly rhizome. The lower leaves are often absent but when present they are generally long-stalked and divided into three leaflets which are more or less sessile. The stem leaves, on the other hand, are sessile or have only short stalks.

The stem usually ends in a single flower but some plants may have two to five flowers. The perianth segments, usually five, are ovate and golden yellow with appressed hairs outside. There are a great many yellow stamens and pistils but the number varies. The fruits are 4- to 5-mm-long achenes covered with short hairs and prolonged into a short curved beak.

This poisonous species is distributed throughout most of the European mainland; it does not grow on the islands and only very occasionally in the Mediterranean region.

Plants that form small, thick cushions and have narrowly cleft leaves, smaller flowers and other different characteristics are described as subspecies *wockeana*.

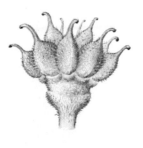

fruits

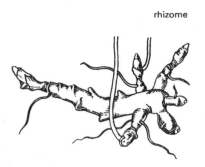

rhizome

Type of plant
dicotyledon

Diploid no.
2n – 32, 30

Flowering period
March – May

Fruit
achene

Heath Anemone

Pulsatilla patens

Syn. *Anemone patens*

This perennial, only 15 cm high when in flower, brightens sunny grassy slopes as well as stony over-grown slopes and open woodlands.

The leaves at its base do not last more than one growing season and appear only after the flowers have faded. They are long-stalked, pinnate, with leaflets that overlap at the margin. The leaves below the flower are deeply incised into linear, hairy, flared segments.

The erect herbaceous stem is likewise covered with hairs. The flowers appear singly at the tips of the stems, and consist of six broadly flared perianth segments coloured pale blue-violet. They are hairy outside and inside contain numerous yellow stamens. The outer stamens are infertile and modified into sessile nectaries sought out by insects, which at the same time gather pollen. The fruit that develops after pollination and fertilization is an achene with a 5-cm-long hairy appendage.

Originally anemones of the genus *Pulsatilla* were grouped together with those of the genus *Anemone,* which they resemble by the arrangement of the three stem leaves below the flower. However, they differ by having club-shaped nectaries and by further growth of the stem after the flowers have faded — *Pulsatilla patens* may be up to 45 cm high in the fruiting stage.

Type of plant
dicotyledon

Diploid no.
2n — 16

Flowering period
March — April

Fruit
achene

fruit

Meadow Anemone

Pulsatilla pratensis

The Meadow Anemone's flowers are a pretty sight on sunny slopes and in woodland and pine groves from lowland to hilly country.

During the flowering period, the herbaceous stem is 7 to 25 cm high but when the fruit is ripening it is nearly 50 cm high. The basal leaves appear after the flowers have faded and die down for the winter. They are long-stalked and pinnate, with deeply cleft leaflets. The leaves below the flower are deeply and irregularly divided, as in all pulsatillas, with linear, hairy segments.

The flowers of the Meadow Anemone are drooping. The bell-shaped perianth is composed of six segments which are recurved at the tip and silky-hairy outside. They are normally blackish-violet, but occasionally may be reddish-violet or even yellowish or whitish. The number of stamens and pistils is large and variable. After the flowers have been pollinated — in this case by insects which they provide with nectar as well as pollen — the peduncles straighten and the achenes thus develop and mature on an upright stem. They are hairy and furnished with an appendage up to 6 cm long.

The Meadow Anemone has two subspecies: subspecies *pratensis* with the inside of the perianth segments coloured pale-violet and greenish-white and subspecies *nigricans* with the inside of the segments coloured dark violet. All members of this genus are on the list of protected species in many central European countries.

Comparison of the distribution of the Heath Anemone *(Pulsatilla patens)* (marked yellow) and Meadow Anemone *(Pulsatilla pratensis)* (marked red)

Type of plant
dicotyledon

Diploid no.
2n — 16

Flowering period
April — May

Fruit
achene

Meadow Buttercup

Ranunculus acris

This perennial, which reaches a height of 50 cm to 1 metre, is common and widespread in meadows, fields and pastureland both in lowland country and in mountain regions.

The stem rising from a short, stout rhizome is erect, greatly branched and carries several flowers. The basal leaves are long-stalked and palmatifid with five to seven lobes. The stem leaves are similar to the basal ones, the upper leaves are sessile.

The rounded flower-peduncles carry flowers with green sepals that fall off early. The petals are golden-yellow and twice as long as the sepals, and have at the base of each petal a nectary covered by a scale. The number of stamens and pistils is large and variable. The receptacle is glabrous. After pollination and fertilization the flowers develop into flattened, ovate-orbicular achenes with a short beak.

This species is found in most of Europe and in western Siberia.

Fresh plants are poisonous because they contain cyanogenic compounds. These, however, are broken down and rendered harmless by drying and hay containing the dried plants is not harmful.

Type of plant
dicotyledon

Diploid no.
2n — 14

Flowering period
May — September

Fruit
achene

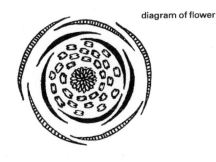

diagram of flower

aggregate fruit

Creeping Buttercup

Ranunculus repens

The Creeping Buttercup is a perennial with creeping to ascending stems 20 to 50 cm long and creeping runners that root at the nodes. It grows in moist and shady places, in meadows, woodlands and alongside streams.

The basal leaves are trifoliolate and long-stalked, the stalks of the stem leaves are successively shorter the farther up they are, and the upper leaves, which are more or less attached to the stem, are each divided into three narrow, tapering segments.

The flower-peduncles are grooved and hairy. There are five green sepals, which are also hairy and are flared and caducous. The five petals are glossy golden-yellow and have nectaries at the base covered by scales. The number of stamens and pistils is large and variable. The flowers measure 2 to 3 cm in diameter. The mature fruits, achenes, that develop on the bristly receptacle, are slightly flattened, smooth, and furnished with a short beak.

Like all other buttercups, this one is also poisonous. It is found throughout all of Europe except for Crete and the Balearic Islands, and has also been introduced to places where it was previously unknown, for instance the Azores, Spitzbergen and North America. In north Africa, where it is also found, it apparently belongs to the native flora.

fruit

Type of plant
dicotyledon

Diploid no.
2n — 32

Flowering period
May — August

Fruit
achene

Lesser Spearwort

Ranunculus flammula

Lesser Spearwort is relatively abundant in damp meadows, near springs and in most ditches in both lowland country and mountains.

The 15- to 40-cm-long, smooth stem rises from a short, underground stem. It often lies flat along the ground and forms roots. The leaves at the base of the plant may be oval or heart-shaped and are long-stalked; the stem leaves are directly attached to the stem and are narrow and tapering.

The flowers are small and have striated peduncles. The spreading green sepals are smooth and caducous. The golden-yellow petals are ovate. The number of stamens and pistils is large and variable. Following pollination the pistils develop into ovate, short-beaked achenes arranged in a globe-like cluster on the smooth receptacle.

Lesser Spearwort is distributed throughout most of Europe but only sparsely around the Mediterranean. It is an extremely variable species embracing three subspecies that differ in the position of the stem and shape of the leaves. Subspecies *flammula* is the most common, subspecies *minimus* grows in western Scotland and Ireland, and subspecies *scoticus* is endemic to northern Scotland.

Type of plant
dicotyledon

Diploid no.
2n — 32

Flowering period
June — October

Fruit
achene

fruit

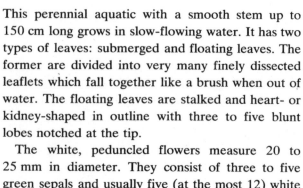

Water Crowfoot

Ranunculus aquatilis

Syn. *Batrachium aquatile*

This perennial aquatic with a smooth stem up to 150 cm long grows in slow-flowing water. It has two types of leaves: submerged and floating leaves. The former are divided into very many finely dissected leaflets which fall together like a brush when out of water. The floating leaves are stalked and heart- or kidney-shaped in outline with three to five blunt lobes notched at the tip.

The white, peduncled flowers measure 20 to 25 mm in diameter. They consist of three to five green sepals and usually five (at the most 12) white ovoid petals with a nectary at the base. The stamens are numerous and longer than the pistils. The achenes are wrinkled transversely, short-beaked, and may be either smooth or hairy.

Ranunculus aquatilis is distributed throughout all Europe.

Found in central Europe are other related species, e.g. *Ranunculus baudotii* with yellow blotch at the base of the petals and *Ranunculus tripartitus* with pure white petals distinguished from *Ranunculus aquatilis* by having less than 10 stamens.

petal with nectary

Type of plant
dicotyledon

Diploid no.
2n – 48

Flowering period
July – September

Fruit
achene

Lesser Celandine

Ranunculus ficaria

Syn. *Ficaria verna*

This perennial herb, 5 to 20 cm high, may be seen in spring in open woodlands, on the outskirts of forests, in thickets and beside streams.

The bottom leaves rise from club-shaped tubers. They are glossy, fleshy, and may be heart- or kidney-shaped in outline with the entire margin of the leaves irregularly notched or toothed. The stem leaves are similar but with shorter stalks. The subspecies *bulbifer* has tiny bulbils in the axils of the lower leaves whereby the plant multiplies by vegetative means. The ascending stem is branched and often roots along its length.

The flowers are hermaphroditic. They are usually composed of three yellow-green sepals that fall off early and 6 to 13 glossy, golden-yellow petals. At the base of each petal there is a nectarial hollow covered by a scale. The number of stamens and pistils is very variable. The fruit is an achene; in the subspecies *bulbifer,* however, it is generally absent.

Native to central Europe is the subspecies *bulbifer* and also the subspecies *calthifolia,* which thrives in a warmer climate and has erect, unbranched stems that do not root. The subspecies *ficaria* is apparently found only in Great Britain and western Europe.

Type of plant
dicotyledon

Diploid no.
2n — 16, 32

Flowering period
March — May

Fruit
achene

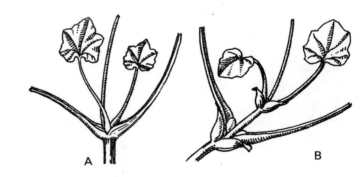

A — subsp. *calthifolia* (without bulbils)   B — subsp. *bulbifer* (with bulbils in leaf axils)

Noble Liverleaf

Hepatica nobilis

Syn. *Anemone hepatica*

This is one of the first spring-flowering herbs to be seen scattered here and there in broad-leaved groves and woodlands as well as at the edge of coniferous forests.

From the creeping rhizome rises a 5- to 15-cm-high stem covered with spreading hairs and bearing a single flower followed by long-stalked, three-lobed leaves with a heart-shaped base. The colour of the leaves is in great measure indicative of the type of soil in which the plant grows: plants growing in humus-rich soils have deep green leaves whereas those growing in mineral-deficient soils have yellow-green leaves. The stem leaves are small and arranged in a whorl of three immediately below the flower so that they resemble a calyx.

The regular, hermaphroditic flowers appear at the top of the stem. The perianth is not differentiated into a calyx and corolla; instead, it is composed of 4 to 10 segments normally coloured dark or pale violet, but occasionally pink or almost white. The flowers are pollinated by insects, though they may also be self-pollinated.

A characteristic feature is the beak on the achenes which contain oily substances fed on by ants, thereby aiding in its dispersal.

Noble Liverleaf, which is slightly poisonous, is widespread throughout most of Europe.

aggregate fruit

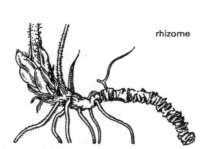

rhizome

Type of plant
dicotyledon

Diploid no.
2n — 14

Flowering period
February — May

Fruit
achene

Spring Pheasant's Eye

Adonis vernalis

Syn. *Adonanthe vernalis*

This perennial herb reaches a height of 10 to 60 cm. It grows on limestone, sometimes also on sandy substrates, on sunny slopes, and in forest-steppe.

The top parts rise from a thick cylindrical rhizome. The leaves are 2- to 4-pinnate and thread-like. The striking golden-yellow flowers measure 3 to 7 cm in diameter. The calyx is composed of five softly-hairy sepals pressed tightly to the corolla, which consists of 10 to 20 petals. There are numerous stamens and pistils as well. The flowers are without fragrance and without nectar but insects are attracted by the large amounts of pollen, thereby serving as agents of pollination. Of interest is the fact that they open before 9 a.m. and follow the movement of the sun across the heavens until 5 p.m. when they close again. When it starts raining the flowers close to form a roof so the water runs off and does not penetrate inside. The achenes are distributed mainly by ants.

Spring Pheasant's Eye contains poisonous glycosides which have medicinal value and is thus cultivated for pharmaceutical purposes.

It is found in central, southeastern and eastern Europe, in the Cévennes in France and in northeastern Spain. The two Swedish islands Öland and Gotland in the Baltic mark the northernmost limit of its range. It is rigidly protected in many countries.

Type of plant
dicotyledon

Diploid no.
2n — 16

Flowering period
April — May

Fruit
achene

aggregate fruit

achene

59

Summer Pheasant's Eye

Adonis aestivalis

This annual herb is a common weed of fields in warm regions from lowland to hilly country. It is partial to lime-rich soils.

The erect, little-branched stem reaches a height of 20 to 50 cm. The lower leaves are short-stalked whereas the upper leaves are sessile and three- to four-pinnate and threadlike.

The flowers are erect and have red petals, often with a black blotch at the base. The smooth sepals are pressed tightly to the corolla. There are a great many dark violet stamens. The fruits are achenes which develop on the conical receptacle after pollination and fertilization.

This species is distributed throughout most of Europe but is not found in the north of the region.

Often grown for garden decoration in central Europe is the related *Adonis annua,* native to southern Europe and distinguished by smooth, flaring sepals that fall off early. The large petals are dark red and also have a conspicuous black blotch at the base. They are arranged in a semi-globe-shaped cluster.

Type of plant
dicotyledon

Diploid no.
2n — 32

Flowering period
May — July

Fruit
achene

seed

Green Hellebore

Helleborus viridis

This perennial, which reaches a height of 15 to 40 cm, grows in open woods, as it is partial to lime-rich soils.

The erect stem is only slightly branched and is leafless. The lower part is often spotted red and is usually smooth; only below the point where it branches is the stem sometimes hairy. The lowest leaves do not last the winter; they are pedate with long stalks and blades. The upper side is a lighter colour, more or less hairy, and has prominent veins. The stem leaves have sheaths at the base.

The flowers are long-peduncled and drooping. The green calyx is composed of broadly-ovate sepals, the corolla of 8 to 12 yellow-green cup-shaped petals with nectaries at the base. The number of stamens is large and variable as in the other members of the buttercup family. The pistils, from 3 to 5, are fused at the base. The fruit is a many-seeded, beaked follicle that opens along a single suture.

Green Hellebore is found chiefly in western and central Europe, and is grown in many gardens in central Europe, where it is one of the first flowers to bloom in early spring.

Type of plant
dicotyledon

Diploid no.
2n — 32

Flowering period
March — April

Fruit
follicle

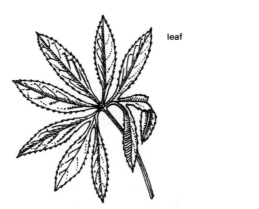

leaf

nectary

Asarabacca

Asarum europaeum

This inconspicuous plant, only 5 to 10 cm in height, grows in the layer of decaying leaves in woods and thickets from lowland to high ground.

It has a slender, branched rhizome from which rises an ascending, hairy stem with two to four, nearly opposite, long-stalked leaves that last the winter. The leathery, glossy green blades are orbicular in outline with a deeply-cut heart-shaped base; the underside is a lighter green.

The flowers are solitary, short-peduncled, slightly drooping and have a peppery scent. They are small and pressed close to the ground so they easily escape notice. The perianth is pitcher- or bell-shaped with three lobes, greenish-brown outside and dark purplish-violet inside. There are 12 stamens. The ovary is inferior and terminated by a six-lobed stigma. Asarabacca is self-pollinated.

This poisonous plant was formerly used as a home remedy to provoke vomiting.

Asarabacca is distributed from southern Scandinavia to southern France, central Italy and Macedonia.

European populations are divided into four varieties according to the substances they contain. Recently it was discovered that Asarabacca may also be divided into four morphologically different groups. Only further research can tell us if there is any link between the botanically and the phytochemically differentiated taxons.

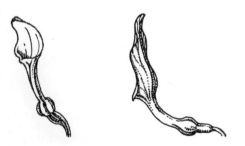

flowers of the related *Aristolochia clematitis* − different views

Type of plant
dicotyledon

Diploid no.
2n − 26

Flowering period
March − May

Fruit
capsule

Field Poppy

Papaver rhoeas

This plant is a weed of fields and wasteland from lowland to hilly country.

It is an annual reaching a height of 15 to 30 cm. The lower leaves are stalked, the upper leaves sessile and bristly. They are elliptic in outline, pinnate and with sharply-toothed segments. The stem is erect and covered with spreading bristles; white milk oozes from the stem when bruised.

The flowers are solitary, with long axillary peduncles covered with spreading bristles. The green calyx, composed of two sepals, is also bristly and falls off very early. The four red petals are rounded with an almost entire margin and sometimes a black blotch at the base. The stamens are black and numerous. The pistil is rounded at the base and the stigma is generally ten-lobed. The fruit is a capsule that is obovate, 1 to 2 cm long, and smooth.

Like other poppies the Field Poppy contains morphinic alkaloids though far less than the Opium Poppy which is an important drug plant used by the modern pharmaceutical industry.

Type of plant
dicotyledon

Diploid no.
2n — 14

Flowering period
May — September

Fruit
capsule

seed

fruit

Greater Celandine

Chelidonium majus

This undemanding perennial grows in wasteland, thickets and locust groves.

The erect, branched stem which reaches a height of 30 to 50 cm, is rounded, covered with scattered hairs and oozes orange latex when bruised. The lower leaves are stalked whereas the upper ones are sessile. The leaves are almost pinnate, with five to seven leaflets.

The yellow flowers are up to 2 cm across. The calyx is composed of two yellow sepals that soon fall, as do the four petals. The stamens are yellow and numerous with filaments swollen below the anthers. The prolonged linear pistil is composed of two carpels. The fruit is a linear capsule up to 5 cm long greatly resembling a siliqua. The seeds are black, egg- or kidney-shaped, and up to 15 mm long.

This species is very variable, mainly in the shape and division of the leaves. More than twenty intraspecific taxons have been described.

Greater Celandine is slightly poisonous and is often used as a home remedy for removing warts. It is widespread throughout Europe but is not indigenous in the north.

cross-section of stem with oozing orange milk

seed

Type of plant
dicotyledon

Diploid no.
2n – 12

Flowering period
May – October

Fruit
capsule

Bulbous Fumewort

Corydalis cava

Syn. *Corydalis bulbosa*

This perennial brightens woodlands with its flowers in early spring. Concealed from view underground is a hollow, brown tuber about the size of a walnut.

The stout, erect stem, 10 to 30 cm high, carries two leaves both of which are stalked, broadly triangular in outline, twice trifoliolate and coloured greyish-green.

The stem ends in flowers arranged in a dense, upright raceme. They grow from the axils of ovate, entire bracts and are coloured blue, dingy pink or yellowish white. The calyx, composed of two sepals, falls off early or is entirely absent. Of the four petals the two inner ones are prolonged, the two outer ones form an upper and lower lip. The upper lip is prolonged into a long recurved spur containing nectar which attracts insects. There are only two stamens. The ovary is superior and develops into a capsule with numerous glossy, round seeds furnished with an appendage.

The Bulbous Fumewort, which is poisonous, is distributed throughout most of the European continent excepting the northern parts and most of the Mediterranean region.

The related Solid-rooted Fumewort *(Corydalis solida),* which looks very similar at first glance, differs by having palmately-divided bracts beneath the flowers and a solid underground tuber.

Type of plant
dicotyledon

Diploid no.
2n — 16

Flowering period
March — May

Fruit
capsule

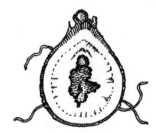

longitudinal section of tuber

Charlock or Wild Mustard
Sinapis arvensis

This annual plant, reaching a height of 20 to 60 cm, is often found growing in fields and wasteland.

The vivid green stem usually carries undivided leaves. Those at the bottom are sometimes lyrate pinnatifid, whereas the stem leaves are ovate or elliptic and irregularly toothed.

The flowers, with their four bright-yellow petals, are eye-catching. The yellow-green sepals are expanded. The fruit is a siliqua, which may be humpy or constricted and opens by valves when ripe. It is furnished with a short beak. The seeds are dark red and smooth, becoming mucilaginous when moistened.

Charlock is probably native to the Mediterranean region but is found throughout most of Europe. It is a very troublesome weed because the seeds retain their viability for up to 50 years. However, only those seeds that are near the surface germinate. Those deeper in the ground have to wait, sometimes for several years, before they are brought up by ploughing.

Wild Radish *(Raphanus raphanistrum)* is a similar species. However it differs by having a bluish stem and sepals pressed tightly to the corolla, also the four yellow petals are generally patterned with violet veins. The fruit of Wild Radish is a loment, a dry schizocarpic fruit that separates into as many as eight segments when ripe.

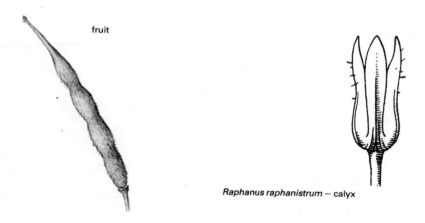

fruit

Raphanus raphanistrum — calyx

Type of plant
dicotyledon

Diploid no.
2n – 18

Flowering period
June – October

Fruit
siliqua

Hoary Cress

Cardaria draba

Syn. *Lepidium draba*

This 20- to 40-cm-high perennial herb grows in wasteland, fallow land and loamy-sandy soils where it often forms spreading masses.

The basal leaves are stalked and elliptic with a lobed margin. The stem leaves are shallowly-toothed and sessile. The whole plant is covered with grey down.

The flowers are small, fragrant and numerous. The calyx is open, the petals twice as long as the sepals and coloured white; there are six stamens. The fruits that develop after pollination and fertilization are wingless, slightly flattened siliculas faintly heart-shaped in outline. They have two locules, each containing one or two smooth brown seeds.

Hoary Cress is probably native to southern Europe or central Asia but is now a common weed in all of Europe.

It was formerly classed in the genus *Lepidium* but its flowers are arranged in dense corymbose panicles and it has a heart-shaped indehiscent silicula with a long persistent style whereas members of the genus *Lepidium* have the flowers arranged in terminal racemes and siliculas that open by two valves and generally have a shorter persistent style.

Type of plant
dicotyledon

Diploid no.
2n – 64

Flowering period
May – July

Fruit
silicula

fruit

Shepherd's Purse

Capsella bursa-pastoris

This common weed of wasteland, wayside ditches and fields as well as parks and gardens, grows to a height of 5 to 50 cm.

It is either an annual or biennial, anchored in the ground by a tap root that later becomes slightly woody and from which rise one or more upright stems. The basal leaves are arranged in a rosette and are stalked and runcinate pinnatisect. The stem leaves are arrow-shaped with wavy toothed edges.

The small flowers are arranged in thick racemes that later become lengthened. They are composed of four ovate sepals and four obovate petals with short claws. The latter are coloured white and measure 2 to 3 mm in length. The fruits are triangular, obovate siliculas 6 to 9 mm long. The seeds are three-sided, heart-shaped and flattened, almost smooth, and coloured light brown. A single plant may produce as many as 75,000.

This species is widespread throughout Europe. Distinguished from it is the species *Capsela heegeri* with its greatly-branched stem and rounded, unflattened siliculas which formerly grew in western Germany (Pfalz) and may still be found in Moravia.

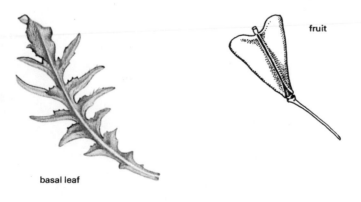

fruit

basal leaf

Type of plant
dicotyledon

Diploid no.
2n — 32

Flowering period
March — November

Fruit
silicula

Field Pennycress

Thlaspi arvense

This annual is a common and widespread weed growing in fields and wasteland from lowland to mountain elevations. It reaches a height of 30 to 40 cm. The lower leaves are stalked and spatulate. The stem is smooth, angled and striated. The stem leaves are coarsely toothed, arrow-shaped at the base and clasping the stem (they are without stalks).

The sepals are yellow-green, the petals, which are twice as long as the sepals, are whitish. The siliculas are 10 to 15 cm long, flat and have a wide rim. They resemble a coin, which explains their common name in English and certain other languages. Each locule contains five to seven wrinkled seeds coloured blackish-brown to grey-brown. The seed coat does not become mucilaginous when moistened.

The plant has a marked pungent flavour but is not poisonous.

This species is found in practically the whole of Europe but is less common in the northern parts and absent in most of the Mediterranean region.

The related *Thlaspi alliaceum* has stems that are hairy near the base, obcordate leaves and garlic-like fragrance. It is found in southern and central Europe, its range extending north as far as Salzburg and south to Bavaria.

Type of plant
dicotyledon

Diploid no.
2n — 14

Flowering period
May — October

Fruit
silicula

diagram of flower

fruit

Golden Alison

Alyssum saxatile

Syn. *Aurinia saxatilis*

This perennial is found only in the warmest parts of Europe on silicic substrates. It is anchored in rock crevices by a persistent rhizome from which grows a rosette of basal leaves and a branched stem 10 to 30 cm high. The basal leaves are narrowly-lanceolate, entire and grey-felted with stellate hairs.

The inflorescence is corymbosely branched and composed of tiny, bright-yellow flowers arranged in short, dense racemes. The calyx falls soon after the flowers are spent. The four petals are up to 5 mm long, short-clawed, shallowly lobed and glabrous. There is a nectary on either side of each stamen. The flowers are pollinated by insects. The siliculas are elliptical and hairless at first with two narrowly-winged seeds in each locule.

This species is divided into the following three subspecies according to the shape and size of the silicula and length of the stigma: the type subspecies *saxatile* with siliculas usually longer than wide which is found in central Europe and the northern Balkans, subspecies *megalocarpum* with siliculas measuring more than 1 cm in diameter and stigma up to 3 mm long, and subspecies *orientale* with nearly oval siliculas measuring 5 to 8 mm in diameter and stigma only 1 mm long. The latter two are distributed from the Balkans to Asia Minor.

Golden Alison is sometimes grown in the rock garden or in dry walls in parks and gardens. It is very pretty with its golden-yellow flowers making bright splashes of colour against the dark rocks.

fruit

diagram of the inflorescence

Type of plant
dicotyledon

Diploid no.
2n — 16

Flowering period
April — May

Fruit
silicula

Lady's Smock

Cardamine pratensis

Lady's Smock, a 20- to 40-cm-high perennial, is widespread in damp meadows from lowland to mountain elevations.

It has a creeping rhizome and an erect, unbranched stem that is hairless. The basal leaves are long-stalked, odd-pinnate and arranged in a rosette. The terminal leaflet is the largest and is usually divided into three lobes. The leaves have five times more Vitamin C than a lemon!

The inflorescence is a terminal raceme composed of 7 to 20 flowers. The four sepals are yellow-green with violet tip and whitish margin. The faintly violet-tinged petals with conspicuous violet veins are also four in number. The flowers are rich in nectar. The six stamens have yellow anthers. During fruition the ovary develops into a siliqua up to 4 cm long.

This extremely variable species is usually divided into as many as six minor species: *Cardamine crassifolia* — native to the Pyrenees; *Cardamine nymani* — found in northern Europe, *Cardamine matthiolii* — growing in central Europe and the northern Balkans; *Cardamine palustris* and *Cardamine rivularis* — found in northwestern and central Europe.

The separate minor species differ in the shape of the leaves and leaflets, the position and branching of the stem, the number and size of the leaflets, and the coloration of the corolla.

Type of plant
dicotyledon

Diploid no.
2n — 28—34, 38—44, 48

Flowering period
April — June

Fruit
siliqua

fruit

basal leaf

Garlic Mustard or **Hedge Garlic**

Alliaria petiolata

This biennial or perennial plant reaches a height of 30 cm to 1 metre, and is found in hedgerows, the outskirts of woodland, and in shady gardens.

The erect, usually unbranched stem is generally smooth or covered with spreading hairs at the bottom so that it appears to be covered in hoar frost. The leaves are stiff and glabrous; the lower ones are kidney-shaped and long-stalked, the stem leaves are short-stalked and triangular-ovate with a heart-shaped base.

The small flowers are coloured white, and their petals are 5 to 6 mm long with a short claw. The ripe fruits – siliquas – are either erect or inclined. The seeds are arranged in a single row inside the locules.

Garlic Mustard is distributed throughout all Europe, although it is less common in the south, in the mountains of north Africa and in the temperate regions of Asia. In general it has no special requirements and grows even on shaded walls, in river meadows and shaded overgrown screes. The other four species of *Alliaria* have more demanding site-requirements and are found only in Asia.

Alliaria has an apt generic name for *Allium* is the generic name for garlic and the leaves of Garlic Mustard smell of garlic when bruised. That is why it was formerly used as a medicinal plant in the same way as garlic.

seed

Type of plant
dicotyledon

Diploid no.
2n – 36, 42

Flowering period
April – June

Fruit
siliqua

Ragged Robin

Lychnis flos-cuculi

This 20- to 60-cm-high herb with its smooth, upright stem is common in meadows from lowland to high ground.

The stem, rising from a rosette of leaves on the ground, is slightly angular, sparsely covered with leaves, sticky beneath the nodes and branching bifurcatedly at the top. It is often reddish. The lower leaves are long and tongue-shaped, pointed at the tip and narrowing at the base into a long stalk. The stem leaves are lance-shaped.

The individual flowers, clustered in a loose dichasium, are 2 to 4 cm in diameter and grow from the axils of membranous bracts. The calyx is a tubular bell shape with five distinct teeth. The rosy-red petals (very occasionally they are white) and the corona are deeply cleft into linear segments. The mature capsule is broadly ovoid. This species is distributed throughout most of Europe.

Often grown for decoration is the Rose Campion *(Lychnis coronaria)* with purple, undivided petals and white silky-woolly leaves. It is indigenous in southern Europe and has become naturalized in many parts of western and central Europe.

Lychnis flos-jovis, native to the Alps at elevations of more than 1,000 metres, is a lovely white-felted plant with bilobed petals which has become naturalized in parts of central Europe.

Type of plant
dicotyledon

Diploid no.
2n — 24

Flowering period
May — July

Fruit
capsule

petal with deeply cleft corona

fruit

Red German Catchfly

Lychnis viscaria
Syn. *Viscaria vulgaris, Viscaria viscosa,*
    Steris viscaria

Grassland, sandy soils, screes and sunny slopes are the habitats of this 30- to 60-cm-high perennial.

It forms a ground rosette of leaves from which rises a smooth, reddish, upright stem with sticky zones beneath each pair of upper leaves. The stem leaves are opposite, glabrous, ciliate at the base, with pointed tips and entire margins. The basal leaves are inversely lanceolate narrowing into a long stalk, whereas the stem leaves are sessile and lanceolate.

The inflorescence is a dichasium usually composed of three flowers. These are divided into five parts, short-peduncled and subtended by reddish, ciliate bracts. The calyx is tubular-funnel-shaped, about 10 mm long and glabrous. The petals are large and coloured red, though they may sometimes be white. They are obovate and faintly bilobed; the corona is bidentate. The peduncled capsules are ovoid and open by five teeth.

This species is widespread throughout most of the European continent but is only sparsely distributed in southwestern Europe.

The similar Alpine Catchfly (*Lychnis alpina*) has a short stem that is not sticky, an inflorescence composed of as many as 20 flowers and calyx only about 5 mm long. It grows in the Alps, the Pyrenees and perhaps also in one locality in the Apennines.

seed

Type of plant
dicotyledon

Diploid no.
2n − 24

Flowering period
May − July

Fruit
capsule

White Campion

Silene alba

Syn. *Lychnis alba, Melandrium album*

This annual to perennial herb, 40 cm to 1 metre high, is found chiefly in wasteland by the wayside and at the edges of thickets.

The erect stems are softly hairy at the bottom, glandular and branched at the top. The bottom leaves are obovate and stalked, the others are lanceolate to ovate-lanceolate with long tapering points and are sessile.

The inflorescence is a dichasium composed of short-peduncled, pendent flowers. Unlike the related Red Campion *(Silene dioica)* which has flowers that remain open the whole day, the flowers of this species do not open until the afternoon. White Campion is a dioecious plant. Both the male and female flowers have a calyx composed of five fused sepals and five separate white petals. The corona is usually bidentate. The male flowers have ten stamens, the female flowers a single pistil composed of five united carpels. The fruit is a broadly-ovoid capsule enclosed by the persistent calyx.

White Campion is a common and widespread species distributed throughout Europe.

The similar *Silene glutinosa* from the Iberian Peninsula has very sticky stems, as its name indicates. The flowers open in the daytime as do those of *Silene dioica*.

Type of plant
dicotyledon

Diploid no.
2n — 24

Flowering period
June — September

Fruit
capsule

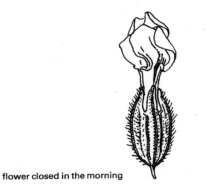

flower closed in the morning

fruit

Red Campion

Silene dioica
Syn. *Melandrium rubrum, Melandrium dioicum, Melandrium sylvestre*

This robust, 40- to 80-cm-high perennial grows in mountain meadows, at the edges of thickets and on the outskirts of forests.

It is anchored in the ground by a rhizome from which rise erect stems covered with soft hairs but without glands. The leaves are dark green with short hairs; the bottom leaves are stalked, ovate and pointed, while the others are sessile.

The red flowers are arranged in dichasiums. They are short-peduncled and open the whole day. The five-toothed calyx is greenish-red with long hairs or wool. The calyx of the female flowers is inflated with twenty pronounced ribs whereas the calyx of the male flowers is longish-cylindrical with ten ribs. The five, separate, red petals are obovate in outline and bifid; the corona has four teeth. The capsule contains seeds arranged on a central columella as in all members of the Caryophyllaceae family.

This species is distributed throughout most of Europe but not the east; however, it is rare in the south.

Plants from different mountain regions often differ in appearance. For example, plants growing in exposed situations, such as on rocks, may even form creeping specimens.

Red Campion often interbreeds with White Campion and hybrids with light rose or rose-tinted flowers are fully fertile.

fruit

petal with small toothed corona

Type of plant
dicotyledon

Diploid no.
2n — 24

Flowering period
May — September

Fruit
capsule

Bladder Campion

Silene vulgaris

Syn. *Silene inflata, Silene cucubalus*

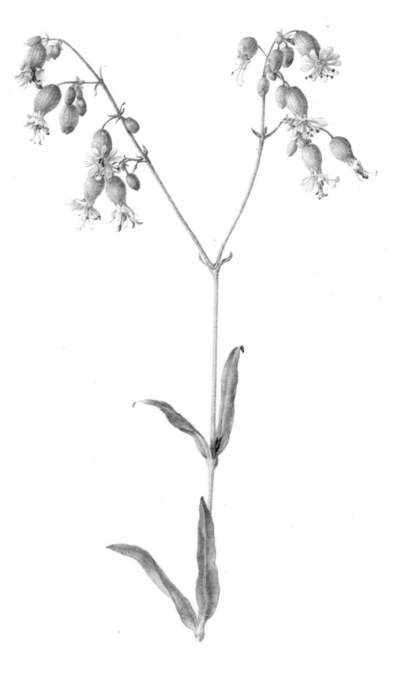

Bladder Campion, 10 to 50 cm high, grows in grassland, pastureland, wasteland and screes.

The basal leaves form a ground rosette from which rises an erect or ascending stem. The leaves are lance-shaped or elliptic, entire, up to 6 cm long, and covered with a white bloom or greyish-green. The bottom leaves are short-stalked, the upper stem leaves are sessile.

The inflorescence is a many-flowered dichasium. The bottom flowers are long-peduncled, the upper ones have short peduncles. The calyx is inflated with 20 distinct ribs, up to 15 mm long, and coloured yellowish-white or pinkish. The corolla is white but may also be tinted pink and usually without a corona; the petals are bilobed. After pollination and fertilization the ovary develops into a broadly ovoid capsule enveloped by the calyx.

Bladder Campion is widespread throughout all Europe, and is morphologically very variable. Plants growing on the Atlantic coast have an ascending, greatly branched stem whose branches generally end in a single flower. They are classified as subspecies *maritima*. Plants with prostrate stems and two- to four-flowered dichasiums are classified as subspecies *prostrata;* they are found in the Alps and Carpathians, usually on limestone substrates.

Type of plant
dicotyledon

Diploid no.
2n — 24

Flowering period
June — September

Fruit
capsule

diagram of flower

unripe fruit

German Pink

Dianthus carthusianorum

Syn. *Dianthus sanguineus*

The blossoms of this perennial, 15- to 60-cm-high plant brighten sunny slopes and grassland from the lowlands to the foothills.

It is a thickly tufted herb with smooth, erect and practically unbranched stems growing from a rhizome. They are of two kinds: short, non-flowering stems and longer, flowering stems. The leaves are opposite, linear, pointed at the tip and joined to form a sheath at the base.

The almost sessile flowers are clustered in heads (capitula). The leathery bracts below the calyx have a long, awn-like point; they are coloured light or dark brown. The calyx is cylindrical, up to 18 mm long and five-toothed. The petals have claws, are toothed at the tip and coloured red. The related Maiden Pink (*Dianthus deltoides*) differs by having distinctive markings on the petals. The 10 stamens have dark violet anthers. The flowers are pollinated by insects.

The German Pink is distributed throughout most of Europe. It is a variable species: tall, robust plants with greater profusion of dark purple flowers and 3- to 5-mm-wide leaves are described as subspecies *latifolius*. These grow in the Alps and Carpathians, usually on limestone. Low plants from the Alps that avoid limestone are designated as subspecies *vaginatus;* these have leaves that measure only 2 to 3 mm in width.

flower of *Dianthus deltoides*

seed

Type of plant
dicotyledon

Diploid no.
2n — 30

Flowering period
May — August

Fruit
capsule

Fringed Pink

Dianthus superbus

The Fringed Pink, 30 to 60 cm high, may be encountered in mountain meadows as well as in groves at lower elevations in humus-rich soil.

It has a woody underground rhizome and smooth, rounded stems which are upright and branched at the top. The leaves are opposite, narrowly-lanceolate and rough on the margin. The basal leaves have blunt tips, the stem leaves are pointed at the tip.

The flowers are very fragrant, up to 4 cm across, and arranged in dichasiums composed of as many as twelve blossoms. The calyx is narrowly-cylindrical and tinted violet. The pinkish petals narrow at the base into a white claw and are deeply incised — only the middle section is elongate and undivided. The fruit is a capsule.

This continental-Mediterranean species is found in practically all of Europe except for the extreme west and extreme south. It is usually divided into three subspecies differing in the length, shape and colour of the petals as well as in the habit of growth. Subspecies *superbus* is a grass-green herb of lower elevations. Subspecies *alpestris* is a taller, robust plant of mountain regions. Subspecies *autumnalis* grows in open groves and woodlands and flowers about a month later than the typical subspecies.

Type of plant
dicotyledon

Diploid no.
2n — 30

Flowering period
June — August

Fruit
capsule

fruit (with persistent calyx and bracts)

Soapwort

Saponaria officinalis

This 30- to 80-cm-high, robust perennial herb grows in wasteland, by roadsides and beside waterways.

It has a creeping rhizome and smooth, upright, rounded stems, usually branched in the upper part. The leaves are opposite, elliptic, pointed, three-veined and rough on the margin.

The short-peduncled flowers, 2 to 3 cm across, are arranged in dense dichasiums. Beneath each flower are two lance-shaped bracts. The calyx is cylindrical, up to 25 mm long, coloured green or reddish, and hairy. The five petals are pale pink to white, up to 40 mm long, shallowly notched at the tip and with a long claw at the base. The longish, cylindrical ovary develops into a capsule containing numerous, conically reniform seeds.

This slightly poisonous plant was formerly grown not only for decoration but also as a medicinal herb. It derives its name from the fact that when rubbed between the fingers and moistened it truly becomes soapy because of the saponins it contains, which are foamy as well as poisonous.

Saponaria officinalis is distributed in Europe from Belgium, northern Germany and the central part of the European USSR southward.

The related Rock Soapwort (*Saponaria ocymoides*) is a mountain plant of southwestern Europe with a low, prostrate stem and pretty red flowers. It is often grown for garden decoration.

flower

Type of plant
dicotyledon

Diploid no.
2n – 28

Flowering period
June – September

Fruit
capsule

Lesser Stitchwort

Stellaria graminea

Lesser Stitchwort, which is 10 to 30 cm high, is found in meadows, grassland and by waysides.

The stems are prostrate at the base, 4-angled and smooth.

The leaves are lance-shaped or linear, pointed at the tip and ciliate at the base but otherwise smooth and coloured grass-green.

The inflorescence is a very scanty, spreading dichasial cyme. The bracts are ciliate on both sides. The flowers measure up to 11 mm in diameter. The sepals are lance-shaped, smooth and marked with three distinct ribs. The white petals are as long as the sepals but are blunt at the tip. Whereas the sepals and petals number five each, the number of styles is only three. The capsule is narrowly-elongate, and is longer than the calyx. The seeds have a grainy surface.

This species is widespread throughout all of Europe and is slightly poisonous.

The similar Marsh Stitchwort (*Stellaria palustris*), which grows chiefly in peat meadows and marshy places, has smooth, grey-green leaves, bracts with unfringed margin, and erect stems. It is interesting to note that all members of this species are perfectly hermaphroditic. Some specimens have partly or completely atrophied sterile anthers. The flowers of such plants are distinctly smaller than hermaphroditic flowers of the same population.

Type of plant
dicotyledon

Diploid no.
2n — 52

Flowering period
May — July

Fruit
capsule

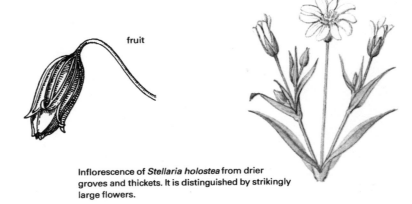

fruit

Inflorescence of *Stellaria holostea* from drier groves and thickets. It is distinguished by strikingly large flowers.

Field Mouse-ear

Cerastium arvense

This 5- to 30-cm-high, sparsely tufted perennial herb grows in sandy soils on sunny slopes and at the edges of woods.

The numerous semi-creeping or ascending stems, which often root in the ground, are covered with narrowly-elliptic or linear-lanceolate short and hairy leaves which are longish-ciliate at the base. Growing from the axils of the leaves are sterile leafy shoots. The uppermost pair of leaves is distant.

The inflorescence is a dichasium composed of 5 to 15 5-merous flowers. The ovate bracts are blunt and generally have a wide membranous margin. The flower peduncles spread apart and outward when the flowers have faded. The sepals are ovate-lanceolate, blunt, downy to hairy, and with a wide, white membranous margin. They, too, are outspread in the fruit. The corolla is funnel-shaped and composed of white bilobed petals double the length of the sepals. The ripe capsule is up to three times as long as the sepals.

This species is distributed throughout most of Europe except for the extreme north. It embraces several subspecies. Subspecies *arvense* is found in central Europe, subspecies *strictum* in southwestern Europe and in the Alps, subspecies *glandulosum* is endemic to the Tatra Mountains, and subspecies *lerchenfeldianum* is found in the eastern Carpathians.

seed

Type of plant
dicotyledon

Diploid no.
2n — 72

Flowering period
April — July

Fruit
capsule

Field Violet

Viola arvensis

This annual or biennial herb is a weed of fields, hedgerows, waste places and waysides.

The smooth or sparsely-hairy stem, reaching a height of 10 to 20 cm, is semi-creeping or ascending and often greatly branched. The leaves are ovate-elliptic, and indeed the lower ones are nearly orbicular, with petioles up to 3 cm long. The terminal lobe of the stipules is ovate to lanceolate and notched, but the middle lobe resembles the leaves.

The flowers, measuring up to 15 mm, are long-peduncled with petals shorter than or the same length as the sepals. They are pale yellow with a violet spur and the upper petal is also partly violet. The spur, which contains nectar, is about the same length as the calyx appendages and corresponds to the length of the proboscis of the insects that are the agents of pollination. The mature capsule is smooth and ovoid, and is the same length as the calyx.

The Wild Pansy or Heartsease (*Viola tricolor*) and the Field Violet are closely related and were formerly often considered subspecies of the same species. In *Viola tricolor* the middle lobe of the stipules is lanceolate and entire and thus not exactly like the leaves. The flowers are two-coloured: the lower petals are yellowish, the upper ones often violet-tinged, blue-violet or very occasionally (mostly in large-flowered mountain specimens) pure yellow; the spur is double the length of the calyx appendages.

Type of plant
dicotyledon

Diploid no.
2n — 34

Flowering period
June — October

Fruit
capsule

seed

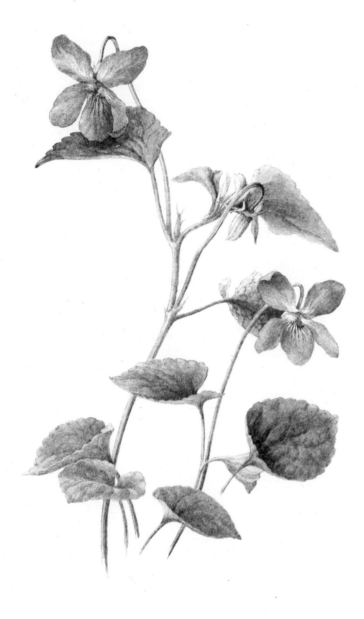

Common Violet

Viola riviniana

This 'dainty', spring-flowering perennial, which reaches a height of 5 to 15 cm, grows in woods, thickets and slopes.

The nearly upright stem bears long-stalked leaves with blades as long as they are wide. The stipules are lance-shaped and sparsely fringed.

The flowers are up to 25 mm in length, the sepals broadly lance-shaped with long appendages, the petals obovate and coloured pale violet with a white spot at the base, the spur stout, blunt and whitish. The mature capsule is up to 10 mm long.

The Common Violet is distributed throughout most of Europe and is also found in Asia. It is often mistaken for other violets and because it readily interbreeds with these other species identification is sometimes difficult. However, a distinctive characteristic that is not passed on to any hybrid is the white spur — in hybrid offspring it is always tinted blue or violet.

Viola riviniana has two subspecies which are readily distinguished from each other.

Subspecies *riviniana* has flowers up to 25 mm long, leaves up to 30 mm long, and capsules usually more than 10 mm in length.

Subspecies *minor* has smaller flowers, barely 15 mm long, leaves only 20 mm long, and capsules always less than 10 mm in length. It forms short, thick masses and usually does not grow in woods.

bract

Type of plant
dicotyledon

Diploid no.
2n — 40

Flowering period
April — May

Fruit
capsule

Common Sorrel

Rumex acetosa

The Common Sorrel, a perennial herb 20 to 60 cm high, is a common sight in meadows, pastureland and by waysides.

The basal leaves are hastate to sagittate and twice to four times longer than they are wide. They have a slightly sour taste and are often eaten, mostly by children.

The flowers are clustered in a panicle-like inflorescence. The six perianth segments are an unobtrusive green and become enlarged and membranous in the fruit. Their shape at this stage is an important means of identification. In Common Sorrel they are broadly ovate, up to 5 mm long, and usually furnished with appendages that are round to four-angled. The mature achenes are 2 mm long and three-angled.

Common Sorrel is widespread throughout most of Europe but is less common in the south where it occurs only in mountains.

The taller Racemose Dock (*Rumex thyrsiflorus*) has much narrower leaves, and flowers at least a month later. It grows in dry places and wasteland, spreading chiefly alongside railway tracks.

Type of plant
dicotyledon

Diploid no.
♀ 2n − 14
♂ 2n − 15

Flowering period
May − August

Fruit
achene

diagram of flower

fruit

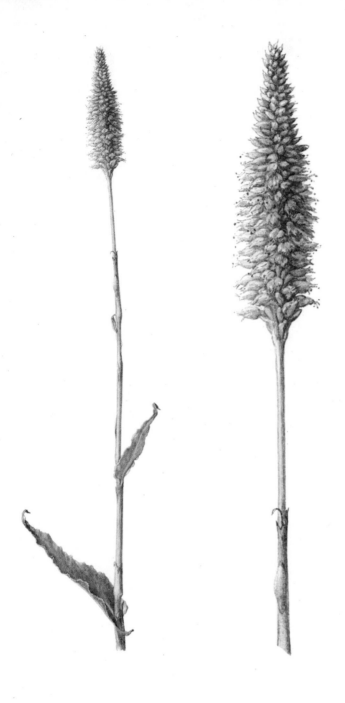

Bistort or Snake Weed

Polygonum bistorta

Bistort is a perennial up to 1 metre high growing in damp and peat meadows found on high ground. It may also be a temporary visitor in lowlands where it is sometimes washed down from higher altitudes.

Its dark green stem rises from a stout rhizome. The basal leaves are elliptic-ovate to longish-lanceolate, the stem leaves distant, slightly heart-shaped to truncated at the base, with a winged stalk. The uppermost leaves are nearly linear and sessile. The ochrea, a membranous sheath formed by the fusion of the stipules and embracing the stem where it joins the leaf-stalk, is cylindrical, brown and smooth.

The small, pink, occasionally whitish flowers are arranged in a terminal spike-like inflorescence up to 9 cm long and 15 mm across. The perianth segments are only about 3 mm long. The eight stamens protrude from the flower. The fruit is a sharply triangular, glossy dark brown achene which is longer than the persistent perianth.

Polygonum bistorta is distributed throughout most of Europe; in Scandinavia it is not indigenous but was introduced there. In southern Europe it grows only in the mountains.

ochrea

Type of plant
dicotyledon

Diploid no.
2n — 48

Flowering period
May — July

Fruit
achene

Redleg

Polygonum persicaria

Redleg, which grows to a height of 20 to 70 cm, is an annual weed of fields, gardens, wasteland and fallow land.

It branches profusely from the ground up. The entire plant is smooth except for the ochreae, which are ciliate on the edge. The leaves, all of one kind, are longish-ovate to lanceolate.

The hermaphroditic flowers are clustered in erect, unbroken, spike-like inflorescences. The five perianth segments are arranged in a spiral. The fruit is a black lenticular achene.

This plant is slightly poisonous and is widespread throughout all of Europe.

The related *Polygonum brittingeri* (syn. *Polygonum danubiale*) is a pioneer plant of alluvial deposits and exposed river beds and lake bottoms in the region of the upper Rhine and Danube, Lake Constance (Bodensee) and other parts of central Europe. It is characterized by a prostrate, much-branched stem with short internodes. The leaves are usually covered with fine grey hairs on the underside and always with colourless glands.

Polygonum is represented by some 25 species in central Europe. One, the Water-pepper (*Polygonum hydropiper*) is distinguished by leaves that have a burning to peppery taste and by a five-segmented perianth without glands; another, the Tasteless Water-pepper (*Polygonum mite*) by non-peppery leaves, a four-segmented perianth and ochreae dotted with glands.

Type of plant
dicotyledon

Diploid no.
2n — 44

Flowering period
July — October

Fruit
achene

ochrea

Common Rock-rose

Helianthemum nummularium

This plant, reaching a height of 6 to 50 cm, grows on sunny slopes, in grassland and in dry thickets.

It is a perennial shrub with numerous prostrate or ascending stems covered with bristles or tufted hairs. The leaves, with linear stipules, are opposite, linear-lanceolate to ovate-orbicular, hairy and on the underside covered with short, soft hairs.

The inflorescence is a raceme composed of 2 to 15 peduncled flowers. The two outside sepals are linear-lanceolate, the three inner ones longer (up to 10 mm) and ovate with four ribs. The five broadly-ovate petals, up to 15 mm long, are vivid yellow, very occasionally pale yellow or orange. The pistil, which is ovoid-conical and densely tomentose, develops into a trilocular capsule after pollination by insects.

This species, which is widely distributed throughout Europe excepting the extreme north, occurs in four subspecies in central Europe — subspecies *nummularium*, subspecies *obscurum* (thermophilous), subspecies *grandiflorum* and subspecies *glabrum* (both mountain forms) — which differ in the indumentum of the leaves and in the length and indumentum of the sepals.

diagram of flower

Type of plant
dicotyledon

Diploid no.
2n — 20

Flowering period
May — August

Fruit
capsule

Stinging Nettle

Urtica dioica

This robust perennial, 50 to 150 cm high, is often found near human habitations but grows also in thickets and damp woods.

The erect, four-angled stem rises from a creeping rhizome. The leaves are stalked, long and pointed, with a heart-shaped base and sickle-toothed margin. The upper side is covered with long stinging hairs which are narrowly-conical cells whose cell membranes have become silicified. Their sharp tips are very fragile and break off readily; when touched they become embedded in the skin and part of the cell contents enters the wound.

Stinging Nettle is dioecious, in other words some plants have only male flowers and some only female flowers. The staminate or male inflorescence is an upright panicle with short branches whereas the branches of the pistillate or female inflorescence are longer and drooping. The perianth is greenish and the flowers are pollinated by the wind.

Stinging Nettle is distributed throughout most of Europe.

The related Small Nettle *(Urtica urens)* is smaller and monoecious. It, too, is covered with stinging hairs.

Type of plant
dicotyledon

Diploid no.
2n — 48, 52

Flowering period
June — October

Fruit
achene

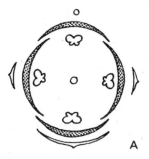

Diagram of flower: A — male flower
B — female flower

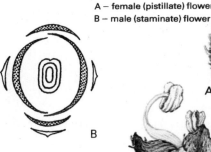

A — female (pistillate) flower
B — male (staminate) flower

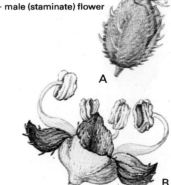

Common Sundew

Drosera rotundifolia

The Common Sundew grows in heather moors, moss moors and wet meadows in foothills and mountains, mostly in slightly acid, but sometimes even in very acid soils.

It is a carnivorous plant with long-stalked basal leaves arranged in a ground rosette. The leaf blades are circular and covered on the upper side with red, stalked glands. These are of two kinds: one secretes a sweet sticky fluid, the other a fluid that breaks down proteins. Small insects get stuck when they alight on the sweet drops and are trapped by the stalked glands which curve downward and hold them fast to the leaf. When the plant has absorbed the nitrogenous substances it needs from the dissolved bodies of the insects the stalked glands straighten and the undigested remnants are removed by the wind or washed off by rain.

In summer a stem up to 20 cm high and ending in a loose monochasial cyme (cincinnus) of small white flowers rises from the centre of the leaf rosette. The 5-merous flowers open in succession from the bottom up and soon fade, so that there are usually only one or two open flowers in an inflorescence at one time, with ripening or fully mature capsules below and unopened buds of diverse size above.

The sundew is a victim of man's interference in the world of nature (draining, drying and liming of meadows, application of artificial fertilizers). Today protecting the plant itself is not enough; it is necessary to protect its natural habitat.

Longitudinal section of insect-trapping gland

Leaf of *Drosera anglica* found in the same situation as *Drosera rotundifolia*

Type of plant
dicotyledon

Diploid no.
2n — 40

Flowering period
July — August

Fruit
capsule

Orpine or Livelong

Sedum telephium

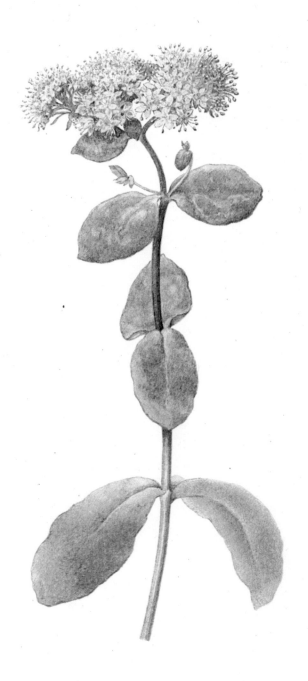

The 50- to 80-cm-high Orpine grows in dry, sandy places and in thickets.

The stem is stiff, upright and sometimes reddish. The leaves are alternate, opposite, or sometimes in whorls of three. They are cordate-obovate, or circular to broadly oblong and sessile with a heart-shaped base clasping the stem.

The inflorescence is a prolonged monochasial cyme (cincinnus) composed of pale yellow-green, sometimes rose-tinted or purple flowers. They are hermaphroditic with 5 sepals, 5 petals, 10 (5 + 5) stamens with brownish-yellow anthers, and 5 pistils. The fruit is a follicle.

Sedum telephium embraces the following three microspecies: *Sedum maximum* with yellow-green petals and upper leaves sessile to slightly semi-clasping and entire. It is found in practically all of Europe.

Sedum telephium (viewed as a narrow species) with rosy-red petals, upper leaves opposite, toothed and sessile with wedge-shaped base. It is found in central and eastern Europe.

Sedum fabaria with dark purple petals and upper leaves alternate and sessile with a narrowed base (almost resembling a stalk). It is found in western and central Europe. Plants of this species are generally smaller and avoid limestone.

Type of plant
dicotyledon

Diploid no.
2n — 24

Flowering period
July — September

Fruit
follicle

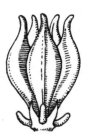

ovaries with glandular nectaries

flower of *Sedum fabaria*

91

Common Stonecrop or **Wall-pepper**

Sedum acre

This tufted perennial herb, 5 to 15 cm high, is found on overgrown rocks, dry sandy slopes and sandy wasteland.

Two types of stems rise from the much-branched rhizome. Non-flowering stems only 2 to 5 cm long thickly covered with overlapping leaves and flowering stems which are simple, 5 to 15 cm long and less densely leaved. The leaves are alternate, fleshy, smooth and broadly ovate with rounded edges and a sac-like base attached directly to the stem. They are up to 10 mm long and have a sharply burning taste.

The inflorescence is composed of two or three monochasial cymes.

The individual flowers are short-peduncled and 5-merous. The yellow ovoid sepals are blunt and up to 3 mm long, the petals are pointed, lance-shaped, 6 to 10 mm long, and expanded. The flowers are followed by follicles.

This species exhibits marked variability in genetic makeup, which is also reflected in the diversity of the morphological features.

Common Stonecrop is distributed throughout Europe. It is often mistaken for the similar Insipid Stonecrop (*Sedum sexangulare*, syn. *Sedum boloniense*), which, however, differs by the presence of a spur at the base of the leaves and by the absence of the bitter substances so characteristic of *Sedum acre*.

mature, burst fruit

Type of plant
dicotyledon

Diploid no.
2n — 40, 48, 60, 80, 100, 120

Flowering period
June — July

Fruit
follicle

Meadow Saxifrage

Saxifraga granulata

Meadows, pastureland and banks, usually with soils rich in lime, are the habitats of this perennial which grows to a height of 10 to 50 cm.

It is a loosely tufted plant with a ground rosette of leaves from which rises a little-branched, sparsely-leaved, pubescent stem. The leaves forming the basal rosette are rounded-reniform with a scalloped or lobed margin and a heart-shaped or truncate base abruptly narrowing into a stalk that is twice to five times as long as the blade; they have bulbils growing from the axils. The lower stem leaves are also long-stalked with scalloped or lobed margins whereas the upper leaves are undivided and nearly sessile or sessile. There are no bulbils growing from the axils of the stem leaves.

The branches of the inflorescence are erect, glandular and sparsely flowered. The flowers are subtended by linear bracts. The calyx is composed of five sepals joined at the base with the petals and stamens into a funnel-shaped hypanthium. The white petals are three times longer than the sepals. There are ten stamens. The capsule is broadly ovoid and contains small seeds covered with tiny warts.

Saxifraga granulata is distributed throughout the whole of Europe and so it is not surprising that it exhibits marked variability in its pattern of growth, branching of the stem and indumentum.

Type of plant
dicotyledon

Diploid no.
2n — 52

Flowering period
May — June

Fruit
capsule

diagram of flower

bulbils in the axils of the leaves of the basal rosette

Silver Saxifrage

Saxifraga paniculata

Syn. *Saxifraga aizoon*

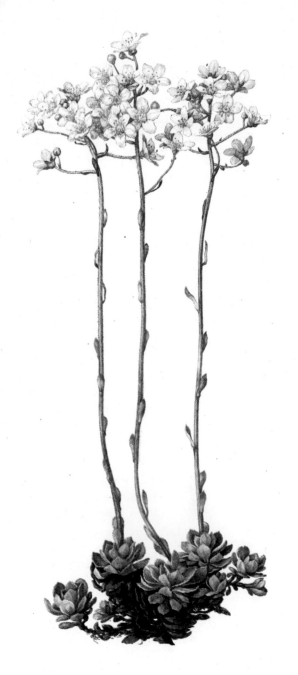

This fleshy, tufted perennial grows on rocks, screes and stony slopes, chiefly in lime-rich soil.

The stiff, grey-green, lance-shaped leaves form a dense rosette from which rises a 4- to 30-cm-high stem sparsely leaved and branching at the top. The edges of the lower leaves have pointed teeth covered with scales of calcium carbonate which have a lime-secreting gland at the base. If we hold the leaf up to the light the gland is visible as a pale spot to the unaided eye. Several vascular bundles conveying water that contains large amounts of calcium carbonate end at this point. The water evaporates but the calcium carbonate remains in the form of scales that serve to prevent excessive evaporation — a very important thing for this plant which grows in extremely hot and dry situations.

The flowers are arranged in dense panicles. The petals are white or sometimes spotted red. The stamens ripen before the pistils. The flowers are pollinated by insects that suck the nectar secreted on the disc-like surface of the ovary. The plant also multiplies by means of shoots.

The Silver Saxifrage is widespread throughout Europe but is often dug up to be planted in rock gardens and so has been put on the list of protected species.

section of leaf with exuded calcium carbonate

flower

Type of plant
dicotyledon

Diploid no.
2n – 28

Flowering period
June – July

Fruit
capsule

Alternate-leaved Golden Saxifrage

Chrysosplenium alternifolium

This perennial herb, which reaches a height of 5 to 20 cm, is common in moist and shaded woodland soil, in riverine meadows and beside springs, not only in lowland country but also in mountains.

It has a long, slender, scaly rhizome and forms loose tufts. The three-angled stem divides into two at the top. The lower leaves are long-stalked, thinly covered with appressed hairs or glabrescent, and glossy. The blade is heart- or kidney-shaped in outline with a broadly scalloped margin. The two to four stem leaves are shallowly heart-shaped, short-stalked and alternate.

The small flowers are yellow and subtended by yellow-green bracts. The sepals have rounded lobes, the corolla is absent. There are eight stamens. The mature fruit, an ovoid capsule, is enclosed by the persistent calyx.

This species is distributed throughout most of Europe excepting the extreme northern parts of western Europe and the Mediterranean region.

The related *Chrysosplenium tetrandrum* always has only four stamens and hence its scientific name. It is usually rather small, almost completely glabrous, and found only in Scandinavia.

The Opposite-leaved Golden Saxifrage *(Chrysosplenium oppositifolium)* of central Europe truly has opposite leaves and is found near mountain springs, on shady heath moors and sweating rocks, chiefly limestone.

Type of plant
dicotyledon

Diploid no.
2n — 48

Flowering period
April — June

Fruit
capsule

flower

Grass of Parnassus

Parnassia palustris

This perennial grows in damp habitats such as peat meadows where it reaches a height of 5 to 30 cm.

The lowest leaves, growing from a thick rhizome and arranged in a rosette, are long-stalked and cordate-ovate. Also growing from the rhizome is an erect, smooth stem with only a single sessile, amplexicaul leaf.

The stem ends in a solitary flower 2 to 3 cm in diameter. There are five sepals and the same number of petals, which are coloured white or very occasionally reddish. Five stamens alternate with five longish-obovate staminodes whose yellowish expanded shovel-shaped middle section secretes nectar. The flowers are pollinated by insects. The pistil is derived from four carpels. The capsule that develops after fertilization opens by four valves.

This species is distributed throughout all Europe as the only European representative of the Parnassiaceae family. Only few like species exhibit such variability in appearance, site requirements and horizontal as well as vertical distribution. Its numbers include small as well as large plants, and plants that grow in moss moors in the lowlands as well as ones that grow on sweating rocks in the Alps and Carpathians.

petal with stamen and staminode

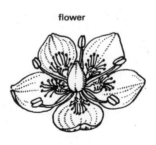

flower

Type of plant
dicotyledon

Diploid no.
2n — 18 (36)

Flowering period
June — September

Fruit
capsule

Wood Goatsbeard

Aruncus dioicus

Syn. *Aruncus sylvestris, Aruncus vulgaris*

Shaded ravines, thickets and long-stemmed grass-lands are the habitats of this perennial herb which grows to a height of 100 to 180 cm.

The leaves are up to 1 metre long, twice tripinnate, irregularly serrate, and without stipules.

The tiny flowers are arranged in dense panicles. They are short-stalked and unisexual. Wood Goatsbeard is usually dioecious, with male and female flowers on separate plants. The former are yellowish, the latter pure white. They are composed of five sepals and five petals, plus three pistils in the female flowers and 20 to 30 stamens in the male flowers. Pollination, by insects, is followed by the development of follicles.

Wood Goatsbeard is widespread in all of central Europe. Close relatives include members of the genus aptly named *Sibiraea*, whose centre of distribution is located in central Asia — one locality in the Altai and another in the Tien-Shan mountains. A third area of distribution of *Sibiraea altaiensis* was discovered in Europe at the turn of the century. Nowadays it is found only in a few localities in Yugoslavia. Inasmuch as the Yugoslav localities are more than 5,000 km distant from the Asian localities it means that the European localities are the remnants of the former wider distribution of the species and that *Sibiraea altaiensis* is a prominent relict of the Tertiary Age; proof of this is supplied by palaeobotanical finds.

Type of plant
dicotyledon

Diploid no.
2n — 18

Flowering period
June — July

Fruit
follicle

longitudinal section of ovary

follicles

Meadowsweet

Filipendula ulmaria

This robust perennial, reaching a height of 100 to 150 cm, grows in damp meadows, ditches, beside springs and in tall-stemmed grasslands.

It has a jointed, creeping rhizome from which rises a stiff, glabrous, erect stem covered with leaves and branching slightly at the top. The leaves are odd-pinnate with interjected leaflets: the two to five paired leaflets are broadly-ovate and pointed, the terminal leaflet is palmately three- to five-lobed. The stipules are broadly heart-shaped and short-toothed.

The small flowers are arranged in dense clusters. The sepals are inconspicuous, the broadly-ovate petals with claw are yellowish-white and fragrant. The stamens are twice as long as the petals. The pistils number six to ten. The flowers are pollinated by insects and after fertilization develop into smooth, 2-mm-long follicles.

This species is distributed in practically all of Europe except the islands and the Mediterranean region.

In central Europe there are two races: the type subspecies *ulmaria,* up to 2 metres high, with loose inflorescence and glabrous follicles, which is found throughout most of Europe, and the subspecies *picbaueri,* only 1 metre high, with dense inflorescence and hairy follicles, which is found in the area extending from east Austria and Czechoslovakia to Bulgaria.

flower

Type of plant
dicotyledon

Diploid no.
2n — 14

Flowering period
June — September

Fruit
follicle

Dropwort

Filipendula vulgaris

Syn. *Filipendula hexapetala*

This perennial, reaching a height of 30 to 60 cm, grows on dry slopes in lime-rich soils.

It has a short rhizome from which rises an erect, usually rounded stem that is leafy below and practically leafless near the top. The pinnate leaves with interjected leaflets are composed of more than twenty paired, deeply incised leaflets, larger pairs alternating with smaller pairs; the stipules are kidney-shaped and toothed.

The dense inflorescence is composed of 6-merous flowers. The petals are white but may also be tinted pink. The stamens are the same length as the petals. The pistils number nine to twelve. The mature follicles are up to 4 mm long and hairy.

This species is distributed throughout most of Europe as far north as Trondheim in Norway.

This and the preceding Meadowsweet (*Filipendula ulmaria*) are the only species found in Europe. However certain North American and Asian species with whitish, pink or red flowers are grown for garden and park decoration.

Type of plant
dicotyledon

Diploid no.
2n — 14

Flowering period
June — July

Fruit
follicle

flower

Marsh Cinquefoil

Potentilla palustris

Syn. *Comarum palustre*

This perennial, 30- to 80-cm-high subshrub grows in wet meadows, bogs and marshes.

It has two of stems — non-flowering, smooth, unbranched stems and flowering, sparsely-branched stems covered with random hairs. The leaves are odd-pinnate, dark green and more or less glabrous above, grey-green and hairy on the veins below. The stipules are half the length of the leaf-stalk and sometimes completely fused with it.

The flowers, which are subtended by bracts, are arranged in a loose corymb. They are large and 5-merous, the terminal flower is often 7-merous. The calyx is green outside, purple inside, up to 18 mm long, and covered with appressed hairs; it is expanded in the flower and erect in the fruit. The epicalyx is green with lanceolate segments. The petals, up to 8 mm long and pointed, are purple and do not fall off. The stamens, twenty in number, are likewise purple. Pollination is by insects. The numerous pistils are located on a semi-globular, hairy receptacle which becomes fleshy as the achenes ripen. The achenes are ovoid and hooked.

This species is found throughout most of Europe from central Spain, northern Italy and southern Bulgaria northward.

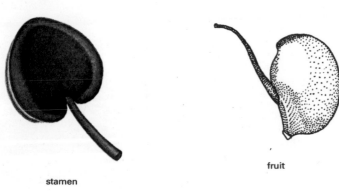

stamen

fruit

Type of plant
dicotyledon

Diploid no.
2n — 42

Flowering period
June — July

Fruit
achene

Silverweed

Potentilla anserina

Wasteland, damp meadows and fields are the habitats of this perennial which has creeping, rooting stems up to one metre long.

The stem rises from a thick tuberous rhizome. The odd-pinnate leaves with interjected leaflets are white-felted below and sometimes also on the upper side. The leaflets, which may number as many as 26, are deeply serrate to pinnatisect.

The flowers grow from the axils of the leaves, are relatively long-peduncled, and measure about 2 cm in diameter. The epicalyx is composed of three segments, the calyx of five. The golden-yellow corolla is also composed of five segments which are twice as long as the sepals. The twenty stamens have ovoid anthers.

Silverweed is widespread in Europe excepting the extreme northeastern parts and most of southern Europe. In the Alps it grows up to elevations of nearly 2,500 metres.

The subspecies *egedii* is distinctive of the north European coast of Sweden and Finland. It has only about 10 leaflets per leaf and these are nearly glabrous on the underside. White flowers distinguish the two species *Potentilla rupestris*, with leaves likewise odd-pinnate, and *Potentilla alba*, which, however, has leaves palmately 5- to 7-lobed, somewhat like those of the strawberry.

Type of plant
dicotyledon

Diploid no.
2n − 28

Flowering period
May − September

Fruit
achene

fruit

flower

Spring Cinquefoil

Potentilla verna

Syn. *Potentilla tabernaemontani*

This perennial plant, reaching a height of only 5 to 20 cm, flowers in spring on sunny slopes and in dry, sandy grasslands.

It has hairy, prostrate stems rising at the tip and often rooting at the nodes. The basal leaves are 5-foliolate to 7-foliolate, long-stalked and covered with simple hairs.

The flowers are short-peduncled and up to 2 cm across. The epicalyx segments are shorter than the sepals. The petals are twice as long as the sepals, notched and coloured golden to sulphur yellow. The corolla, calyx and epicalyx have five lobes each. There are many stamens and pistils.

This species is distributed throughout most of Europe excepting the Baltic region, Byelorussia and Bulgaria.

Potentilla verna is the name of a group of microspecies of which the following two are examples.

Potentilla neumanniana is the designation for central and west European plants with only simple, appressed or spreading hairs and basal leaves with narrowly-lanceolate to linear stipules. *Potentilla pusilla* includes plants with random stellate hairs on the underside of the leaves. There are more than ten such microspecies of Spring Cinquefoil in Europe.

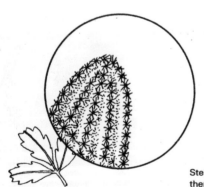

Stellate hairs on the leaf of the related and more thermophilous *Potentilla arenaria*

Type of plant
dicotyledon

Diploid no.
2n – 42

Flowering period
March – June

Fruit
achene

Wild Strawberry

Fragaria vesca

The Wild Strawberry, 5 to 20 cm high, is a common plant of forest margins and woodland clearings.

From the axils of the basal leaves, arranged in a rosette, grow creeping, rooting stolons and upright stems the same length or only slightly longer than the leaves. The leaves are long-stalked and trifoliolate with lanceolate, entire stipules. The stems, flower-stalks, leaves and stipules are all hairy.

The flowers have long peduncles and epicalyx about the same length as the calyx. The sepals are recurved in the fruit. The petals are broadly obovate, up to 8 mm long, and pure white. There are twenty stamens in the flower. After pollination by insects and fertilization the receptacle develops into the fleshy accessory fruit known to everyone as the 'strawberry' covered with numerous achenes which are the true fruits. Ripe strawberries measure up to 2 cm in length, are red and sweet and fall readily.

This species is widespread throughout most of Europe. The very similar Hautbois Strawberry (*Fragaria moschata*) has stems distinctly longer than the leaves and fruits that do not fall readily and are coloured greenish flushed with red only on the sunny side. The Green Strawberry (*Fragaria viridis*), with yellowish-white flowers, has a persistent calyx pressed tightly to the fruit; the fruit is yellowish-white and flushed red only at the tip.

Type of plant
dicotyledon

Diploid no.
2n — 14

Flowering period
May — August

Fruit
aggregate fruit of achenes

longitudinal section of strawberry

Common Agrimony

Agrimonia eupatoria

This 30- to 100-cm-high perennial grows on sunny slopes, at the edges of woods and in open thickets. It is partial to lime-rich soil.

It is a hairy, glandular plant with a thick rhizome and simple or little-branched stem. The stem is scaly at the base. The leaves farther up the stem are odd-pinnate with interjected leaflets; the leaflets, numbering 5 to 9 larger ones and 6 to 10 smaller ones to each leaf, are ovate to rhombic, coarsely toothed, dark green above and lighter green beneath. The stipules resemble the leaves.

The flowers are arranged in a prolonged, spike-like raceme which may be up to 30 cm long. The calyx is 5-merous with conical base and ten prominent ribs. Instead of an epicalyx this species has a hyer-anthium edged with a ring of bristles. The five yellow petals have net venation. The fruit is one or two achenes enclosed in the hyer-anthium.

Common Agrimony is found in practically all of Europe excepting the extreme north.

It is a medicinal plant with anti-inflammatory properties. Its healing properties were supposedly discovered by Mithridates Eupator, King of Pontus (132 − 63 B.C.) and that is the derivation of its Latin name *eupatoria*.

hypanthium

bud

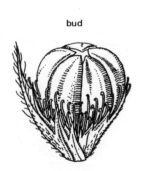

Type of plant
dicotyledon

Diploid no.
2n − 28

Flowering period
June − August

Fruit
achenes enclosed in a hypanthium

Great Burnet

Sanguisorba officinalis

Syn. *Poterium officinale*

This perennial, which reaches a height of 20 cm to 1 metre, grows in damp meadows.

It has a thick rhizome from which rises a rosette of basal leaves and an erect, smooth stem that branches at the top. The leaves are odd-pinnate and up to 40 cm long. The membranous stipules are joined to the long stalks. The toothed leaflets, numbering three to seven pairs, are long-stalked, glossy dark green above, and lighter green with prominent veins beneath. The three or four stem leaves resemble the basal leaves.

The dark red flower heads borne on long, erect peduncles are ovoid-oblong and up to 2 cm long. They are composed of five to ten hermaphroditic flowers that open in succession from the bottom upward. The calyx is a dark brownish-red and serves as a substitute for the absent corolla. The four stamens have long red filaments and yellow anthers. The calyx is winged in the fruit.

This species was formerly collected as a medicinal plant used to treat excessive bleeding and diarrhoea.

It is found in the British Isles and in Europe from Scandinavia to central Spain, the Appenines, Montenegro and Bulgaria.

The related *Sanguisorba dodecandra* has large flower heads, green calyxes, and always more than four stamens. It grows only in the north Italian Alps.

Type of plant
dicotyledon

Diploid no.
2n — 28, 56

Flowering period
July — September

Fruit
achenes enclosed in a hypanthium

flower

Salad Burnet

Sanguisorba minor

This 20- to 60-cm-high perennial grows on sunny slopes and overgrown screes.

The stem, which rises from the thick, fleshy rhizome, is usually erect but sometimes ascending, rounded, branched and coloured violet. The leaves are odd-pinnate and short-stalked with small stipules that are joined to the stalks. The leaflets are likewise short-stalked, broadly-ovate, coarsely toothed on the margin, and glabrous.

The globular flower heads are composed of staminate flowers at the base, hermaphroditic flowers in the middle and pistillate flowers at the top. The calyx is brownish-red, the corolla is absent. The stamens have red filaments and yellow anthers.

This species is found in southern, western and central Europe.

Also found in central Europe, where it has become naturalized, is the south European species *Sanguisorba muricata* which has an enlarged hypanthium that is winged and covered with irregular ridges in the fruit.

Native to the Iberian Peninsula are two further related species: *Sanguisorba hybrida* — sticky, with glandular hairs, and *Sanguisorba ancistroides* — without glandular hairs and with flower heads only about 1 cm across.

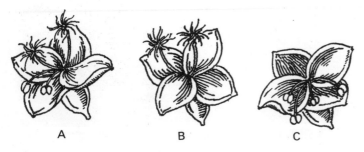

Three types of flowers: A — hermaphroditic B — female C — male

Type of plant
dicotyledon

Diploid no.
2n — 28

Flowering period
May — July

Fruit
achenes enclosed in a hypanthium

Dyer's Greenweed

Genista tinctoria

This shrub, up to 60 cm high, grows in open woods, sunny forest margins and dry heaths.

The alternate, oval or lance-shaped leaves are almost sessile and have atrophied stipules. They are dark green and glabrous above, a lighter green and ciliate beneath with prominent lateral veins. The stem is short, ascending and much branched.

The flowers are arranged in racemes. The peduncles are the same length as the calyx and carry two lance-shaped bracts. The calyx is smooth, five-lobed, and falls off early. The corolla is smooth and golden yellow with an ovoid standard. The flower is followed by a smooth pod containing six to ten seeds.

The area of distribution of this species includes most of Europe. The many populations exhibit slight differences and so numerous deviations have been described.

Dyer's Greenweed contains flavonoid glycosides, e.g. luteolin, for which reason the leaves and flowers were formerly collected for use as a yellow dye.

German Greenweed (*Genista germanica*) differs from Dyer's Greenweed chiefly by having thorny branches, sessile leaves and hairy pods, plus the fact that it flowers about a month earlier.

Type of plant
dicotyledon

Diploid no.
2n — 48, 96

Flowering period
June — August

Fruit
pod

seed

White Melilot

Melilotus alba

This biennial, which reaches a height of 20 cm to 2 metres, is found in dry, stony and overgrown wasteland as well as on railway embankments. It is also sometimes grown as fodder and to stabilize roadside embankments.

It may have many stems, usually more or less upright. The trifoliolate, toothed leaves with stipules fall soon after the flowers have faded.

The flowers are arranged in narrow racemes up to 6 cm long, each composed of 40 to 80 flowers. The flowers are short-peduncled, up to 5 mm long, and drooping. The caducous calyx is five-toothed. The corolla is white with three to six veins; the standard is longer than the wings. The pods are blunt, glabrous, blackish when ripe and contain one or two but sometimes three seeds.

This species is widespread in Europe.

In central Europe *Melilotus alba* is the only white-flowering species but there are several with yellow flowers. Most often seen is the Common Melilot (*Melilotus officinalis*) — a biennial with glabrous pods, and the plural-yearly Golden Melilot (*Melilotus altissima*) with pubescent pods.

flower of *Melilotus officinalis*

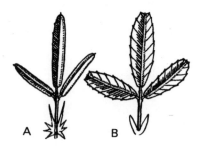

Leaves: A — *Melilotus dentata* with 18—20 lateral veins
B — *Melilotus alba* with 6—12 lateral veins

Type of plant
dicotyledon

Diploid no.
2n — 16

Flowering period
May — August

Fruit
pod

White Clover

Trifolium repens

This perennial clover, 10 to 30 cm high, occurs in meadows, pastureland, fallow land and by roadsides. It is sometimes added to lawn mixtures.

The stems are creeping, rising at the tip and rooting at the nodes. The stalked, trifoliolate leaves are sometimes as much as 20 cm long and have large membranous stipules. They are patterned with fine veins and a light, angled, horizontal band towards the base.

The inflorescence has a longer peduncle than the leaves. It is a globose head about 2 cm across and is composed of 40 to 80 flowers. The individual flowers are up to 12 mm long and drooping when they are spent. The calyx is green and bell-shaped, the membranous corolla is white, but may be tinted green or pink and light brown when the flower has faded. The upper petal is pointed and a third longer than the two lateral petals. The two lower petals are joined and form a keel. There are usually ten stamens. The pod is held fast in the persistent calyx.

White Clover is widespread throughout Europe to Cape Nordkyn in Norway, the northernmost point of the European mainland. In central Europe there are two subspecies: One is the type subspecies *repens* which has glabrous stems reaching a height of more than 30 cm and flowers usually coloured white. The other is subspecies *prostratum*, found in the Rhine region, southern France and the entire Mediterranean region; this has short, hairy stems and flowers tinted pink.

Type of plant
dicotyledon

Diploid no.
2n — 32

Flowering period
May — September

Fruit
pod

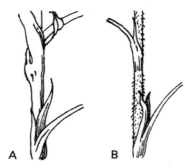

A — section of the glabrous stem of *Trifolium repens* B — section of the hairy stem of *Trifolium montanum*, another, white-flowered clover found in hilly districts

flower

Red Clover

Trifolium pratense

This perennial herb, 20 to 50 cm high, is widespread in meadows, pastureland, dry grassland and by roadsides. It is also widely grown as a forage crop.

The stems, growing from a rhizome, are angled and hairy, erect or ascending, and composed of three to five segments. The lower leaves are long-stalked, the upper leaves are short-stalked or sessile. The stipules are joined with the stalk and bristle-pointed. The leaflets are glabrous and patterned with a whitish to reddish-brown crescent-shaped spot on the upper surface, hairy on the underside, and ciliate on the margins.

The flower heads are globose to ovoid with base enfolded in the large stipules of the subtending leaves. The head is usully composed of 30 to 60 flowers which are sessile and do not grow from the axils of bracts. They are up to 18 mm long and erect. The calyx has five teeth. The corolla is pale carmine-red or meaty-red; it is fused at the base. The standard is longer than the wings. The pod is ovoid and contains only a single seed.

This is an extremely variable species – plants that are strikingly hairy are classified as varieties or subspecies and sometimes even as separate species.

longitudinal section of flower

Type of plant
dicotyledon

Diploid no.
2n – 14

Flowering period
June – September

Fruit
pod

Large Hop Trefoil

Trifolium aureum

Syn. *Trifolium strepens*

This 10- to 30-cm-high biennial grows on sunny slopes, embankments and by roads.

The stem is erect or slightly ascending, branched and very leafy. The leaf-stalks are 1 cm long and the stipules about the same length; the latter are longish-ovate, pointed and strongly veined. The leaflets are short-stalked and covered with appressed hairs on both sides.

The flower head is borne on a stout, upright peduncle either the same length or longer than the subtending bract and up to 5 cm long in the fruit. The individual flowers are short-peduncled and pendent after they have faded. The corolla is deep yellow, but after flowering it is yellowish-brown and membranous. The standard is spoon-shaped and up to 6 mm long.

This species is distributed throughout most of Europe except the extreme north. Central Europe has a great many yellow-flowering species with small heads that usually turn brown later. One is the Hop Trefoil (*Trifolium campestre*) in which the terminal leaflet has a strikingly long stalk. The flowers are pale yellow and the corolla about 4 to 5 mm long. It grows in grassy, sandy meadows but only on silicic substrates.

Type of plant
dicotyledon

Diploid no.
2n — 14

Flowering period
June — August

Fruit
pod

diagram of flower of the pea family

Common Bird's-foot Trefoil, Bacon-and-Eggs

Lotus corniculatus

This 5- to 40-cm-high perennial herb grows in meadows, pastureland, grassland and the edges of thickets.

The stems that grow from the rhizome are prostrate or ascending, sparsely branched, and may be glabrous or covered randomly with hairs as are the leaves. The latter are pinnate with five leaflets and coloured grey-green on the underside.

The flowers are arranged in sparse 3- to 6-flowered umbels longer than the subtending bract and with a peduncle up to 10 cm long. The individual flowers are short-peduncled and up to 13 mm long. The calyx is five-ribbed, the corolla is deep yellow and often reddish outside; in dry weather it is sometimes tinted green. The standard is rounded-ovate, the wings broadly ovate and the keel has an upturned beak in front. The pods are chestnut-brown when ripe and the valves coil in a spiral after they open.

Lotus corniculatus is widespread in most of Europe. In central Europe there are two subspecies differing in the pubescence of the stems and leaves: subspecies *hirsutus,* which is partial to rather dry, lime-rich meadows, and subspecies *corniculatus,* which is more common in damp, lime-deficient meadows.

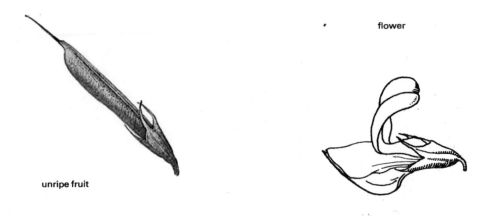

unripe fruit

flower

Type of plant
dicotyledon

Diploid no.
2n – 24

Flowering period
May – September

Fruit
pod

Common Crown Vetch

Coronilla varia

Pastureland, hedgerows, meadows, forest margins, embankments and wasteland are the habitats of this perennial herb which grows to a height of 30 cm to 1 metre.

It has a branched rhizome and an ascending twining stem. The long-stalked pinnate leaves are 5 to 10 cm long and have up to 10 pairs of leaflets. The latter are short-stalked and have a spiny point. The stipules are very small and are not fused.

The flowers, arranged in ten- to twenty-flowered umbels, are short-peduncled and subtended by small bracts. The calyx is bell-funnel-shaped with short teeth. The corolla is pink or white; the standard is dark pink or violet and shorter than the white wings as well as the beaked keel coloured dark violet at the tip. The fruit is an upcurved loment with 3 to 6 faintly constricted segments.

Common Crown Vetch is found mainly in central and southern Europe. It is also frequently cultivated and introduced into western and northern Europe. It is poisonous.

Related species growing in central Erope are all yellow-flowering, e.g. *Coronilla emerus* − a shrub attaining a height of more than 1 metre with two-flowered heads, the herbaceous *Coronilla vaginalis* with heads numbering up to ten flowers, and *Coronilla coronata* with heads of as many as 20 flowers.

Type of plant
dicotyledon

Diploid no.
2n − 24

Flowering period
June − August

Fruit
loment

leaf (odd-pinnate)

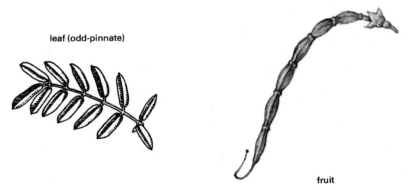

fruit

Spring Vetchling

Lathyrus vernus

Syn. *Orobus vernus*

Spring Vetchling, which reaches a height of 20 to 40 cm, is one of the plants growing in the herbaceous layer of woods.

The erect or ascending stems are angled and un-branched, scaly at the base and leafy above. The leaves are odd-pinnate with 2 to 3 pairs of pointed, ovate leaflets. These are smooth, glossy on the underside and a lighter green underneath than above. The axis of the leaf ends in a point. The stipules are up to 2 cm long and semi-sagittate.

The inflorescence is a scanty raceme. There may be only a single terminal cluster on a plant with perhaps two or three more in the axils of the leaves. The flowers have a bell-shaped, five-segmented calyx usually tinted brown or violet and a zygomorphic, 5-merous corolla. This is coloured reddish-violet (the wings are more bluish), later blue to blue-green. The flower is followed after fertilization by an erect, chestnut-brown pod with tip inclined downward at an angle. It contains 8 to 14, smooth, globular or len-ticular, streaked seeds.

Spring Vetchling is distributed throughout most of Europe, as is the similar Black Pea (*Lathyrus niger*), which has leaves with 4 to 6 pairs of leaflets that turn black when dry.

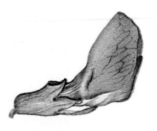

faded flower

leaf with long-pointed rachis

Type of plant
dicotyledon

Diploid no.
2n – 14

Flowering period
April – May

Fruit
pod

114

Sanfoin

Onobrychis viciifolia

This 20- to 50-cm-high perennial occurs on dry slopes and in meadows but is chiefly grown for fodder.

It has a short, branched, woody rhizome from which rises an erect, grooved stem bearing odd-pinnate leaves with elliptic to linear leaflets.

The flowers are clustered in ovoid to cylindrical, pointed racemes borne on erect, axillary branches up to 20 cm long. The individual flowers, up to 14 mm in length, grow from the axils of bracts which are longer than the flower peduncles. The bell-shaped calyx has lanceolate, ciliate teeth. The dark or deep pink petals terminate in a short claw at the base. The standard is patterned with dark-violet veins. There are ten stamens. The pod is orbicular and flat with prominent ridges.

Opinions differ as to whether this species is indigenous to central Europe with some authorities believing it to have originated from southeastern Europe. Definitely native to central Europe are the lime-loving *Onobrychis arenaria* with leaves composed of as many as 14 paired leaflets and the mountain species *Onobrychis montana* with 3 to 7 pairs of leaflets per leaf. Both have a prostrate stem and are morphologically variable.

Type of plant
dicotyledon

Diploid no.
2n – 28

Flowering period
May – August

Fruit
pod

seed

fruit

Tufted Vetch

Vicia cracca

This 20- to 50-cm-high perennial is often found in fields, pastureland as well as by the edges of woods.

It has a thick, creeping rhizome from which rise stiff, angled and branched, climbing stems. The leaves are sessile, up to 15 cm long, composed of six to fifteen pairs of leaflets and usually terminated by two long tendrils. The underside is more or less hairy.

The one-sided racemes, which may be up to twice as long as the nearest leaf, are usually composed of as many as thirty, short-peduncled, pendent flowers. The sepals are fused into a bell-shaped calyx with shortly-lanceolate teeth. The corolla is three to four times as long as the calyx and coloured blue-violet to red-violet, although very occasionally it is whitish. The standard is obovate to obcordate. The keel is short. The pods are glabrous when ripe.

This species is distributed throughout most of Europe.

Very similar is the related *Vicia tenuifolia* which differs chiefly by having larger flowers and pods.

The prostrate Mountain Vetch, only about 25 cm high with lanceolate leaflets and an inflorescence shorter than the nearest leaf, occurs in the mountains of central Europe and Scandinavia and is described as *Vicia oreophila*.

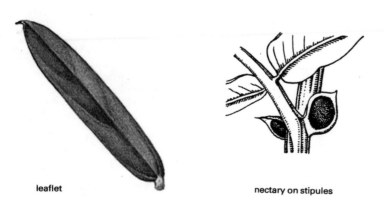

leaflet

nectary on stipules

Type of plant
dicotyledon

Diploid no.
2n — 14 (28)

Flowering period
June — August

Fruit
pod

Milk Vetch

Astragalus glycyphyllos

The edges of woods, sunny, open thickets and woodland clearings is where we will encounter the 50- to 150-cm-high Milk Vetch.

The stems are angled, prostrate or creeping, and glabrous. The odd-pinnate leaves have four to seven paired leaflets and resemble the leaves of the locust tree.

The dense racemes are shorter than the leaves. The flowers are short-peduncled and up to 14 mm long. The bracts subtending the flowers are ciliate and longer than the flower peduncles. The calyx is broadly bell-shaped, whitish, and more or less glabrous. The corolla is greenish-yellow and pale though later creamy-brown. The pods are sickle-shaped and contain a number of seeds.

This species is found in most of Europe excepting the extreme north, but is chiefly found in the mountain regions of southern Europe.

Central Europe has more than twenty-five species of vetch. Several others occur even on the overgrown lava fields of Mount Etna, in the stony semi-deserts of southern Spain and in the Aitos mountain range of eastern Bulgaria. Vetches growing in these extremely dry and warm localities are thorny shrubs with flowers growing from the axils of the leaves concealed inside the woody 'hemisphere'.

Type of plant
dicotyledon

Diploid no.
2n — 16

Flowering period
June — July

Fruit
pod

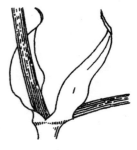

stipules

Herb Robert

Geranium robertianum

The edges of woods, forest clearings, thickets and overgrown screes are the habitats of this 20- to 40-cm-high annual herb, which shows a preference for nitrogen-rich soils.

It is somewhat foetid and has reddish, brittle stems covered with spreading hairs. The lowest leaves dry very early. The stem leaves are opposite, long-stalked and triangular in outline; they are composed of three to five pinnatipartite or bipinnatipartite leaflets.

The two-flowered dichasiums are longer than the subtending leaves. The flowers are short-peduncled and erect. The calyx tightly enfolds the base of the flower and later also the fruit. The corolla is composed of five, pale carmine-red, obovate petals each with a long claw. Inside are 10 stamens with reddish-brown anthers and orange pollen. The superior ovary is derived from five carpels. The ripe fruit is schizocarpic and beaked, splitting from the base into five one-seeded segments.

Herb Robert is found from lowland to mountain elevations in most of Europe, excepting the extreme north.

The related *Geranium purpureum* has smaller flowers with dark purple corolla and bright yellow anthers and pollen. It is distributed in southern and western Europe including Great Britain.

leaf

Type of plant
dicotyledon

Diploid no.
2n – 64

Flowering period
May – October

Fruit
schizocarp

Meadow Cranesbill

Geranium pratense

This perennial herb, 30 to 50 cm high, grows in hedgerows, meadows and pastureland.

It has a short, thick rhizome from which rises a roughly hairy stem, branched and glandular at the top. The lowest leaves, arranged in a ground rosette, are long-stalked. The stem leaves are short-stalked and palmatipartite with obovate segments. The stipules are ovate-lanceolate and coloured reddish-brown.

The dichasiums are on long branches with four lanceolate bracts. The sepals, tapering to a long point, are a lighter colour on the margin. The blue-violet petals are up to 20 mm long, ciliate at the base and spread out flat. The fruits are beaked; at maturity they split into one-seeded segments that are ejected up to two metres from the plant.

Meadow Cranesbill is distributed throughout most of Europe except the extreme north.

The related Wood Cranesbill (*Geranium sylvaticum*) is usually readily identified by its reddish-violet flowers. Despite its name, this species grows only in meadows, especially mountain grasslands.

Type of plant
dicotyledon

Diploid no.
2n – 28

Flowering period
June – September

Fruit
schizocarp

leaf

beaked fruit

Common Storksbill

Erodium cicutarium

The Common Storksbill is an annual or biennial plant, 10 to 40 cm high, that grows in fallow land, sandy fields, wasteland, vineyards and ruderal pastureland.

The erect stem is often branched and hairy, although very occasionally it is glandular-hairy. Unlike other members of the family, the leaves are odd-pinnate. The lowest leaves are arranged in a rosette, the stem leaves have short stalks.

The inflorescence is composed of from three to eight flowers with peduncles twice to three times as long as the subtending bracts. The bracts are fused at the base. The sepals are three- to five-ribbed with a short point. The petals are up to twice as long as the sepals and coloured carmine-red or violet. The fruit is as much as 4 cm long, beaked and ciliate.

This species is distributed throughout most of Europe. It is very variable and its division into a number of microspecies is problematic; the individual microspecies, sometimes classed as mere subspecies, differ in inconspicuous characteristics, chiefly in the fruit or number of chromosomes. Besides *Erodium cicutarium* proper there are three other microspecies found in sandy soils and sand dunes, chiefly on the northwestern and west European coast — *Erodium lebelii* (syn. *Erodium glutinosum*), *Erodium danicum* and *Erodium balii*.

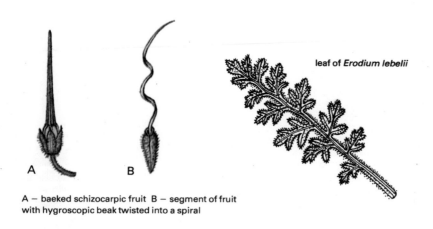

leaf of *Erodium lebelii*

A — baeked schizocarpic fruit B — segment of fruit with hygroscopic beak twisted into a spiral

Type of plant
dicotyledon

Diploid no.
2n — 40

Flowering period
April — October

Fruit
schizocarp

Common Wood Sorrel

Oxalis acetosella

This 5- to 15-cm-high perennial grows in open woods and forests with developed herb layer and in sub-alpine tall-stemmed grasslands.

The delicate, long-stalked leaves which are borne on a creeping rhizome, are trifoliolate and reddish on the underside; the stem is atrophied.

The flower-peduncle is hairy and bears two scale-like bracts. The calyx is longish-oval and hairy outside, the petals are white with violet-red veins. There are 10 stamens. The pistil is derived from five carpels and develops into a capsule. The ripe seeds are ejected a distance of up to several decimetres.

In sunny weather the flowers usually open between nine and ten in the morning and as a rule close between five and seven in the afternoon. However, they close at any time of the day if rain threatens; at the same time the peduncles curve downward so the flowers are protected from damp. The separate leaflets likewise fold along the midrib and their stalks droop.

Wood Sorrel is widespread in all Europe and occurs also in Asia, north Africa and North America.

It is sometimes eaten by children who like its somewhat sour taste; however it is slightly poisonous and may therefore be dangerous if eaten in greater quantities.

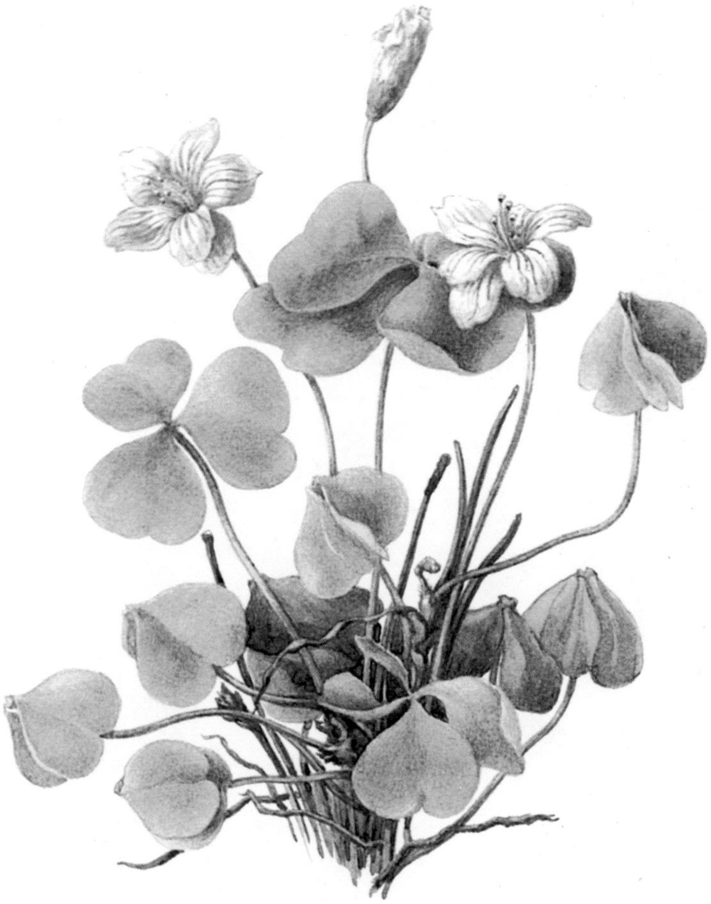

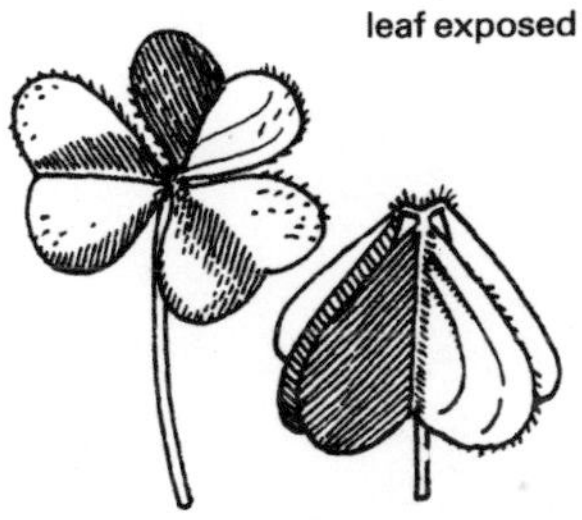

leaf exposed to light and shaded leaf

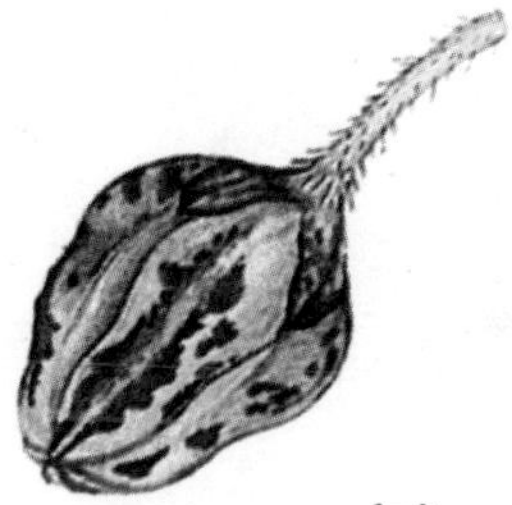

fruit

Type of plant
dicotyledon

Diploid no.
2n – 22

Flowering period
April – May

Fruit
capsule

Burning Bush

Dictamnus albus

This perennial, with its characteristic woody, whitish rhizome from which it takes its Latin name *albus*, occurs in open woods, on sunny, shrubby slopes and in forest steppe, but only on limestone.

The erect, unbranched and softly-hairy stem reaches a height of 60 to 120 cm. The upper part is covered with black oil glands. The lower leaves are simple and sessile, the upper ones odd-pinnate and stalked. They are covered with fine hairs and translucent dots, visible when held up to the light, which are vessels containing lemon-scented volatile oil.

The flowers, which are regular and arranged in racemes, are not borne until the sixth year. The stamens mature before the pistils. The five pistils, consisting of a single carpel each, develop into five follicles, which, however, are reminiscent of a capsule by their shape and arrangement. As the fruit matures and dries the walls burst and the seeds are ejected a comparatively long distance — sometimes even more than 2 metres from the plant.

This is a thermophilous, Eurasian species.

Burning Bush has a typical lemon scent which is especially pronounced in bright sun. It is produced by the fragrant substances secreted by the glands that cover practically the whole plant. The volatile oils, which evaporate and turn into a gas in hot weather, may even be ignited under such conditions.

mature fruit

diagram of flower of the rue family

Type fo plant
dicotyledon

Diploid no.
2n — 36

Flowering period
May — June

Fruit
follicle

Box-leaved Milkwort

Polygala chamaebuxus

Syn. *Chamaebuxus alpestris*

This much-branched shrub, up to 30 cm high, occurs in open woods and forest margins with thick vegetation.

The branches, which turn woody, root where they lie on the ground and rise in a curving arc at the tip. The leaves are leathery, persistent and evergreen.

On each branch there are one or two, less often three peduncled flowers, coloured yellow and up to 15 mm in length. The sepals are yellowish-white during the flowering period, later they are reddish-brown to purple. There are only three petals; the middle one is like a tubular sac and resembles the keel of the papilionate corolla, the other two are smaller. The corolla is whitish to pale yellow at first, yellow to orange in full bloom, and often almost reddish when spent. The flowers are pollinated by insects. The capsules contain seeds up to 5 mm long with an appendage, which is a favourite food of ants, that is responsible for the dispersal of the seeds, sometimes quite far from the parent plant.

This species often flowers a second time – in autumn. It is common in western Europe, the Alps and central Europe. The Vltava River in Czechoslovakia marks the eastern boundary of its range.

Type of plant
dicotyledon

Diploid no.
2n – 46

Flowering period
March – June

Fruit
capsule

fruit

faded flower

Dog's Mercury

Mercurialis perennis

This dioecious perennial, 10 to 40 cm high, grows in open woods, thickets and forest margins.

It has a creeping rhizome that turns dark violet in dry conditions. The stem rising from the rhizome is erect, four-angled, scaly at the base and unbranched. The stalked leaves are longish-ovate to elliptic-lanceolate, narrowing abruptly towards the base and toothed on the margin. The stipules are approximately 2 mm long.

The greenish flowers are small and unisexual. The male flowers are in small clusters and form slender, sparse racemes, whereas the female flowers are either solitary or in twos on long peduncles. The staminate flowers are composed of three sepals and nine stamens, the pistillate flowers of three sepals and a superior ovary — there are no petals. The fruit is a bristly capsule.

Dog's Mercury is a poisonous plant containing saponins. An interesting sidelight is that this is the species where the sexuality of plants was first discovered.

It is distributed throughout Europe almost to the Arctic Circle.

fruit

Type of plant
dicotyledon

Diploid no.
2n — 42, 64, 66, 80, 84

Flowering period
April — May

Fruit
capsule

Cypress Spurge

Euphorbia cyparissias

The Cypress Spurge is a 10- to 30-cm-high perennial growing on sunny slopes, in open thickets and in dry waste places.

It has a woody, branched rhizome from which rise tufted stems that ooze milk containing poisonous glycosides when bruised. The stems are red and leafless at the base, higher up they are thickly covered with sessile alternate leaves which are linear, glabrous and spreading.

The inflorescence is very complex and is called a cyathium. The involucral bracts are broadly ovate, pointed and yellow, becoming reddish in the fruit. The inconspicuous false 'flowers' are perched singly amongst the smaller bracts. In reality they are small inflorescences with a single peduncled female flower reduced to a mere pistil and encircled by eight to twelve male flowers. The latter are also reduced – in this case to a single stamen. On the margin of the inflorescence there are four orbicular, two-horned, yellowish glands that later acquire a brown tint.

The trilocular, peduncled ovary (the reduced pistillate flower) has three styles and develops into a finely warty capsule that bursts when ripe, ejecting the seeds far from the parent plant.

This species is widespread in almost all of continental Europe except the extreme north and south.

Type of plant
dicotyledon

Diploid no.
2n – 20, 40

Flowering period
April – May

Fruit
capsule

inflorescence

Sun Spurge

Euphorbia helioscopia

This annual, reaching a height of 5 to 40 cm, grows in loamy fields, gardens, vineyards and wasteland.

The erect, rounded stem is sparsely covered with alternate leaves that fall off during the fruiting period. The wedge-shaped-obovate to rounded-spatulate leaves with their narrowed bases rise directly from the stem. The lower ones are smallest, those farther up are increasingly larger the closer they are to the top. The subtending bracts are large.

The inflorescence (a cyathium) is the same as in the preceding species, the only difference being that the involucral bracts are slanting obovate and blunt. The inflorescences contain yellow, elliptic glands. The developing capsules are glabrous, smooth and finely spotted.

Sun spurge is probably a native of the Mediterranean region. It is found in most of Europe except the extreme north, also in Asia, and north Africa. It has been introduced to Australia and New Zealand.

Like *Euphorbia cyparissias* it oozes a white fluid when bruised, this being a typical characteristic of spurges. It is also a reliable means of distinguishing certain African desert spurges from cacti, which they resemble at first glance.

Some species of the spurge family are tree forms reaching a height of 20 metres. One example is the Rubber Tree (*Hevea brasiliensis*) which is the source of the caoutchouc of commerce, obtained by coagulating the milky juice (latex) from the plant.

fruit

inflorescence

Type of plant
dicotyledon

Diploid no.
2n — 42

Flowering period
May — September

Fruit
capsule

One-flowered Wintergreen

Moneses uniflora
Syn. *Moneses grandiflora, Pyrola uniflora*

This small perennial plant, reaching a height of 5 to 10 cm, grows in coniferous woods.

The stem growing from the rhizome is erect and angled. There are only three basal leaves which are persistent, up to 2.5 cm long, and circular in outline with a finely crenate margin.

The stem carries a single, drooping, rotate flower with a pronounced fragrance. The calyx lobes are up to 3 mm long, rounded-ovate and ciliate. The capsules are erect, not pendent, and dehisce from the top at maturity.

One-flowered Wintergreen, though inconspicuous, is a beautiful plant when viewed close up and it is only thanks to its unobtrusiveness that it escapes the notice of rock garden enthusiasts. As a rule it is not as rigidly bound by a mycorhizal association with its host as are the other members of the wintergreen family, which can only rarely be grown in cultivation, and can be readily grown from seeds sown under conifers. Adult plants, however, should not be moved because even though it grows throughout most of Europe, chiefly in mountain regions, it is on the list of rigidly protected species in some countries.

Type of plant
dicotyledon

Diploid no.
2n — 26

Flowering period
May — August

Fruit
capsule

diagram of flower

fruit

Yellow Birdsnest

Monotropa hypopitys

This 10- to 25-cm-high perennial grows in shady coniferous as well as mixed woods.

Inasmuch as it does not contain chlorophyll it is not able to carry on photosynthesis from which it is evident that it lives as a parasite. The richly-branched rhizome has a vanilla-like scent. From this rises an erect stem coloured waxy yellow, whitish or brownish, and covered with ovate scale-like leaves.

The flowers are arranged in a drooping raceme which later straightens. They are sessile and grow from the axils of semi-clasping, longish-ovate bracts. The bracts beneath the flowers are a substitute for the calyx, which is absent in this plant. The pale yellow petals are up to 16 mm long, narrowly bell-shaped and nodding. The stamens are ciliate. The capsules are up to 8 mm long.

Members of the wintergreen family, which often live in symbiosis with other plants, include among their derived relatives plants that live solely as parasites. In the northern hemisphere the only such relatives are plants of the genus *Monotropa*. Besides the Yellow Birdsnest, also found in Europe is the species *Monotropa hypophegea*, which is entirely glabrous even during the flowering period. It occurs in broad-leaved woodlands, chiefly beech woods.

fruit

diagram of flower

Type of plant
dicotyledon

Diploid no.
2n — 48

Flowering period
May — August

Fruit
capsule

Marsh Andromeda

Andromeda polifolia

This small shrub, up to 40 cm high, is a very rare plant found only in some high mountain heaths in central and northern Europe.

It has a creeping, woody rhizome which bears rooting, prostrate or ascending, little-branched stems. The leaves have revolute margins and are covered with a greyish bloom beneath; the upper surface is dark green.

The flowers are pendent and have striking red peduncles. The calyx is deeply divided into five segments, the urceolate corolla is 4 to 6 mm long, pale pink, with short, recurved lobes coloured a darker hue. There are ten stamens. The fruit is a dark blue-green capsule.

This poisonous plant is a central European glacial relict, i.e. a species widespread in the northern regions at the end of the Tertiary and forced to retreat by the spreading ice sheet to central Europe where it has survived in certain high mountain localities to this day.

Relatives of Marsh Andromeda include the Bearberry (*Arctostaphylos uva-ursi*), a prostrate shrublet reminiscent of the Cowberry. However, its leaves are persistent and without the translucent dots found in Cowberry. The fruit of Bearberry, a berry-like drupe with five pyrenes, is coloured red.

Type of flower
dicotyledon

Diploid no.
2n — 48

Flowering period
May — June

Fruit
capsule

longitudinal section of flower

Wild Rosemary
or **Marsh Tea**

Ledum palustre

This evergreen shrub reaching a height of 150 cm grows in heath moors and open pine woods from lowlands to foothills, very occasionally also on shaded, moss-covered sandstone rocks.

The leaves are rust-felted on the underside, as are the young branches. Normally spread out horizontally, the leaves droop during lengthier periods of drought, thereby reducing to the minimum the surface area exposed to the sun. The white flowers contain nectar, and are arranged in dense umbels. The stamens are longer than the petals, which, unlike those of other members of the heath family, are entirely separate, not joined. The flowers are pollinated by insects which are attracted not only by their appearance but apparently also by the plant's strong spicy fragrance. The fruit resembles a fountain with 10- to 15-mm-long peduncled capsules hanging from the arching sprays. The numerous seeds falling from the capsules at maturity are dispersed by the wind.

Wild Rosemary reaches an age of thirty years. It contains poisonous substances and was formerly used in folk medicine as well as against troublesome insects. Nowadays, it is on the list of protected species in many countries. It is found in northern and central Europe but has already become extinct in many places.

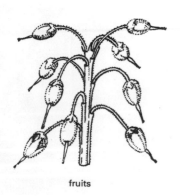

fruits

Type of plant
dicotyledon

Diploid no.
2n — 52

Flowering period
May — July

Fruit
capsule

Heather or Ling

Calluna vulgaris

Heaths, dry, overgrown moss moors, pine woods and forest margins are the habitats of this plant.

The stems of this prostrate, 25- to 50-cm-high shrublet are densely leafy. The leaves are prickly with conspicuously revolute margins, seemingly hollow, and furnished with two small teeth at the base.

The pendent flowers are arranged in terminal racemes. They grow on short peduncles from the axils of bracts. The violet-pink calyx is 4-merous, membranous, glossy and does not fall when the flowers are spent. The corolla is not evident at first glance because it is shorter than the calyx (half its length). There are eight stamens and the ovary is composed of four carpels. The fruit is a brownish capsule that opens by four valves. It contains a great many tiny seeds.

This species is widespread throughout most of Europe and is also found in Asia Minor and western Siberia, as well as in North America where it was introduced.

Beech woods, spruce woods, high-stemmed mountain grasslands, etc. are composed not only of beech, spruce, grasses, etc. but also of diverse plant species in various parts of the northern hemisphere. Heaths, however, are all composed of a single, albeit variable species – Heather (*Calluna vulgaris*). The genus *Calluna* has only the one species. The related genus *Erica* (Heath), on the other hand, embraces at least 500 species, of which some 15 to 20 are found in Europe, the remainder in South Africa.

Type of plant
dicotyledon

Diploid no.
2n – 16

Flowering period
July – October

Fruit
capsule

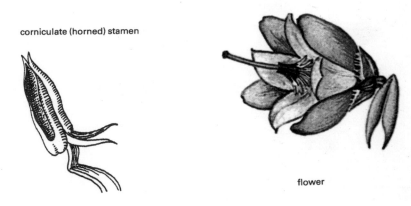

corniculate (horned) stamen

flower

Flesh-coloured Heath

Erica herbacea

Syn. *Erica carnea*

This richly-branched shrublet, reaching a height of 50 cm, grows in mountain pine woods and overgrown screes, being partial to lime-rich soils.

The ascending to erect stems are thickly covered with narrowly-linear, acicular leaves that are hairless, glossy and evergreen.

The flowers are arranged in dense terminal racemes. They are drooping and flesh-coloured but may sometimes be white. The four sepals are joined, the teeth pointed and reddish. The narrowly bell-shaped corolla, up to 50 mm long (longer than the calyx), is composed of four petals joined to form a tube ending in four short teeth. The eight stamens have purple anthers. The pistils are dark red and glabrous. The long style protrudes from the flower. Pollination is by insects.

This species is an Atlantic element and is found chiefly in southwestern and western Europe.

Both names — *Erica carnea* and *Erica herbacea* — were given to the plant by Linné, who first described spring-flowering specimens according to the flesh-pink colour of the blossom and then autumn specimens after the flowers had faded. Even though it is a shrublet, Flesh-coloured Heath was given the name *herbacea*, meaning herbaceous, to underscore the difference between this and the best-known member of the genus Brier (*Erica arborea*) — its large woody root is used to make the tobacco pipes called briars — which is of tree-like habit (*arborea* is Latin for 'tree-like').

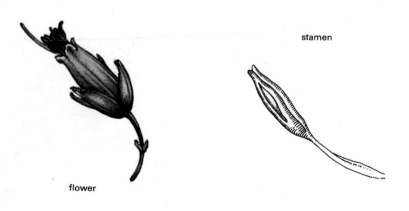

stamen

flower

Type of plant
dicotyledon

Diploid no.
2n — 24

Flowering period
March — June

Fruit
capsule

Cowberry

Vaccinium vitis-idaea

This thickly-branched shrub, up to 20 cm high, grows in coniferous woods and heaths but avoids soils containing lime.

The twigs are rounded and erect. They are covered with short, rather soft hairs in youth; later they are glabrescent. The leaves are persistent, evergreen and stiff, with a revolute margin. They are glossy dark green above and pale green dotted brown on the underside.

The flowers are arranged in terminal racemes. The calyx is composed of five joined sepals with triangular ciliate teeth. The corolla is whitish-pink, faintly scented and divided one-third to halfway to the base into four or five pointed, recurved petals. There are ten stamens. The stigma protrudes from the drooping flower. The fruit is a berry, coloured red when ripe and with a pleasant, slightly bitter taste. The berries are a popular food and collected for both home use as well as industrial processing; Cowberry is also used as a medicinal plant, particularly in treating diarrhoea.

This species is distributed in northern and central Europe. Found in the European part of the Arctic, in arctic Asia and artic North America is a Cowberry with stems that are always less than 10 cm high, scanty racemes composed of only two to five flowers, and smaller berries; it is a subspecies designated as subspecies *minus*.

Type of plant
dicotyledon

Diploid no.
2n — 24

Flowering period
June — August

Fruit
berry

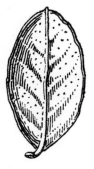

leaf

Common Bilberry or **Whortleberry**

Vaccinium myrtillus

The Common Bilberry, a thickly-branched shrub up to 50 cm high, is found in coniferous woods and heaths, where it often makes thick spreading masses.

The twigs are angled and covered with soft, alternate deciduous leaves with a finely serrate margin.

Growing from the axils of the leaves are peduncled, drooping flowers. The calyx is bluntly lobed and coloured pale green. The rose-tinted corolla is globosely-urceolate with short teeth. Like the calyx it is formed by the fusion of four to five segments. There are eight to ten stamens. After fertilization the flowers develop into berries coloured blackish-blue when ripe and often covered with a frost-like bloom.

This species is found in most of Europe, but in southern Europe it grows only in the mountains.

The berries are used in cooking to make pies, compotes, etc. and also for their medicinal properties. They contain substances that lower the sugar level in the blood, besides which they are rich in Vitamin A, B, and above all C. That is why they are of such great value from the viewpoint of diet, and are even beneficial where diabetics are concerned. They likewise alleviate symptoms in diarrhoea.

The blue, pruinose berries of the related Bog Bilberry (*Vaccinium uliginosum*), on the other hand, though edible may cause nausea in some people. This species with greyish-green, prominently-veined leaves grows in mountain moorland.

fruits

cross-section of stem

Type of plant
dicotyledon

Diploid no.
2n – 24

Flowering period
April – July

Fruit
berry

Mezereon

Daphne mezereum

Humus-rich woodlands with a thick herb layer, thickets, and high-stemmed grasslands is the location of this perennial, 30- to 150-cm-high shrub, generally found on limestone substrates to which it is partial.

The relatively sparse branches are firm and flexible; the alternate leaves are clustered at the tips of the branches.

Mezereon flowers in early spring so that the previous year's leaves are still on the branches. From the axils of these leaves grow scant clusters of rosy-purple, 4-merous flowers with a heady fragrance. The coloured calyx resembles a corolla and its segments are joined at the base to form a tube. The heterostylous flowers are pollinated by insects, which are attracted not only by their fragrance but also visually. The pollen germinates only on the stigma of another type of flower. The leaves appear on the twigs after the flowers fall. The fruits, red drupes, are eaten by some birds, who then distribute undigestible seeds throughout the neighbourhood in their faeces.

Mezereon is an extremely poisonous plant. It is on the list of protected species in many European countries.

It is often grown in the garden — both the typical rosy-purple variety and the white form (var. *alba*) with yellow drupes. The related south- and west-European species (*Daphne pontica, Daphne alpina,* and others) are very decorative elements in the rock garden. Found in a single locality in central Europe, where it is endemic, is the species *Daphne arbuscula*, whose deep rose blossoms brighten the limestone rocks of the Muráň Highlands in middle Slovakia.

Type of plant
dicotyledon

Diploid no.
2n — 18

Flowering period
February — March

Fruit
drupe

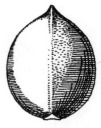

seed

Touch-me-not

Impatiens noli-tangere

This annual herb, 50 to 120 cm high, grows in damp broad-leaved and mixed woods and in their margins.

The juicy, hairless stems are upright and branched about a third of their length. The leaves are alternate, long-stalked, longish-ovate and pointed at the tip.

The large yellow flowers are drooping and arranged in racemes. The calyx is usually composed of three sepals, one of which is prolonged into a down-curved spur. The corolla is generally composed of five petals dotted red inside; the lower petal is largest. The five stamens have fused filaments and the five carpels are likewise fused. After fertilization the flower develops into a large capsule up to 25 mm long with valves. These contract abruptly and eject the seeds far from the parent plant when the capsule is ripe. Although Touch-me-not is distributed throughout most of Europe, this is the only member of the genus native to Europe. All other balsams have been introduced here; some of them occur as garden escapes and others are already well established. The Small-flowered Balsam (*Impatiens parviflora*) is today a widespread weed of damp woods, coastal thickets, parks and gardens. It is a native of central Asia and southern Siberia. Another that is grown in gardens and occurs in large numbers as an escape is *Impatiens glandulifera* (syn. *Impatiens roylei*) from the forests at the foot of the Himalayas. It has up to 2-metre-high stems covered with alternate or whorled leaves and large, rosy-purple flowers.

dehiscing fruit

Type of flower
dicotyledon

Diploid no.
2n — 20

Flowering period
July — August

Fruit
capsule

Common Mallow
Malva sylvestris

This plant, which may be biennial or perennial, reaches a height of 20 cm to 1 metre and is found in dry waste places rich in nitrogen.

The ascending or upright stem is more or less woody at the base. The lowest leaves are long-stalked, the stem leaves have shorter stalks. They usually have from three to seven lobes and gland-dotted veins. Both stem and leaves are thickly hairy. The stipules are triangular-ovate.

The flowers are peduncled and grow in clusters of two to six from the axils of the leaves. They have both a calyx and an epicalyx. The corolla is composed of five obovate, deeply notched petals coloured rose with three darker veins. The stamens are many and variable in number and their filaments are fused into a tube. The pistils are also numerous. The fruit is schizocarpic and splits into one-seeded, half-moon-shaped segments at maturity.

Common Mallow is distributed throughout most of Europe except the extreme north. Because of the large amount of mucilaginous substances in the flowers and leaves, it is used in the preparation of expectorants — medicines provoking the cough reflex.

The robust subspecies *mauritiana* from the Mediterranean region is grown for pharmaceutical purposes.

Type of plant
dicotyledon

Diploid no.
2n — 42

Flowering period
June — September

Fruit
schizocarp

diagram of flower

fruit

Common St. John's Wort

Hypericum perforatum

This 30- to 90-cm-high perennial grows on sunny slopes, in grassland, heaths, thickets and open woods.

The greatly-branched underground rhizome bears an upright, more or less glandular flowering stem branching at the top and several, much-branched, non-flowering stems. The elliptic leaves are thickly covered with translucent dots. The lower leaves are sessile and rounded at the base, the upper leaves narrow at the base into a short stalk. In dry weather they curl slightly at the edge. The calyx is spotted black and pointed, and the golden-yellow corolla is also spotted black. The stamens, from 50 to 60, are arranged in three bundles. The fruit is a capsule.

This species is distributed throughout most of Europe excepting the northernmost islands. Therefore it is not surprising that it exhibits such marked variability and that many intraspecific taxons and seemingly different species have been described. The currently recognized subspecies *veronense*, subspecies *angustifolia* and subspecies *latifolium* differ from the type subspecies *perforatum* in the size of the leaves, length of the calyx lobes and size of the flowers.

fruit

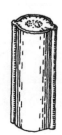

cross-section of stem

Type of plant
dicotyledon

Diploid no.
2n — 32

Flowering period
July — August

Fruit
capsule

Purple Loosestrife

Lythrum salicaria

Purple Loosestrife grows to a height of 30 cm to 2 metres, and is found by waterways and in wet meadows and ditches.

The stems are erect and simple or else branched in the lower half, sharply four-angled or winged, and shortly-pubescent. The lower leaves are opposite, the upper leaves alternate, sessile, with narrowly- to ovate-lanceolate blade and rounded or heart-shaped base.

The flowers are arranged in short dichasiums, which grow from the axils of bracts and these in turn form spike-like inflorescences at the tips of the stems. The flowers are subtended by two bracteoles. The calyx is composed of six joined sepals. The corolla is bluish-violet, red or whitish. The hypanthium, formed by the union of the lower part of the calyx and corolla, is tubular, twelve-ribbed and pubescent. Self-pollination is prevented by the differing lengths of the stamens and styles in the individual flowers − heterotristyly. The fruit is a capsule.

This species is distributed throughout most of Europe except the extreme north.

Other, related species such as *Lythrum hyssopifolia* which has small violet flowers and *Lythrum virgatum* which has red flowers are found in central Europe.

Type of plant
dicotyledon

Diploid no.
2n − 60

Flowering period
July − September

Fruit
capsule

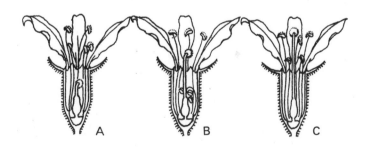

Heterostyly: A − short-styled flower B − median-styled flower C − long-styled flower

fruit

fruit

Rosebay Willow-herb or **Fireweed**

Epilobium angustifolium

Syn. *Chamaerion angustifolium, Chamaenerion angustifolium*

This perennial, reaching a height of 60 to 120 cm, grows in woodland clearings and subalpine grasslands, but avoids soils with a calcareous substrate.

It has a creeping rhizome which bears simple, upright, more or less rounded stems that are usually almost hairless. The leaves are thin, alternate, linear-lanceolate, and short-stalked with indistinctly toothed, more or less revolute margins. The underside has prominent veins. The leaves of this species were formerly used to adulterate tea.

The flowers are arranged in dense racemes that are leafy at the base. The flower buds are elliptic and pointed, the open flowers may be more than 1 cm across. The calyx is composed of four sepals and is red and pubescent outside. The petals are obovate and coloured red, very occasionally white. The capsules are longish-linear and covered with thick down. They contain a great many seeds which are furnished with a cottony tuft of hairs facilitating their dispersal by the wind. This species is widespread in all Europe.

The species *Epilobium dodonaei*, which is a pioneer plant of sandy shores, sand dunes, quarries and the like, differs by having stiff leaves narrowly-linear to linear-lanceolate in outline and pink flowers borne until September.

Type of plant
dicotyledon

Diploid no.
2n − 36

Flowering period
June − September

Fruit
capsule

Broad-leaved Willow-herb

Epilobium montanum

This 20- to 80-cm-high perennial occurs in open woods and woodland clearings.

The stems growing from the short rhizome are rounded and branched at the top, the tips drooping at first and erect during flowering. There are two rows of hairs running down the length of the stem (one on either side), the upper part of the stem is pubescent with interspersed glands. The lower leaves are opposite, the upper leaves alternate. They are ovate, with a rounded wedge-shaped base, pointed tip, irregularly toothed margin, and veins covered with down on both the upper and under surface.

The bracts are narrow, lanceolate and sharply serrate. The flowers are arranged in terminal racemes. The calyx is composed of four green sepals, the corolla of four upright petals coloured various shades of red with dark veins and twice as long as the sepals. The stamens are arranged in two rings of four each. The mature capsules are glandular-pubescent.

This species is distributed throughout most of Europe.

The related species *Epilobium collinum* has stems branching from the base, smaller, grey-green leaves, and capsules that are pubescent but without glands. It grows on sunny, stony slopes and rocks, in open woods and in thickets, usually avoiding chalky soil. Found in mountain grasslands is the species *Epilobium alpestre*, distinguished by having the leaves arranged in whorls of three to four leaves.

Type of plant
dicotyledon

Diploid no.
2n — 36

Flowering period
June — September

Fruit
capsule

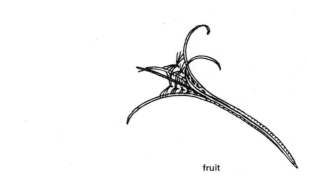

fruit

Common Evening Primrose

Oenothera biennis

Sandy and gravelly banks by the waterside, sandy waste places and railway embankments are the habitats of this 50- to 150-cm-high herb, which, as its Latin name indicates, is a biennial.

The first year it produces a basal rosette of obovate leaves pressed close to the ground, the second year an erect, usually angled, glandular-pubescent stem that is often branched at the top. The stem leaves are short-stalked, elliptic or longish-cordate, with a finely and irregularly toothed margin.

The large flowers are arranged in terminal racemes. The four sepals are lanceolate and reflexed. The four petals, coloured pale yellow, are obcordate and slightly notched. The sepals and petals are joined at the base in a hypanthium. There are eight stamens and the ovary is derived from four carpels. The fruit is a slender, long, four-angled capsule, often felted, which is enclosed by the hypanthium.

This species is native to North America, but it is now found in practically all of Europe. In central Europe it occurs as a collective species embracing a number of microspecies. *Oenothera parviflora*, another collective species (comprising more than five microspecies) differs by having the leaf rosette 5 to 10 cm above the ground and an inflorescence more or less drooping before the flowers open.

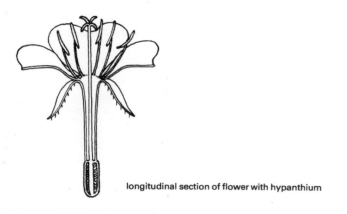

longitudinal section of flower with hypanthium

Type of plant
dicotyledon

Diploid no.
2n — 14

Flowering period
June — August

Fruit
capsule

Water-chestnut

Trapa natans

This annual floating weed occurs in calm, and slow-flowing sun-warmed water.

The root often disappears shortly after germination and the plant is anchored in the soil at the bottom by adventitious roots. When the tip of the stem reaches the surface and the floating leaves appear, the bottom part of the stem either rots or the plant is torn from its moorings by a storm. New, pinnately-branched stems then grow in at the nodes in place of the former roots, but they are green (due to the presence of chlorophyll) and carry on photosynthesis, thereby functioning partly as leaves.

The flowers are hermaphroditic and grow on long peduncles from the axils of the upper leaves. They are composed of four sepals, four white petals, four stamens and a single pistil. They may be fertilized by the pollen from their own stamens (autogamy) or from the stamens of other flowers (allogamy) usually brought by aquatic insects. Shortly after pollination the flower peduncles submerge and the fruit develops below the surface. It is a one-seeded 'nut' enclosed by the calyx which has become enlarged and woody. When it falls its four spikes or horns serve to anchor the fruit in the mud at the bottom, where it overwinters. The seeds are edible and rich in starch.

This species occurred in Europe as far back as the Tertiary as testified to by the fossil finds of fruits.

Type of plant
dicotyledon

Diploid no.
2n − (40),48

Flowering period
June − September

Fruit
'nut'

leaf with inflated petiole

fruit

Ivy

Hedera helix

The trunks of trees in broad-leaved and mixed woods as well as rocks and walls are sometimes covered by Ivy which may reach a length of up to two metres. It is often grown for decoration in a number of cultivated forms.

This evergreen climber climbs by numerous adhesive roots. Its leaves are leathery, without stipules and of two distinct kinds. Those on the flowering twigs are longish-ovate, whereas those on the non-flowering twigs are three- to five-lobed.

The flowers are arranged in small, semi-globose umbels with peduncles growing from the axils of scale-like bracts. They are regular, divided into five parts, and hermaphroditic. The petals, brownish outside and green inside, fall when spent. The fruits are round black berries up to 1 cm across containing three to five seeds.

Ivy is distributed throughout most of Europe and in north Africa.

Both cultivated as well as natural populations are relatively variable. The subspecies *poetarum* found in France and Italy has yellow berries. Grown in parks and gardens is the species *Hedera colchica* from the Caucasus and Anatolia which was not discovered until the eighteenth century.

fruits

two types of leaves

Type of plant
dicotyledon

Diploid no.
2n — 48

Flowering period
September — October

Fruit
berry

Wood Sanicle

Sanicula europaea

This perennial, reaching a height of 25 to 45 cm, grows in mixed woods, and particularly in lime-rich soils.

It has a short creeping rhizome from which rises a simple, erect, sharply angled stem. The lowest leaves are long-stalked and are each divided into from three to five leaflets. In general, there are no stem leaves, but occasionally one or two may exist. When they are present, they are small, less divided and sessile.

The flowers are arranged in scanty, terminal umbels composed of tiny heads (capitula). They are of two kinds: more or less sessile, hermaphroditic flowers and short-peduncled male flowers. The latter are composed of five sepals, five whitish or reddish petals and five stamens. The hermaphroditic flowers are the same except that in addition they have a pistil composed of two carpels. The mature fruit, a double achene, is globose or shortly-ovate, up to 5 mm long, and covered all over with hooked spines which catch in the fur of animals thereby aiding in the plant's dispersal.

Wood Sanicle is distributed throughout Europe, except the Azores, Balearic Islands, Crete, Iceland and the southwestern USSR.

Type of plant
dicotyledon

Diploid no.
2n – 16

Flowering period
May – June

Fruit
double achene

A – male flower B – hermaphroditic flower

Field Eryngo

Eryngium campestre

This prickly perennial herb, which forms globose tufts and reaches a height of 20 to 50 cm, grows on sunny slopes and in sandy grasslands.

The stems are thick, erect, glabrous and finely grooved. They branch out loosely from about a third of their length up. The basal leaves of young plants are simple, elongate and spiny. The lower stem leaves of flowering plants are long-stalked and pinnatisect. The segments are broadly linear, sharply spiny on the margin, and continue on down the rachis. The upper stem leaves are sessile, more simple and smaller.

The flowers are clustered in dense spherical heads (capitula). The bracts are spiny, and the outer bracts are longer than the flower heads. The sepals are also spiny. The petals, only half as long as the sepals, are either white or greenish. The fruits are flattened, obovate and scaly. When these mature whole spherical clumps of Eryngo (tumbleweeds) break off and are blown about by the wind, sometimes for great distances.

Field Eryngo is found in central and southern Europe. There are more than 25 species of Eryngo in Europe, some of which would be very pretty in the rock garden. *Eryngium giganteum* from central Asia is a striking plant with its huge heads of flowers and *Eringium maritimum* is a decorative element of coastal sands.

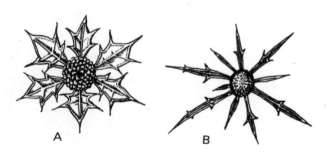

Head: A – *Eryngium maritimum* B – *Eryngium campestre*

Type of plant
dicotyledon

Diploid no.
2n – 14, 48

Flowering period
July – August

Fruit
double achene

Longleaf

Falcaria vulgaris

This 30- to 100-cm-high plant, which may be a biennial or perennial, grows on sunny slopes and in dry hedgerows.

The erect, rounded, finely-grooved stems have spreading branches. The leaves are stiff with segments that are often sickle-shaped and sharply serrate. The lower leaves are usually simple or ternate, those in the middle of the stem 1- or 2-ternate.

The tiny white flowers are arranged in loose umbels with four to eight linear bracts and bracteoles. The fruit is a double achene reminiscent of caraway; it is brownish-yellow and measures up to 4 mm in length.

This species is distributed from northern France and central Russia to southern Europe but is absent on the islands (Crete, Corsica, Sicily, etc.). It was introduced into Holland and Belgium as well as North and South America.

One may often come across non-flowering plants as late as July, when most members of this species are already in full bloom. The leaves of such plants are covered with the tiny, usually orange fruiting bodies of the parasitic rust fungus *Aecidium falcariae*. Plants attacked by rust do not flower, but their leaves usually die before the onset of autumn; this is an instance of a plant that is only seemingly annual, for under normal circumstances it requires at least two years for full development.

Type of plant
dicotyledon

Diploid no.
2n — 22

Flowering period
July — September

Fruit
double achene

sickle-shaped leaf

Cowbane

Cicuta virosa

This perennial, which reaches a height of 50 to 150 cm, grows on muddy shores, in flooded places and in ditches.

The stem is tuberous at the base, upright, and with transverse cavities. It branches in whorls at the top. The large leaves on the lower part of the stem are long-stalked, 2- or 3-pinnatisect and rough on the upper surface. The upper leaves are short-stalked or with sheath-like stalks. They are also less divided.

The flowers, usually whitish, are arranged in long-peduncled umbels without a set of bracts or with only one or two linear bracts. The umbellets are many-flowered and dense. The fruits are broadly ovoid and narrowly ribbed.

Cowbane is widespread in almost all of Europe, roughly from Madrid, Naples and Salonica northward.

This faintly foetid plant, smelling of mice according to some, contains a number of very poisonous alkaloids, principally cikutoxin. Although once the cause of cattle poisoning, this rarely occurs now as cultivation and drainage have been responsible for its disappearance from meadows. Cowbane is the only member of this genus but its relatives include plants that are equally as poisonous, e.g. Hemlock (*Conium maculatum*).

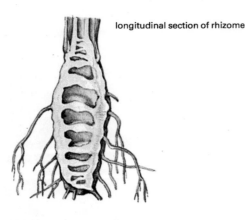

longitudinal section of rhizome

fruit

Type of plant
dicotyledon

Diploid no.
2n — 22

Flowering period
July — September

Fruit
double achene

Caraway

Carum carvi

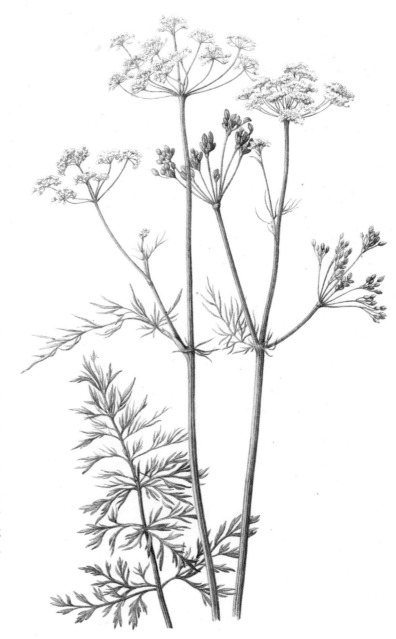

This annual, which reaches a height of 20 to 80 cm, is found in fields, meadows, pastureland and hedgerows from lowland to mountain districts. It is also grown domestically for its strongly scented fruits which are used as a kitchen herb in cooking.

The upright, sparsely-branched stem is grooved and angular and grows from a branched root which smells like a carrot. The leaves are 2- to 3-pinnatisect with linear to thread-like segments.

The branches end in umbels composed of eight to sixteen dense umbellets with peduncles of varying length. Bracts and bracteoles are generally absent. The calyx has indistinct teeth, the corolla is composed of whitish or rose-tinted, deeply-notched petals. The fruit is a double achene up to 5 mm long and grooved on the back.

Caraway is distributed throughout practically all of Europe except the Mediterranean region; it is widely established as a cultivated plant. All other European species of *Carum* generally have smaller fruits; some grow on rocks in the mountains, chiefly in the Balkans, Italian Alps and Apennines. However, the only one that is cultivated is *Carum carvi,* its fruits being used in many ways in cooking and its essential oils in the preparation of certain medicines and liqueurs.

Type of plant
dicotyledon

Diploid no.
2n – 20

Flowering period
May – July

Fruit
double achene

fruit

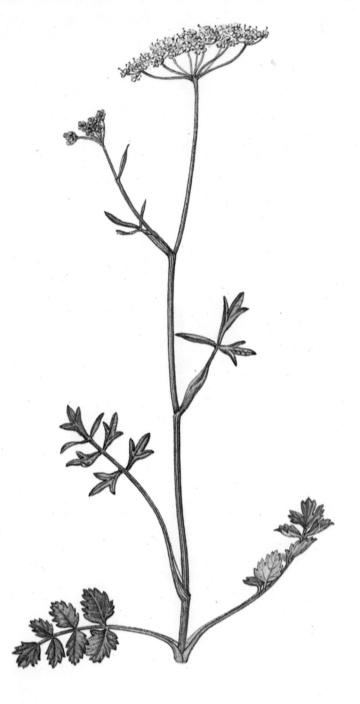

Burnet Saxifrage

Pimpinella saxifraga

Sunny slopes, pastureland and dry heaths are the habitats of this 15- to 50-cm-high perennial.

The spindle-like root, which has an unpleasant odour, bears round, finely-grooved, upright stems that branch at the top. The lower leaves are long-stalked, simply odd-pinnate with toothed, sessile leaflets, and the terminal leaflet is divided into three lobes. The upper leaves have sheath-like stalks and smaller, more divided leaflets.

The minute flowers are arranged in umbels composed of six to fifteen umbellets; bracts and bracteoles are usually absent. The flowers are white, tinted rose or yellowish, and are divided into five parts. The achenes are narrowly-ribbed on the back and about 2 mm long.

This species is widespread in nearly all of Europe but is absent in the southernmost parts and on the islands. It is also found in Asia Minor and western Siberia as well as in North America, where it was introduced. It exhibits marked variability within this extensive range; the various forms are sometimes classed as microspecies and sometimes only as subspecies or varieties.

fruit

flower

Type of plant
dicotyledon

Diploid no.
2n — 36

Flowering period
July — September

Fruit
double achene

Goutweed

Aegopodium podagraria

This perennial, which reaches a height of 50 to 90 cm, grows in woodland clearings, forest margins and thickets as well as in neglected lawns and gardens where it is a troublesome weed.

The angled, hollow stems form numerous underground runners by means of which the plant rapidly spreads. Though seemingly glabrous, a look through a magnifying lens reveals that it is covered with short bristles. The lower leaves are long-stalked and twice trifid (in three segments, each divided into three). The upper leaves are simply trifid, the uppermost leaves may be undivided.

The flowers are arranged in umbels composed of more than fifteen umbellets. Bracts and bracteoles are absent. The flower peduncles are roughly pubescent. The corollas are white, very occasionally tinted rose. The achenes are longish ovoid, up to 3 mm long, and coloured brown with pale ribs.

This species is distributed throughout most of Europe though it is rarer in the south. Its range extends to the Caucasus and Siberia. It is not native to Britain, Ireland and Iceland but has been introduced, and to North America as well.

Related species include *Sium latifolium* and Lesser Water-parsnip (*Berula erecta*), plants of swamps, pools and coastal vegetation.

Type of plant
dicotyledon

Diploid no.
2n — 44 (22)

Flowering period
May — September

Fruit
double achene

flower

fruit

Wild Angelica

Angelica sylvestris

This 50- to 150-cm-high plant grows as an annual or perennial in damp meadows, forest margins, thickets and alder groves.

The thick rhizome, which has a carroty smell and a bitter or burning taste, bears a robust, erect stem that is grooved, hollow, glabrous and covered with a frostlike bloom. The leaves are triangular in outline and 2- or 3-pinnate with large, inflated sheaths. The lower leaves are long-stalked and up to 60 cm long; the stalks are shallowly channelled on the upper side. The upper leaves are smaller and less divided, the uppermost have sheath-like stalks.

The flowers are clustered in terminal inflorescences — dense, semi-globose umbels composed of twenty to thirty-five umbellets without bracts but with numerous linear bracteoles. The teeth of the calyx are indistinct, the corollas are white or reddish, the stamens twice as long as the corollas, and the pistils longer than the corollas and curved.

The fruits are flattened, broadly elliptic achenes with three slender ribs on the back and two broad wings.

This species is found in most of Europe.

fruit

Type of plant
dicotyledon

Diploid no.
2n — 22

Flowering period
July — September

Fruit
double achene

Wild Carrot

Daucus carota

This plant, reaching a height of 30 to 80 cm, grows in rather dry meadows, hedgerows, pastureland and on embankments.

It has a characteristic root and a distinctive scent. The stem is erect, grooved and covered with bristly hairs. The leaves each have from two to four leaflets. The lower leaves are stalked and the upper leaves are sessile. All have small sheaths.

The flowers are arranged in dense flat umbels, which are funnel-shaped to spherical in the fruit, with numerous pinnatisect bracts and bracteoles. The central flower of the inflorescence is often dark violet, the others are normally white or yellowish. The marginal flowers are radiate.

The fruits are elliptic to ovoid achenes, up to 4 mm long, with three main ribs covered with short bristles and four subsidiary ribs covered with long, hooked spines.

This species is distributed in all of Europe except the Faeroe Islands, Iceland and Spitzbergen.

Cultivated forms belonging to the subspecies *sativus* have a large, sweet root, coloured red or orange to whitish, which is eaten as a vegetable. There are about ten related taxons in Europe.

Type of plant
dicotyledon

Diploid no.
2n – 18

Flowering period
June – September

Fruit
double achene

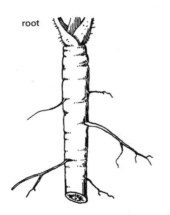

root

inflorescence with dark flower in centre

Hogweed

Heracleum sphondylium

This 50- to 250-cm-high perennial occurs chiefly in damp ditches, damp meadows and by the waterside.

The erect stems are angled, grooved and hollow and covered with recurved bristly hairs; only rarely are they glabrescent. The lower leaves have channelled stalks, the upper ones are smaller with inconspicuous sheath-like stalks.

The stems are terminated by large umbels usually composed entirely of hermaphroditic flowers. The lateral umbels, which are often smaller, are in the main composed solely of male flowers. Each umbel consists of from 15 to 30 umbellets. Bracts are either entirely absent or the lateral umbels may have from one to six. The calyx teeth are broad. The corollas are radiate and usually coloured white, though they may also be tinted yellow, green or pink. The fruits are glabrous, elliptic achenes with three ribs on the back and narrow wings.

This species is common in northwestern Europe, and is found in most of the rest of the continent.

The related *Heracleum mantegazzianum* from southwest Asia is a striking robust plant up to five metres high. It contains prominent photosensitive substances that cause blisters when they come in contact with the skin in the presence of sunlight.

fruit

flower

Type of plant
dicotyledon

Diploid no.
2n — 22

Flowering period
June — September

Fruit
double achene

Oxlip

Primula elatior

This perennial, which reaches a height of 30 cm, occurs mostly in meadows but is also found in open broad-leaved woods and thickets.

The leaves, arranged in a basal rosette, are at first curved underneath and more or less wrinkled; they are ovate to longishovate with an irregularly crenate. margin and narrow at the base into a winged stalk.

The scape is terminated by a one-sided umbel. The peduncles of the individual flowers are up to 2 cm long. The calyx is narrowly-cylindrical and pressed tightly to the corolla tube; its sharp edges are green, otherwise it is pale yellow and divided halfway to the base into five lanceolate teeth. The corolla is unscented, coloured sulphur yellow and has spreading lobes. After fertilization the flower develops into a cylindrical capsule which is longer than the calyx.

Oxlip is on the list of protected species in many European countries.

It is a medicinal plant, the same as Cowslip (*Primula veris*).The two species often interbreed and the hybrid offspring are classified as *Primula x media*.

Primula elatior is found in most of Europe extending as far north as northern Denmark.

In Europe it occurs in several subspecies, differing in the pubescence of the leaves or size and colour of the flowers.

Type of plant
dicotyledon

Diploid no.
2n — 22

Flowering period
March — May

Fruit
capsule

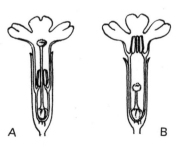

Heterostyly: A — long-styled flower B — short-styled flower

fruit

Cowslip

Primula veris

This perennial, reaching a height of 10 to 30 cm, grows in rather dry meadows, open woods, thickets, grassland and on embankments.

During the flowering period it may be pubescent or even glabrescent; it is sometimes also briefly dotted with reddish glands. The leaves, arranged in a basal rosette, are curved underneath at first and wrinkled; the blade is ovate to elliptic with an undulate margin and narrows at the base into a winged stalk.

The scape is terminated by a one-sided umbel of faintly scented flowers. The calyx, coloured pale yellow or greenish yellow, is slightly inflated and stands off from the corolla which is coloured yolk-yellow. The mouth of the corolla tube, which is the same length or longer than the calyx, is orange. The flowers are heterostylous thereby preventing self-pollination. They are fertilized only if pollen from flowers with a short style is carried by insects to the stigma of flowers with a long style and vice versa. The capsule is ovoid and about half the length of the inflated calyx which remains on the fruit.

Cowslip is slightly poisonous but is at the same time used as a home remedy in treating bronchitis, diseases of the urinary tract, rheumatism and to cause perspiration.

It is distributed throughout much of Europe but not the extreme north or the greater part of the Mediterranean region.

Cowslip is one of the plants where it is necessary to protect chiefly the underground parts.

fruit

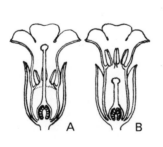

Heterostyly: A — long-styled flower
B — short-styled flower

Type of plant
dicotyledon

Diploid no.
2n — 22

Flowering period
April — June

Fruit
capsule

Purple Sowbread

Cyclamen purpurascens

Syn. *Cyclamen europaeum*

This pretty plant, only 10 to 20 cm high, grows in mountain forests, chiefly in deciduous woods.

The underground tuber bears a short scaly stem and a rosette of fleshy leaves that last the winter. The leaves are long-stalked and rounded-cordate with shallow scallops along the margin. They are dark green above, often spotted white, and reddish to carmine on the underside.

The scape ends in a fragrant flower. The sepals are green, the petals carmine with a slightly darker throat. The latter are sharply reflexed and joined at the base into a tube. The peduncles coil in a spiral and bend toward the ground in the fruit.

This species with its lovely, fragrant flowers is on the list of protected plants in many European countries. Its range extends from southeastern France to the western Carpathians and central Yugoslavia. In central Europe it occurs only in Bavaria, Austria and southern Czechoslovakia. Found in southern Europe are several other species of Cyclamen, all relicts from the Tertiary period and all protected by law.

Type of plant
dicotyledon

Diploid no.
2n — 34

Flowering period
July — September

Fruit
capsule

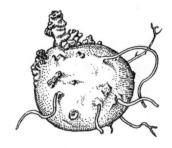

tuber

fruit

Yellow Loosestrife

Lysimachia vulgaris

Waterside thickets, damp woods, wet meadows and the edges of ponds and lakes are the habitats of this perennial which grows to a height of 50 to 150 cm.

It has an underground rhizome with scaly runners bearing reproductive buds and an erect, sparsely branched stem. The latter is bluntly angled and is covered with pubescent leaves dotted with dark red; these may be opposite or arranged in whorls of three, very occasionally four leaves.

The flowers are in terminal panicles which are leafy at the base. The flower peduncles, up to 1 cm long, grow from the axils of linear bracts. The calyx is divided all the way to the base into lanceolate lobes edged with red. The golden-yellow corolla is also divided to the base; the corolla lobes are longish-ovate, blunt and glabrous. The filaments are joined for half their length. The mature capsule is approximately 5 mm long.

This species is distributed throughout most of Europe.

The related *Lysimachia punctata* from southeastern Europe has flowers arranged in axillary verticillasters and leaves usually in whorls of three or four. It was formerly grown for decoration in gardens but because it readily occurs as an escape it has become naturalized and established in many localities in the western and northern parts of central Europe. Also sometimes grown in gardens is *Lysimachia ciliata* from North America which has also become naturalized chiefly in northwestern Europe.

Type of plant
dicotyledon

Diploid no.
2n — 56, 84

Flowering period
June — August

Fruit
capsule

Creeping Jenny

Lysimachia nummularia

This perennial, with 10- to 50-cm-long stems, grows in damp meadows, gardens, ditches and by water.

The 4-angled, creeping stem often roots at the nodes. It is glabrous and covered with opposite, rounded-ovate, black-dotted leaves with short stalks and entire margins.

The short-peduncled flowers grow from the axils of the middle leaves and are usually solitary. The calyx is divided to the base into heart-shaped, pointed lobes. The corolla is deep yellow spotted with dark red inside; the petals are blunt and obovate. The stamens have glandular filaments. The capsules are globose and shorter than the persistent calyx.

This species is distributed throughout most of Europe. Although it was determined that there are four cytotypes (populations differing in the number of chromosomes) it does not appear to be extremely variable. However, sometimes the flowers are not solitary but in twos and there are deviations in the size of the corolla lobes and the flowers, all of which may be viewed as normal intraspecific variability.

Related species found in central Europe include *Lysimachia nemorum* which has pointed-ovate leaves, long-peduncled flowers, linear-lanceolate petals and capsules the same length as the calyx.

Type of plant
dicotyledon

Diploid no.
2n — 32, 36, 43, 45

Flowering period
May — August

Fruit
capsule

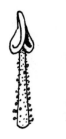

stamens

Tufted Loosestrife

Lysimachia thyrsiflora

Syn. *Naumburgia thyrsiflora*

This perennial, which reaches a height of 30 to 60 cm, is found in overgrown marshes and at watersides.

It has a creeping underground rhizome with shoots bearing reproductive buds and an erect stem which is scaly at the base and densely leaved above the scaly section. It is usually unbranched and woolly-pubescent to glabrescent. The leaves are opposite and decussate, though they may sometimes be in whorls. They are narrowly-lanceolate, up to 10 cm long, and semi-clasping at the base.

The 6- to 7-merous flowers are arranged in dense racemes that grow on long peduncles from the axils of the middle leaves. The calyx is only 2 mm long and divided to the base into linear lobes. The golden-yellow corolla is up to 5 mm long and is also divided to the base into linear, blunt lobes dotted with red. The stamens are glabrous, the pistil covered with red glands. The mature capsule is globose.

Tufted Loosestrife is found in northern Europe including the British Isles.

The family to which this marsh species belongs also includes the Water-violet (*Hottonia palustris*) which grows in still waters and pools. It forms 3- to 6-flowered racemes of whitish to rose-tinted flowers.

diagram of flower

Type of plant
dicotyledon

Diploid no.
2n — 54

Flowering period
May — July

Fruit
capsule

160

Scarlet Pimpernel

Anagallis arvensis

This small annual herb is a weed of fields, gardens, vineyards and wasteland.

The fragile stems are prostrate or ascending, reaching a length of 10 to 20 cm. The leaves, which may be opposite and decussate or arranged in whorls of three, are sessile, broadly-ovate with an entire margin and dotted with red on the underside.

The flowers grow singly on long peduncles from the axils of the leaves. The calyx is composed of five united sepals and deeply cleft into lanceolate lobes. The rotate, five-petalled corolla is slightly longer than the calyx. The corolla lobes are obovate and blunt with finely toothed, ciliate margin. They are coloured carmine but may be pink, violet as well as whitish and very occasionally tinted blue. The five violet-fringed stamens are joined at the base. The capsule is globose, about 5 mm across, and opens by a lid.

This species is distributed throughout Europe except Spitzbergen and Iceland. Also found in like places is the rarer *Anagallis foemina* which is truly difficult to distinguish from *Anagallis arvensis* in the case of specimens with blue-tinted flowers.

Type of plant
dicotyledon

Diploid no.
2n — 40

Flowering period
June — September

Fruit
capsule

fruit

flower of *Anagallis foemina*

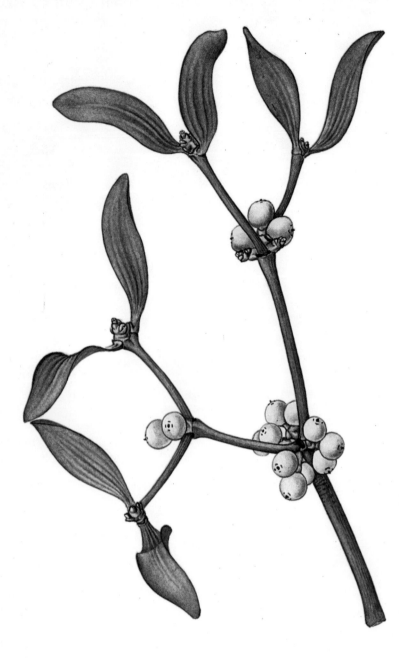

Common Mistletoe

Viscum laxum

This semi-parasitic evergreen shrublet up to 1 metre in diameter grows on the branches of trees in coniferous woods, chiefly spruce and pine woods.

The stems, which branch by repeated forking, are rounded, yellowish-green and brittle. The leaves are nearly sessile, opposite, oblong-ovate, with entire margin and leathery; they are also yellowish-green and do not drop.

The unisexual inflorescence is a dichasium composed of three flowers, growing sessile in the axils of branches. The larger male flowers are composed of four joined perianth segments and four stamens. The female flowers have three or four perianth segments and an inferior ovary. The fruit is a yellowish-white berry about 5 mm in diameter with a very sticky pericarp.

Common Mistletoe is found mainly on pines. Very occasionally one may come across the subspecies *abietis* on firs; this has broader, dark green leaves and whitish berries without the yellow tinge. The very similar White Mistletoe (*Viscum album*) with larger white berries and larger leaves occurs only on deciduous trees. The seeds of Common Mistletoe are greenish and contain only a single embryo, those of White Mistletoe are white and have two or three embryos. Found on the Iberian Peninsula, where it was introduced from North America, is the species *Viscum cruciatum* with red berries; it also grows only on deciduous trees.

Inflorescence: three-flowered dichasium

Type of plant
dicotyledon

Diploid no.
2n – 20

Flowering period
March – April

Fruit
false berry

Milkweed Gentian

Gentiana asclepiadea

The edges of subalpine deciduous woods and thickets and high-stemmed grasslands are the habitats of this lovely perennial which reaches a height of 30 to 60 cm.

It has a slender rhizome and simple, inclined stems thickly covered with opposite leaves. The latter are ovate-lanceolate, long-pointed and sessile. The entire plant is glabrous.

The flowers grow from the axils of the uppermost leaves (two or three in each axil) and form a narrow, one-sided raceme. The bottom flowers are short-peduncled, the upper ones sessile. The calyx is bell-shaped with shallow lobes. The corolla has its petals united at the base and coloured dark azure blue, usually spotted reddish-violet within. Very occasionally it may also be white. The fruit is an elongate, distinctly peduncled capsule with numerous broadly-winged seeds about 2 mm long.

This species is found chiefly in the mountains of central Europe; elsewhere in Europe it is less frequent. In the Alps it occurs at elevations of up to 2,200 metres.

In many localities Milkweed Gentian is on the list of protected species, because frequent picking of its lovely flowers has posed a grave threat to its existence.

Type of plant
dicotyledon

Diploid no.
2n — 44

Flowering period
August — September

Fruit
capsule

diagram of flower

Marsh Gentian

Gentiana pneumonanthe

This 20- to 40-cm-high perennial grows in peat meadows and in damp heaths.

It has a thick rhizome and erect, bluntly angled stems covered with narrow, sessile leaves with a slightly revolute margin.

The flowers grow from the axils of the uppermost leaves (from one to three in each axil). The upper flowers are sessile, the lower ones have short peduncles. The bell-shaped calyx is divided halfway to the base into linear lobes with a leathery membrane in between. The funnel-shaped corolla is coloured deep blue with five green-spotted lines on the outside; it is a paler hue at the base. Very occasionally it may be entirely blue, rose or white. The fruit is a capsule.

Marsh Gentian is distributed throughout most of Europe but is absent on many islands. It and the other gentians are on the list of protected species in many European countries.

Gentians of strikingly different colours include the yellow-flowered *Gentiana lutea, Gentiana punctata* with pale yellow flowers dotted dark violet and *Gentiana pannonica* which has dingy blue-violet to brownish-violet flowers with a dark-spotted throat. All are decorative elements of the mountains of central Europe and all pay dearly for having such beautiful flowers; the yellow gentians also for the medicinal properties of their roots.

bud

Type of plant
dicotyledon

Diploid no.
2n — 26

Flowering period
July — October

Fruit
capsule

Delicate Gentian

Gentianella ciliata

This herbaceous plant, which may be biennial or perennial and reaches a height of 5 to 25 cm, occurs mostly in grassy places in open woods and in thickets. It prefers lime-rich soils.

The slender rhizome bears erect, 4-angled stems. The leaves are opposite, linear to narrowly-elliptic and pointed, with a single vein. The margins are slightly rough.

The flowers are in four parts and borne singly at the tips of the stems or sparse branches. The calyx is cylindrical and divided two-thirds of the way to the base into linear-lanceolate lobes. Each corolla is vivid blue and shaped like a trumpet with expanded lobes that are fringed on the margin; the mouth of the trumpet is glabrous. The fruit is a capsule.

This species is distributed throughout most of Europe but is absent in the north. It is on the list of protected plants in most European countries.

Members of the genus *Gentianella* are noted for their seasonal and ecotypical polymorphism. *Gentianella campestris,* for instance, includes besides the typical autumn-flowering plants of lowland districts also deviations distinguished by spring flowering or mountain distribution. Other similar examples are *Gentianella germanica, Gentianella aspera, Gentianella austriaca* and *Gentianella lutescens.*

Type of plant
dicotyledon

Diploid no.
2n — 44

Flowering period
August — October

Fruit
capsule

petal

Common
or **Lesser Centaury**

Centaurium erythraea
Syn. *Centaurium minus, Centaurium umbellatum*

This 10- to 40-cm-high plant, which may be annual or biennial, grows in forest margins and woodland clearings as well as in rather dry grasslands.

The leaves, in a basal rosette, are obovate and blunt with a broad stalk. Rising from the rosette is an upright, 4-angled stem that branches by forking at the top. The stem leaves are longish-ovate to lanceolate, entire and sessile.

The flowers are peduncled or sessile and arranged in a loose inflorescence. The calyx has five lanceolate lobes. The corolla is hypocrateriform with five rose-red, expanded lobes. The mature capsules are narrowly-cylindrical and up to 10 mm long.

This species is widespread in all Europe and exhibits marked variability in a number of characteristics, for instance in the branching of the stem, the shape and size of the leaves, the density of the inflorescence, etc. European populations are sometimes divided into as many as six subspecies. Despite this there is no difficulty in identifying another central European species – Slender Centaury (*Centaurium pulchellum*), which differs by having the stem greatly branched already from the base, by being without a basal rosette and by having flowers with long peduncles. The most important difference, however, is in the site requirements – Slender Centaury is generally found in wet and peat meadows and moors, more often in lime-rich or salty soils.

longitudinal section of flower

Type of plant
dicotyledon

Diploid no.
2n – 40

Flowering period
July – September

Fruit
capsule

Bogbean
or **Marsh Trefoil**

Menyanthes trifoliata

This perennial, which reaches a height of 15 to 30 cm, is found in marshes, bogs, pools and ditches, wet meadows and moors, from lowland to mountain elevations.

It has a thick, jointed, creeping rhizome from which rise both leaves and long, upright, leafless stems. The leaf stalk widens into a sheath at the base, the blade consists of three leaflets.

The leafless stem ends in a raceme of white flowers. The individual flowers grow on short peduncles from the axils of small bracts. The calyx is composed of five blunt lobes. The corolla, also five-lobed, is broadly funnel-shaped, divided about half-way to the base into fringed lobes and coloured white or faintly pink. The five stamens have violet anthers. The flowers, pollinated by insects, develop into capsules, which at maturity open by two valves.

Bogbean is a medicinal herb with a slightly bitter taste. The bitter principles contain glycosides (e.g. rutin) and stimulate the appetite in the case of minor digestive ailments.

It is distributed throughout most of Europe, where it and the species *Nymphoides peltata* are the only representatives of the small but distinctive family Menyanthaceae. Most members of this family are water or bog plants with prominently stalked, alternate leaves, a characteristic that distinguishes them from members of the Gentianaceae family, in which species of the genus *Menyanthes* and *Nymphoides* were formerly classed.

Type of plant
dicotyledon

Diploid no.
2n — 54

Flowering period
May — June

Fruit
capsule

longitudinal section of flower

Fringed Water-lily

Nymphoides peltata

Syn. *Limnanthemum nymphoides*

This perennial is found in still and slow-flowing waters that do not freeze over completely in winter.

The rigid, creeping rhizome, which is more than 2 metres long and is rooted in the soil at the bottom, bears both long and short shoots. The former develop in the summer, for their growth is promoted by higher temperatures, the latter do not begin to develop until autumn when the temperature drops. The leaves are of two kinds: submerged leaves with a long stalk and a small triangular blade and floating leaves with an entire margin and an orbicular blade that is deeply heart-shaped at the base.

The inflorescence is a four- to eight-flowered umbel. The flower buds are formed underwater, rising to the surface only during the flowering period. The fused sepals have lanceolate, pointed teeth. The five yellowish petals are joined into a funnel-shaped corolla approximately 3 cm in diameter. The flowers are pollinated by insects, self-pollination being prevented by heterostyly. The fruit develops underwater until it is mature, when it separates from the peduncle and floats on the surface. The capsule splits irregularly to release the ripe seeds which are dispersed either by water currents or by water birds. They germinate both in water and on dry land.

The Fringed Water-lily slightly resembles the White Water-lily and is distributed throughout practically all of Europe. It is on the list of protected species in some countries.

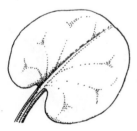

flowing leaf

Type of plant
dicotyledon

Diploid no.
2n — 54

Flowering period
July — September

Fruit
capsule

Lesser Periwinkle

Vinca minor

Open broad-leaved and mixed woods are the locations of this perennial shrub which reaches a height of 15 to 20 cm. It is also widely grown for decoration.

Two types of stems grow from the long, creeping rhizome. The first are non-flowering, prostrate stems that root at the nodes, the second are flowering stems that curve upwards and become woody at the base. The entire plant is glabrous. The longish-lanceolate to elliptic leaves have short stalks. They are leathery and persistent, glossy on the upper surface and paler green beneath with a slightly revolute margin.

The flowers grow singly on relatively long peduncles from the axils of the leaves. The calyx is usually divided into four, or sometimes five, parts and encloses the hypocrateriform corolla with unequal, asymmetrical lobes. The fruit consists of two follicles fused at the base.

Lesser Periwinkle is distributed throughout most of Europe.

It is often grown together with the related *Vinca major* in many multi-coloured varieties. It was introduced by man to many places where it became established as an escape and nowadays it is very difficult to determine the boundaries of its original range.

Type of plant
dicotyledon

Diploid no.
2n — 46

Flowering period
April — June

Fruit
follicle

fruit (two follicles joined only at the base)

Field Bindweed

Convolvulus arvensis

This 30-cm-to 1-metre-high twining perennial is found in fields, vineyards, gardens, wasteland and dunes.

The stem is bluntly 6-angled, prostrate or twining and branched. It is usually pubescent or glabrous. The leaves are long-stalked and shaped like an arrowhead or halberd, with two spreading lobes at the base; the upper leaves are smaller. The flowers grow singly or in twos or threes on long peduncles. The calyx, about 5 mm long, is composed of five fused lobes and is sometimes fringed with white hairs. The broadly funnel-shaped corolla is also composed of five fused lobes which may be white or tinted pink. The filaments are violet. The pistil is surrounded by orange nectaries at the base. The fruit is a globose-ovoid capsule up to 8 mm long enclosed for two-thirds of its length by the persistent calyx.

The flowers open in the morning and fade in the evening of the same day. Field Bindweed is widespread in all of Europe but exhibits marked variability in its growth rate, colour of the flowers, indument and shape of the leaves.

The *Convolvulus tricolor* from the Mediterranean region has a non-twining stem (it is merely ascendent or erect) often covered only with stalkless lanceolate leaves and bearing flowers that are truly three-coloured: blue outside, white in the middle and yellow within. It is sometimes grown for garden decoration.

fruit

leaf

Type of plant
dicotyledon

Diploid no.
2n — 48 (50)

Flowering period
June — August

Fruit
capsule

Hound's-tongue

Cynoglossum officinale

Dry wasteland, overgrown ruderal turf and the edges of thickets are the habitats of this biennial herb which grows to a height of 30 to 80 cm.

The stem is thick and angled, erect and branched and densely covered with hairs. The leafy lateral stems, that later increase in length, grow from the axils of leaves. The lowest leaves are long-stalked and lanceolate in outline, the stem leaves are sessile, semi-amplexicaul, and longish-lanceolate. They are hairy to grey-pubescent on both the upper and under surface.

The inflorescence is a scorpioid cyme that later becomes longer and is without bracts. The individual flowers are peduncled and pendent. The sepals are ovate, the corollas are about 6 mm in diameter and normally coloured dark brownish-red. The four nutlets are ovoid and covered with hooked spines.

This species is distributed throughout most of Europe except the extreme north and south. Other members of the genus found in central Europe are the annual *Cynoglossum columnae* from the Mediterranean region with dark-blue flowers and *Cynoglossum germanicum* with rosy-violet flowers, found only in calcareous soils from southern England and the Midlands through central France and Spain to Italy, Bulgaria and the Ukraine.

Type of plant
dicotyledon

Diploid no.
2n — 24

Flowering period
May — July

Fruit
nutlets

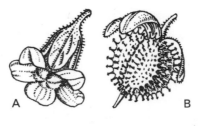

A — flower, B — nutlet of *Cynoglossum germanicum*

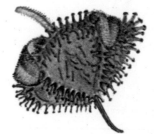

aggregate fruit

Wood Forget-me-not

Myosotis sylvatica

This plant, which may be biennial or perennial, grows in forest margins, woodland groves with tangled vegetation and mountain meadows.

It has a short rhizome and rounded erect or ascendent stems reaching a height of 10 to 40 cm. The basal leaves are obovate, narrowing at the base to a stalk up to five cm long. The stem leaves are sessile, ovate-lanceolate and blunt. The entire plant is light green and covered with soft spreading hairs.

The flowers are arranged in dense, terminal, scorpioid cymes that become longer in the fruit. The calyx is bell-shaped, becoming larger and opening in the fruit, with numerous hooked hairs at the base. The corolla is pink or white at first, but later becomes bright azure blue with a yellow eye. The corolla tube is approximately the same length as the calyx. The nutlets are glossy black-brown, pointed and edged with a narrow border.

Wood Forget-me-not grows throughout most of Europe but is absent in the southwest and the greater part of the north. It exhibits great variability as does the entire genus *Myosotis*.

calyx

Type of plant
dicotyledon

Diploid no.
2n — 18 (20)

Flowering period
August — October

Fruit
nutlets

Viper's Bugloss

Echium vulgare

This biennial herb, reaching a height of 25 to 100 cm, occurs by roadsides, in hedgerows and in dry pasture-land.

The simple, erect stem carries linear-lanceolate leaves covered with spreading bristles which grow from whitish or brownish warts.

The flowers are erect and arranged in scorpioid cymes located in the axils of the leaves and forming secondary racemes. The sepals are bristly-hairy. The corolla is funnel-shaped, more or less bilabiate, up to 12 mm in diameter and 20 mm in length. Before it opens it is coloured pink, in full bloom it is blue. The triangular nutlets are roughly warty and toothed on the edges.

This species is widespread in practically all of Europe.

Also found in central Europe is the related species *Echium lycopsis* (syn. *Echium plantagineum*) with violet flowers. It grows in similar places to *Echium vulgare* but its range extends farther into southern and western Europe. Its diploid number is 2n — 16. *Echium russicum* (syn. *Echium rubrum*), noted for its dark red flowers, extends as far west as Czecho-slovakia from its southeastern range.

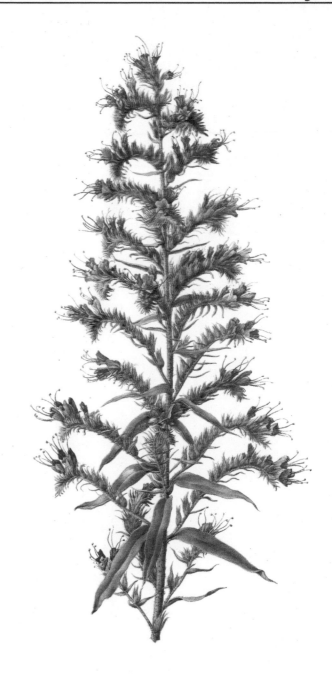

Type of plant
dicotyledon

Diploid no.
2n — 32

Flowering period
May — October

Fruit
nutlets

leaf

True Alkanet

Anchusa officinalis

This plant may be biennial or perennial and reaches a height of 30 to 80 cm. It grows in hedgerows, sandy and sunny places and waste ground.

It has a black tap root and erect, unbranched stem. The basal leaves measure up to 20 cm in the first year but are dry by the time the flowers appear. The stem leaves are sessile, lanceolate in outline with a broadly heart-shaped base and an entire or sparsely toothed margin.

The flowers are in dense scorpioid cymes that become longer after the flowers are spent. The calyx is divided by a cleft into two linear-lanceolate lobes. The corolla is reddish at first, later dark blue-violet. The corolla tube is only slightly longer than the calyx and has rounded lobes and velvety white scales in the throat. These scales, arranged in alternate sequence with the stamens and more or less closing the mouth of the corolla tube, are a characteristic feature of most members of the borage family. The mature nutlets are ovoid, up to 4 mm long, and spotted.

This species is found throughout most of Europe but not the extreme north. Also found in central Europe, where it extends from the Mediterranean region, is the species *Anchusa azurea* (syn. *Anchusa italica*) with azure-blue corollas and hairy scales.

longitudinal section of flower

Type of plant
dicotyledon

Diploid no.
2n — 16

Flowering period
May — September

Fruit
nutlets

Wrinklenut

Nonea pulla

Dry hedgerows, waste ground and fallow land are the habitats of this perennial which grows to a height of 20 to 40 cm and prefers soils with large amounts of calcium carbonate.

The stem is erect and branched at the top. The entire plant is covered with grey hairs. The basal leaves are in a rosette, the stem leaves are semi-clasping and entire on the margin.

The flowers are short-peduncled and arranged in dense scorpioid cymes growing from the axils of the upper leaves. The calyx is bell-shaped (enlarged in the fruit) with an inflated base and five, shallow, triangular teeth. The corolla is dark brownish-violet, but may be dingy pink or whitish or, very occasionally, yellowish-white. The corolla tube has tufts of hairs inside instead of the scales usually found in members of this family. The nutlets are globe-shaped or oval and furrowed.

This species is distributed throughout most of Europe.

The more robust *Nonea lutea* has pale yellow flowers (it is believed to be native to the Caucasus) and is sometimes grown for garden decoration; in southeastern Europe it occurs locally as an escape. *Nonea pallens* is also found in southeastern Europe and also has whitish or yellowish flowers. Members of this genus may be coloured blue, brown or purple, but are most frequently brownish-purple. All are adapted to dry, hot conditions and are found chiefly in waste ground and fallow land.

Type of plant
dicotyledon

Diploid no.
2n — 20

Flowering period
May — August

Fruit
nutlets

seed

Common Lungwort
Pulmonaria officinalis

This perennial, reaching a height of 10 to 30 cm, grows in broad-leaved and mixed woods, meadowland and thickets.

It is perceptibly roughly hairy both to the eye and to the touch. The lower leaves, usually spotted white, appear at the same time as the flowers, and are long-stalked and ovate in outline with a heart-shaped base. The stem leaves are ovate to lanceolate, nearly sessile, and often covered with stalked glandular hairs on the upper side.

The erect stem carries three scorpioid cymes coloured purplish at first, but changing later to blue-violet. The calyx is divided into two parts and up to 8 mm long, reaching a length of up to 12 mm in the fruit. The five stamens are shorter than the corolla tube. The flowers are pollinated by insects but self-pollination is also possible. The mature nutlets are brownish or blackish.

This species is distributed from Holland and southern Sweden to northern Italy and Bulgaria.

It is sometimes quite difficult to distinguish between this and Bark Lungwort (*Pulmonaria obscura*), often considered a microspecies of the *Pulmonaria officinalis* group. It differs by having summer leaves that are narrower, usually without spots or only with light green spots, and often without the glandular hairs. The autumn leaves generally are not persistent, unlike those of the illustrated species which usually last the winter.

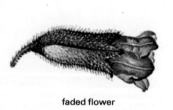

faded flower

diagram of flower

Type of plant
dicotyledon

Diploid no.
2n — 16

Flowering period
March — May

Fruit
nutlets

Common Comfrey

Symphytum officinale

This robust perennial, which reaches a height of 50 to 120 cm, grows by the waterside, in ditches, on damp edges of meadows and in inundated fields.

It has a blackish, head-like rhizome and a winged stem covered with spreading bristly hairs. The stem is rigid and erect, branching only at the top. The leaves are long and decurrent, ovate-lanceolate in outline with prominent venation on the under surface.

The flowers are short-peduncled, drooping, and arranged in dense scorpioid cymes. The calyx is bifid, the calyx teeth lanceolate. The corolla is tubular-urceolate, twice as long as the calyx and reddish-violet, or very occasionally a dingy yellowish-white. The scales in the throat are triangular and curve outward. The five stamens have dark violet anthers that are longer than the filaments. The mature nutlets are up to 5 mm long and coloured greyish-brown.

This species is found throughout Europe but is rare in the extreme south.

The closely related *Symphytum asperum* differs by having stalked, conspicuously hairy leaves and flowers coloured carmine at first, changing later to azure blue. It is grown not only for decoration but also as fodder.

Type of plant
dicotyledon

Diploid no.
2n — 48

Flowering period
May — July

Fruit
nutlets

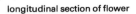

longitudinal section of flower

flower of the related *Symphytum tuberosus*

Upright Bugle

Ajuga genevensis

This perennial plant grows to a height of from 10 to 30 cm, and occurs on the edges of dry woods and in thickets and grasslands.

The stems are simple and ascendent or erect. The basal leaves are obovate to elliptic and arranged in a scanty ground rosette. Both are densely hairy. This plant does not produce stolons.

The bracts subtending the flowers are longer than the flowers. The uppermost are often flushed with blue. The flowers, which are sessile, are arranged in dense, terminal, spike-like inflorescences. Their corollas are usually violet-blue but sometimes pink. The upper lip is short so that the stamens and pistil protrude from the flower. The fruits are nutlets, as is true of all the other members of this family.

This species is distributed from southern Sweden through France, Italy and Macedonia to the Caucasus, and is also found in England.

Growing in mountain meadows are robust plants with short gray hairs classified as var. *arida*; mountain plants with glabrous or randomly hairy stems are classified as var. *elatior*. The two varieties also differ in the shape and size of the leaves and bracts.

diagram of flower of the mint family

Type of plant
dicotyledon

Diploid no.
2n — 32

Flowering period
April — July

Fruit
nutlets

Common Bugle

Ajuga reptans

This perennial, which reaches a height of 10 to 30 cm, grows at the edges of meadows, in forest margins and in open grassy woodlands.

The simple, upright stems are 4-angled and usually hairy on two opposite sides or hairless. Leafy stolons, up to 30 cm long, are produced at the same time as the stem. The basal leaves form a rosette, the stem leaves are short-stalked or sessile and longish-ovate with a margin that may be scalloped or smooth.

The flowers grow from the axils of bracts and are arranged in relatively loose terminal spike-like inflorescences. The calyx is bell-shaped, toothed and more or less pubescent. The corolla, also pubescent, is violet-blue but may sometimes be pink. The corolla tube is straight, the lower lip three times as long as the upper lip and deeply three-lobed. The four stamens are all the same length and pubescent.

This species is widespread in practically all of Europe. In the mountains we may encounter plants that look exactly the same but do not have stolons. These are designated as var. *alpina* and are found chiefly in high-stemmed mountain grasslands. Pyramidal Bugle *(Ajuga pyramidalis)*, closely related to *Ajuga reptans* and *Ajuga genevensis*, differs from both in the shape of the long bracts. All three species readily interbreed, producing hybrid offspring that are very much alike.

Type of plant
dicotyledon

Diploid no.
2n — 32

Flowering period
May — August

Fruit
nutlets

flower

Ground Ivy

Glechoma hederacea

Forest margins, thickets and meadows are the habitats of this perennial which grows to a height of 10 to 40 cm.

It has a creeping rhizome which bears ascending, branched flowering stems with leafy shoots up to 1 metre long at the base. The stems are hairy and root at the nodes. The leaves are stalked and kidney- or heart-shaped.

The flowers, peduncled and up to 2 cm long, grow in twos or threes from the axils of the middle and upper leaves. The calyx is tubular, faintly two-lipped and five-toothed. The corolla is blue-violet and twice to four times as long as the calyx. Inside the tube is a ring of hairs. The upper lip is two-lobed and straight, the lower lip three-lobed, larger than the upper and dark violet.

Ground Ivy is distributed throughout most of Europe as well as in Asia and was introduced to North America.

The young leaves of this pleasantly scented plant are used to flavour stuffings and soups.

Plants thickly covered with long hairs are classified as *Glechoma hirsuta*; this species is further distinguished by larger flowers measuring up to 3 cm. They are found mostly in eastern and southeastern Europe.

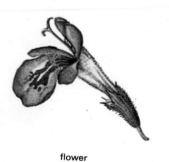

flower

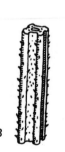

Detail of stem: A – *Glechoma hirsuta*
B – *Glechoma hederacea*

Type of plant
dicotyledon

Diploid no.
2n – 18

Flowering period
April – July

Fruit
nutlets

Common Self-heal

Prunella vulgaris

This perennial, reaching a height of 5 to 30 cm, occurs in meadows, heaths, hedgerows and by road-sides as well as in dry ditches.

The ascending stems, often coloured brown with a violet tinge, are sparsely branched and covered with stalked leaves. The lower leaves, which are ovate-elliptic, form a ground rosette. The uppermost pair of leaves is just beneath the spike-like inflorescence.

The flowers, clustered in small terminal heads, grow from the axils of pointed, ovate bracts, tinted brown or violet. The calyx is 8 mm long and bilabiate with conspicuous teeth. The corolla is twice as long as the calyx and coloured blue-violet; the upper lip of the corolla is high-domed and ciliate. The flowers are usually hermaphroditic but sometimes one may come across flowers with aborted (atrophied) stamens. They are pollinated by insects but self-pollination is not ruled out.

This species is distributed through most of Europe, Asia and north Africa and is often naturalized elsewhere.

Besides the wild plants, there are also pale blue-violet and pink-flowered forms that are grown in the garden.

Type of plant
dicotyledon

Diploid no.
2n — 28

Flowering period
May — September

Fruit
nutlets

flower

White Dead-nettle

Lamium album

This perennial herb, which reaches a height of 20 to 40 cm, occurs in and at the edges of thickets and in ruderal grasslands. It prefers nitrogen-rich soils.

The simple stems are glabrescent at the bottom and often tinted violet. The long-stalked leaves are ovate and long-pointed with a heart-shaped or rounded base and a toothed margin. The bracts resemble the upper leaves but have shorter stalks.

The flowers are sessile and arranged in verticillasters that grow from the axils of the bracts. The calyx is bell-shaped and bifid with spreading lanceolate teeth. The corolla is white or faintly yellowish, the corolla tube is slightly curved. The anthers are dark brown.

This species is found in most of Europe but occurs more sparsely in the south and is absent on the Mediterranean islands. It is also found in Asia and in North America, where it was introduced.

The flowers are used by the pharmaceutical industry and as a home remedy in the form of tea for treating bronchitis.

There are more than fifteen species of dead-nettle in Europe but white-flowered ones are few: in the west Mediterranean region the white, but slightly pinkish *Lamium flexuosum* and in southern Europe *Lamium bifidum.*

fruit

flower

Type of plant
dicotyledon

Diploid no.
2n — 18

Flowering period
April — September

Fruit
nutlets

Spotted Dead-nettle

Lamium maculatum

This 10- to 50-cm-high perennial grows in mixed woods and thickets, exhibiting a preference for nitrogen-rich soils.

It has both underground and surface runners and apart from the colour of the flowers is very similar to White Dead-nettle (*Lamium album*). The simple, 4-angled stems are reddish at the bottom and covered with spreading down at the top. The leaves are pointed and often spotted white on the upper side. The leaf stalks are up to 4 cm long.

The verticillasters grow from the axils of bracts. There are sometimes small bracteoles in the inflorescence itself. The flowers are sessile and up to 3 cm long. The calyx is an open bell-shape with long-pointed teeth. The corolla is normally rose-red; the corolla tube is conspicuously curved. The upper lip is pubescent, the lower lip three-lobed, the middle lobe patterned with violet markings. The anthers are violet-brown or red. The mature nutlets are triangular and coloured green.

This species is widespread in all of Europe.

The related Red Dead-nettle (*Lamium purpureum)* it the same colour, i.e. it has rose-red flowers, but the corolla tube is straight with a conspicuous ring of hairs, the flowers are slightly smaller and the leaves are coarsely dentate.

Type of plant
dicotyledon

Diploid no.
2n — 18

Flowering period
April — September

Fruit
nutlets

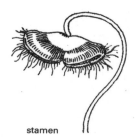

stamen

flower

Yellow Archangel

Galeobdolon luteum

Syn. *Lamium galeobdolon, Lamiastrum galeobdolon*

This perennial, which reaches a height of 15 to 45 cm, is found in mixed woods and thickets.

It is randomly hairy or glabrescent, has leafy, rooting stolons and is very similar to White Dead-nettle. One evident difference, however, is in the colour of the flowers, for those of Yellow Archangel are truly yellow. The stems are simple and leafy. The leaves are long-stalked, ovate in outline with a coarsely toothed margin, and often spotted white. The bracts are short-stalked and pointed.

The flowers, arranged in scanty, six- to eight-flowered verticillasters, are sessile, up to 2 cm long and grow from the axils of distant bracts. They are pale yellow. The calyx is tubular and open, with awn-like teeth. The corolla tube is straight, the upper lip helmet-shaped and the lower lip conspicuously three-lobed. The yellow anthers are glabrous. The mature nutlets are black and possess a white fleshy appendage; these appendages are a favourite food of ants which are the agents of dispersal.

This species is found in most of Europe but is less common in the Mediterranean region and in the north.

Diagram of the runners of the related *Galeobdolon montanum*

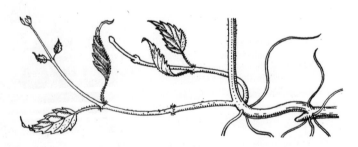

Type of plant
dicotyledon

Diploid no.
2n — 18

Flowering period
April — July

Fruit
nutlets

Wood Betony

Stachys officinalis

Syn. *Stachys betonica, Betonica officinalis*

This perennial, which reaches a height of 30 cm to 1 metre, grows in wet meadows as well as in rather dry woods and their outskirts.

The stems are erect, unbranched and sparsely leaved. The lower leaves are long-stalked and longish-ovate to elliptic with a coarsely crenate margin. They are glabrous above and hairy beneath. The leaves in the middle of the stem have shorter stalks and those farther up are increasingly smaller. The uppermost leaves are narrowly-lanceolate and sessile.

The bracts immediately above the leaves subtend verticillasters of flowers which collectively form terminal, cylindrical, spike-like inflorescences that are dense but slightly looser at the base. The individual flowers are up to 14 mm long. The calyx is bell-shaped and divided by a cleft; it has short awn-like teeth. The corollas are carmine-red, but may sometimes be dark pink or very occasionally whitish. The corolla tube is curved and much longer than the calyx. The upper lip is straight and hairy outside. The lower lip is three-lobed, the middle lobe large and crenate. The stamens, with violet-brown anthers, are anchored near the top of the corolla tube.

This species is found in most of Europe. In the north its range extends to middle Scotland, southern Sweden and the northwestern USSR.

Wood Betony was formerly used as tea chiefly to treat colds.

Type of plant
dicotyledon

Diploid no.
2n — 16

Flowering period
July — August

Fruit
nutlets

longitudinal section of flower

Meadow Clary

Salvia pratensis

This 30- to 80-cm-high perennial herb grows in rather dry meadows and pastureland.

The erect or ascendent stem is glandular and sparsely branched at the top. The leaves, forming a ground rosette, are long-stalked, ovate to longish-lanceolate with a heart-shaped base, and wrinkled on the underside. The stem leaves are either absent or there are three pairs or less. They are very short-stalked or sessile.

The flowers are usually arranged in six-flowered verticillasters. They grow on short peduncles from the axils of small, green, ovate bracts. The bell-shaped calyx is up to 1 cm long, more or less glandular, and covered with spreading hairs. The corolla is blue to blue-violet and covered randomly with down. The corolla tube is slightly longer than the calyx. The upper lip is two-lobed and arched, the lower lip is shorter and three-lobed. Concealed within at the base is a nectary. There are only two stamens. Both stamens and style move freely, and when the flower is visited by an insect both bend so that pollen is wiped off the body of the insect onto the stigma. Besides hermaphroditic flowers, there may also be smaller, pistillate flowers with atrophied stamens on the same plant or on seperate plants.

Meadow Clary is widespread throughout most of Europe. It is often used in folk medicine to treat acne, excessive bleeding and to stimulate the heart and brain.

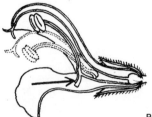

Pollination (the arrow shows the direction of the pressure of the insect on the base of the stamen causing it to bend and at the same time inclining the stigma as well)

Type of plant
dicotyledon

Diploid no.
2n — 18

Flowering period
May — August

Fruit
nutlets

Wild Basil

Clinopodium vulgare

Syn. *Calamintha clinopodium*

This perennial, which reaches a height of 30 to 60 cm, grows in thickets, open woods and their borders.

It has a creeping rhizome and simple or little-branched stems sparsely covered with leaves. These are short-stalked, ovate, entire and slightly woolly.

The flowers are arranged in dense, sessile verticillasters that grow from the axils of the upper leaves and are composed of ten to twenty flowers. These are short-peduncled and up to 15 mm long. The calyx is tubular, hairy and bilabiate. The corolla is carmine-red, although it is sometimes pink and very occasionally even white. The corolla tube is more or less straight and twice as long as the calyx. The lower lip is approximately twice as long as the upper lip.

Wild Basil is widespread in all of Europe extending north almost to the Arctic Circle.

Its relatives include the Common Balm *(Melissa officinalis)* from the east Mediterranean used since ancient times for its medicinal properties. Its characteristic lemon odour is due to the presence of an essence which contains citral. The decoction from the leaves is used as a home remedy for flatulence and as a tonic to stimulate the appetite.

Type of plant
dicotyledon

Diploid no.
2n — 20

Flowering period
July — September

Fruit
nutlets

Stamen of *Salvia officinalis* with prolonged connective attached to the filament by means of a movable joint — example of the stamen of the mint family

Pot or Wild Marjoram, Oregano

Origanum vulgare

Thickets, open woodlands and their borders are the locations of this aromatic perennial which reaches a height of 20 to 50 cm.

The woody rhizome bears leafy, upright stems with short axillary branches ending in a dichasial inflorescence. The leaves are short-stalked, ovate, and entire or faintly scalloped. They have prominent veins and are a lighter colour on the under surface. The bracts, which resemble the leaves, are sessile and often violet-red.

The verticillasters are composed of up to three short-peduncled flowers and are clustered in a practically globose inflorescence resembling a capitulum. The calyx is tubular, bell-shaped and shorter than the bracts. The corollas are usually light red but infrequently they are dingy white. The upper lip is short, straight and shallowly notched; the lower lip longer, curved and three-lobed. The stamens are four in number — two are long and two short — and protrude from the corolla tube. The nutlets are smooth and coloured brown.

Pot Marjoram is used as a home remedy in the form of tea to improve digestion and to treat various digestive disorders, because the drug contains effective substances from the terpene group.

This species is distributed throughout most of Europe.

Type of plant
dicotyledon

Diploid no.
2n — 30

Flowering period
July — September

Fruit
nutlets

leaf

Wild Thyme

Thymus serpyllum

Syn. *Thymus angustifolium*

This perennial, which reaches a height of 10 to 50 cm, grows in rather dry, sandy and grassy situations, chiefly in pine woods.

It is actually a subshrub with slightly woody branches. The stems may be erect, ascendent or creeping, rounded or 4-angled and variously hairy. The leaves are opposite, sessile or short-stalked, elliptic to nearly orbicular in outline and entire.

The flowers are arranged in spike-like inflorescences that are usually clustered in a globose head at the tip of the stem but may sometimes be prolonged and discontinuous towards the base of the inflorescence. The calyx is bilabiate, tubular bell-shaped and ciliate. The corolla is 6 mm long with short tube and usually dark or pale violet-red, less often whitish.

This species is widespread in all of Europe, chiefly north of France, Austria, Hungary and Byelorussia. It is very difficult to distinguish between this and the many other related thymes. Identification is further complicated by the existence of many hybrids. One species that is readily recognized, however, is Garden Thyme *(Thymus vulgaris)* which has erect, branching stems up to 40 cm high and leaves that are white-felted on the underside and revolute on the margin; it is native to the Mediterranean.

Type of plant
dicotyledon

Diploid no.
2n — 24

Flowering period
July — August

Fruit
nutlets

flower

Deadly Nightshade, Belladonna

Atropa bella-donna

This perennial grows to a height of 50 to 150 cm and is found in woodland clearings.

The thick stem is erect and bluntly angled. The leaves are alternate, but those on flowering branches are seemingly opposite. They are ovate to elliptic in outline, narrowing at the base into a short stalk, entire, pubescent and dark green.

The flowers are solitary, peduncled and drooping. The calyx is composed of five fused segments. The corolla, also composed of five segments, is a tubular bell-shape; it is coloured brownish-violet outside and greyish-yellow patterned with red veins within. The corolla lobes are rounded and spreading. The stamens are five in number; the filaments hairy at the base and twisted at the top, the anthers yellow. The fruit is a cherry-sized berry coloured green at first, later black; it is subtended by the enlarged, flared calyx.

Deadly Nightshade grows in the British Isles, central and southern Europe as far east as Iran, and northern Africa.

Although poisonous, it has medicinal uses.

fruit

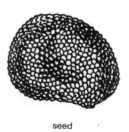

seed

Type of plant
dicotyledon

Diploid no.
2n – 72

Flowering period
June – August

Fruit
berry

Henbane

Hyoscyamus niger

Henbane, which reaches a height from 10 to 50 cm, grows in rather dry waste ground and land left fallow after root crops; it is partial to nitrogen-rich soils.

The stem is erect, bluntly angled and glandular-woolly. The leaves are alternate, with the lower leaves short-stalked and the upper leaves semi-clasping the stem.

The sessile flowers, growing from the axils of the upper bracts, form one-sided monochasial cymes. The calyx is tubular-urceolate with prickly-pointed lobes. The corolla is funnel-shaped, hairy outside and hairless within. The corolla lobes are dingy yellow with violet veins and a reddish-violet eye. The stamens, with pubescent filaments and violet anthers, are five in number — two are shorter than the others. The fruit is a capsule containing up to 200 seeds. There are approximately 50 capsules to a plant, and consequently a single specimen produces some 10,000 seeds. These often remain in the ground several years before they germinate, and for this reason Henbane is a troublesome weed. Furthermore, it is very poisonous, for it contains hyoscyamine and other poisonous alkaloids. It is also very dangerous inasmuch as its seeds resemble those of the poppy and can readily be mistaken for poppy seeds — and only a few can cause a serious case of poisoning.

Type of plant
dicotyledon

Diploid no.
2n — 34

Flowering period
July — October

Fruit
capsule

fruit

Bittersweet, Woody Nightshade

Solanum dulcamara

This prostrate perennial, which reaches a length of from 30 to 200 cm, grows in thickets, alder groves and waste ground.

It has a creeping rhizome and either climbing or prostrate stems that are glabrous and become woody at the base. The stalked leaves are ovate and covered with random hairs on both the upper and under surfaces.

The flowers are arranged in terminal, drooping panicles. The calyx is short; the corolla has lanceolate, reflexed, pointed petals coloured dark blue-violet with two green white-edged spots at the base. The five yellow anthers are fused into a cone. The fruit peduncle is thickened at the end and ends in a drooping, red, ovoid berry with kidney-shaped seeds.

This species is distributed throughout most of Europe excepting the extreme north.

Bittersweet, like most members of the nightshade family, is poisonous. In fact, even the potato *(Solanum tuberosum)* is a poisonous plant! The poisonous alkaloids, however, are concentrated mainly in the stems with slight amounts in the leaves and berries and only negligible traces in the rhizomatic tubers — and only in the skins or green parts that were not completely covered by soil. The concentration increases only when the buds begin to sprout. Potatoes, however, are peeled and cooked before eating so there is no danger of poisoning.

hastate leaf with two basal segments

Type of plant
dicotyledon

Diploid no.
2n — 24

Flowering period
June — August

Fruit
berry

Large-flowered Mullein

Verbascum densiflorum

Syn. *Verbascum thapsiforme*

This biennial, which reaches a height of more than two metres, occurs on sunny and stony slopes, in screes and on stony shores.

The first year it produces basal leaves which are longish-ovate, narrowing at the base into a short stalk, and finely scalloped on the margin. The stem leaves are elliptic to lanceolate and all are decurrent, extending to the leaf below. The entire plant is covered with a layer of thick yellowish-white wool.

The flowers, which are short-peduncled and grow from the axils of ovate-lanceolate bracts, are in clusters and form a long, spike-like inflorescence. The calyx is composed of five joined segments, the flat corolla of five spreading petals; it measures up to 5 cm in diameter. The fruit is a capsule the same length as the calyx.

This robust, profusely-flowering plant is an important medicinal herb as are other mulleins with large flowers and glabrous or white-woolly filaments. The parts collected for the drug market are the flowers, which contain effective substances that act as an expectorant. Small-flowered mulleins with violet-hairy filaments and leaves that are glabrous on the upper side are not suitable for pharmaceutical purposes. The medicinal properties of the substances present in the flowers of Large-flowered Mullein, Common Mullein *(Verbascum thapsus)* and Orange Mullein *(Verbascum phlomoides),* the ones most commonly gathered, are that they ease the bringing up of phlegm from the respiratory passages.

Type of plant
dicotyledon

Diploid no.
2n − 32

Flowering period
July − September

Fruit
capsule

flower

Toadflax

Linaria vulgaris

This perennial herb, reaching a height of 20 to 50 cm, grows by roadsides, and in fallow land, waste ground and fields.

The stem is glabrous, usually simple, and densely covered with leaves which are alternate and sessile, linear-lanceolate and entire.

The stalked flowers, which grow from the axils of bracts, are arranged in a raceme that is conical at first, later becoming longer. The calyx is deeply divided into five segments. The corolla is bilabiate and coloured sulphur-yellow with orange lower palate. The upper lip is two-lobed, the lower lip three-lobed. The palate of the lower lip closes the mouth of the corolla; the other end of the corolla is prolonged into a curving spur. The fruit is an ovoid capsule which is longer than the persistent calyx and contains flat, warty seeds with a broad, wing-like border. Toadflax is extremely prolific since a single plant produces as many as 30,000 seeds.

It is distributed throughout most of Europe except the extreme north; it is also absent from practically the entire Mediterranean region.

Found very occasionally on stony slopes in south-eastern and central Europe is the species *Linaria angustissima* with very narrow leaves. A much commoner weed of fields, chiefly ones with sandy soil, is the Field Toadflax *(Linaria arvensis)* with very small corollas coloured pale blue-violet.

fruit

flower

Type of plant
dicotyledon

Diploid no.
2n — 12

Flowering period
June — October

Fruit
capsule

Common Figwort

Scrophularia nodosa

This perennial, which has a pronounced odour, grows in scrub, fallow land, shady woods and shoreline thickets and reaches a height of 40 cm to 1 metre.

It has a horizontal, tuberous rhizome and an erect stem that is glandular at the top but otherwise glabrous, and four-angled but not winged. The leaves are opposite and short-stalked; the lower leaves are ovate to longish-ovate with broadly wedge-shaped to faintly heart-shaped base, the upper leaves are pointed. All are glabrous.

The peduncled flowers, growing from the axils of narrowly-lanceolate bracts, are arranged in cymose inflorescences. The peduncles are glandular. The calyx is bell-shaped with five lobes. The corolla is brownish-red with a green or sometimes yellow-green throat; it is not spurred and consists of an inflated tube and two short lips. The upper lip is slightly longer than the lower lip; the latter is three-lobed. The fruit is a capsule.

Common Figwort is a slightly poisonous but at the same time medicinal plant. It is widespread in almost all of Europe.

There are more than thirty related species of which the most noteworthy is the Yellow Figwort *(Scrophularia vernalis)* with pale yellow flowers which is often grown by apiarists for its nectar.

Type of plant
dicotyledon

Diploid no.
2n — 36

Flowering period
June — August

Fruit
capsule

longitudinal section of flower

Blue-topped Cow-weed

Melampyrum nemorosum

Open woods, scrub and meadows up to mountain elevations are the habitats of this annual plant which reaches a height of 10 to 50 cm.

The erect stem is more or less branched. The lower leaves are ovate to longish-lanceolate with an attenuated base and a short stalk. The upper leaves are truncate to hastate at the base and toothed.

The flowers are clustered in loose, one-sided racemes. The calyx is woolly with lanceolate, spreading teeth. The corolla is golden-yellow. The corolla tube is faintly funnel-shaped and the two lips form an acute angle. The fruit is a capsule.

The genus *Melampyrum* and several other genera of the figwort family exhibit marked variability in the form of seasonal ecotypes, great differences between plants of mountain and lowland districts, and between plants from diverse territories. In the case of *Melampyrum nemorosum,* there are marked differences between the spring and mountain variants and the autumn type species which is much branched and has long and ascendent branches. The spring ecotype is sparsely branched with very narrow leaves. The mountain ecotype has up to 3 pairs of erect branches and thick, fleshy leaves up to 25 mm wide. Both types are found in almost all of central Europe.

flower

Type of plant
dicotyledon

Diploid no.
2n — 18

Flowering period
July — September

Fruit
capsule

Birdseye Speedwell

Veronica chamaedrys

Meadows, woodland clearings and thickets are the habitats of this small plant which is only 15 to 20 cm high.

A perennial herb, it has a stem that is simple or only sparsely branched and often hairy on two opposite sides. The leaves are opposite, sessile or short-stalked and oval.

The flowers, with peduncles longer than the lanceolate bracts, are arranged in axillary racemes. The calyx lobes are linear-lanceolate. The rotate corollas, with practically no tube, are about 10 to 14 mm across and coloured azure blue; they soon fall. There are two stamens. The ovary develops into a capsule containing flat, ovoid seeds. These are dispersed not only by ants, but also by the wind and rain.

Birdseye Speedwell is found throughout most of Europe except the islands and the Arctic.

In central Europe it occurs in two subspecies. Subsp. *chamaedrys* has dark-green leaves, a more or less hairy stem and a calyx that is only slightly hairy; subsp. *vindobonensis* has yellow-green leaves, stem hairy only on two opposite sides, a densely glandular-hairy calyx and a pale blue corolla that may occasionally be pinkish.

Type of plant
dicotyledon

Diploid no.
2n — 32 (16)

Flowering period
May — June

Fruit
capsule

stem hairy on two opposite sides

fruit

Common
or **Heath Speedwell**

Veronica officinalis

This perennial, which reaches a height of 30 to 50 cm, occurs in woods, forest margins and heaths.

The rooting stem lies along the ground, rising only at the tip. The leaves are opposite, usually elliptic or obovate to broadly-lanceolate, tapered into a short stalk, and toothed on the margin.

The small, short-peduncled flowers, subtended by lanceolate bracts, are clustered in dense racemes in the upper leaf axils. The calyx is the same length as the flower-peduncle. The bell-like rotate corolla measures about 7 mm in diameter and is coloured pale violet. The developing capsule is shallowly notched, glandular, and about 4 mm long.

Common Speedwell is distributed throughout most of Europe. It has medicinal properties — tea brewed from the top parts is used to treat coughs for it acts as an expectorant.

Plants from the southwestern Alps are sometimes classified as a separate species *(Veronica allionii)* because they are more or less glabrous, have shorter stems, smaller leaves and smaller capsules, and are coloured pale blue. However, glabrescent plants with small, nearly glabrous leaves and flowers a paler hue than Common Speedwell proper are also to be found in places other than the Alps.

flower

Type of plant
dicotyledon

Diploid no.
2n — 36 (18)

Flowering period
June — August

Fruit
capsule

Long-hairy Yellow-rattle

Rhinanthus alectorolophus

Grain fields, meadows and mountain meadows are the habitats of this semi-parasitic annual, which reaches a height of from 10 to 80 cm.

A hairy weed, it has an upright stem coloured pale green without black lines (unlike *Rhinanthus minor, Rhinanthus alpinus, Rhinanthus major,* etc.) and leaves that are elliptic-lanceolate to ovate with a serrate margin.

The flowers grow from the axils of broadly-ovate, woolly bracts. The calyx is white-woolly. The corolla is yellow and up to 2 cm long; the corolla tube curves slightly upward. The upper lip has a violet to whitish, pointed tooth up to 2 mm long. The lower lip closes the mouth of the corolla. The capsule is enclosed by the persistent calyx.

This species is distributed from northern France and Holland southward to northern Italy and northern Yugoslavia.

As with members of the genus *Melampyrum,* the problem of how to deal with the variability and seasonal polymorphism of this plant, in other words how to evaluate the ecotypes, poses great difficulties. One of the possibilities is to classify the seasonal ecotypes as subspecies. Spring plants are then classed as subspecies *alectorolophus* proper, summer weeds as subspecies *buccalis,* autumn plants as subspecies *patulus* and mountain plants as subspecies *modestus* and subspecies *kerneri.*

Type of plant
dicotyledon

Diploid no.
2n — 22

Flowering period
June — July

Fruit
capsule

calyx

Lousewort

Pedicularis sylvatica

This 5- to 15-cm-high plant, which may be biennial or perennial, grows in peat meadows and wet heaths.

The stems lie flat along the ground, rising only at the tip, and are arranged in a circle; the middle stem is erect and covered with alternate, short-stalked leaves that are longish-lanceolate in outline and pinnatipartite.

The flowers, growing from the axils of bracts, are arranged in loose, terminal racemes. The calyx is unequally five-toothed, tubular, bell-shaped and patterned with a network of ribs. The corolla is pale pink to reddish-violet. The corolla tube is twice as long as the calyx; its upper lip is straight with tip curved like a sickle, its lower lip is three-lobed. Of the four stamens concealed by the upper lip, two are longer and two shorter. Pollination is by insects. The fruit is a capsule enclosed by the persistent calyx.

Lousewort is slightly poisonous. It is distributed throughout most of Europe.

There are more than fifty *Pedicularis* species in Europe, many of them glacial relicts and attractive elements of some of the mountain ranges in central Europe. One example is Sudeten Lousewort *(Pedicularis sudetica)* with simple, short, sparsely-leaved stem and purplish-red flowers found only in the Krkonoše (Giant) Mountains, the arctic regions of Europe and Siberia, the northern and middle Urals and arctic North America.

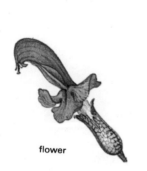

flower

A

B

A — five-lobed calyx of *Pedicularis sylvatica*
B — two-lobed lower lip and three-lobed upper lip of calyx of *Pedicularis palustris*

Type of plant
dicotyledon

Diploid no.
2n – 32

Flowering period
May – July

Fruit
capsule

Purple Foxglove

Digitalis purpurea

This striking, biennial herb, which reaches a height of 40 to 140 cm, occurs in forest margins and at the edges of thickets.

The stem is simple, upright and felted. The basal leaves as well as lower stem leaves are large and have long, winged stalks. The blade is ovate to ovate-lanceolate with a tapering base. The leaves farther up the stem are increasingly smaller and sessile, the uppermost leaves giving way to bracts.

The large flowers are in dense, one-sided racemes. They are drooping and grow on short peduncles from the axils of bracts. The inflorescence is rarely terminated by a radially symmetrical flower. The calyx is composed of five lobes that are joined into a tube. The corolla is a tubular bell shape with an indistinctly four- to five-lobed edge. It is coloured red with dark, pale-edged spots within. The mature capsules are ovoid, hairy and enclosed by the persistent calyx.

This species is a medicinal but at the same time extremely poisonous plant (it has a high concentration of cardiotonic glycosides).

Purple Foxglove is found in western and southwestern Europe. Because it is grown both for pharmacological reasons and for garden decoration, it has sometimes become established in eastern districts as well.

It is an extremely variable species. Noteworthy are plants from the Iberian Peninsula with white, pale-yellow or pinkish flowers (subspecies *heywoodii*).

Type of plant
dicotyledon

Diploid no.
2n — 56

Flowering period
June — July

Fruit
capsule

diagram of flower

Yellow Foxglove

Digitalis grandiflora

Syn. *Digitalis ambigua*

This striking, 60- to 120-cm-high herb grows as a perennial in open woods, thickets, and their margins as well as in woodland clearings from lowland to mountains.

The stem growing from the rhizome is simple, erect and glandular-pubescent at the top. The basal and lower stem leaves are alternate, longish-lanceolate in outline and tapered at the base into winged stalks. The upper leaves are smaller and sessile, the uppermost giving way to bracts.

The flowers are arranged in dense, one-sided racemes. The corolla is pale ochre spotted with brown within and glandular-sticky outside. The four stamens are joined to the corolla and are didynamous (two are longer and two shorter). The flowers are pollinated by insects but self-pollination may also occur. The bilocular capsule contains small seeds coloured orange.

This species contains medicinal substances, as does *Digitalis purpurea,* and is therefore grown for this purpose as well as collected in the wild, this likewise being the reason why it is on the list of protected plants in many European countries.

Also cultivated for its medicinal properties is the Balkan species *Digitalis lanata* which also contains very effective cardiotonic glycosides essential to modern medicine. A word of warning, however — it should never be used as a home remedy! Even a few seeds may cause serious poisoning.

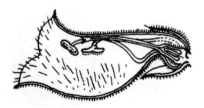

longitudinal section of flower

Type of plant
dicotyledon

Diploid no.
2n — 56

Flowering period
June — September

Fruit
capsule

Toothwort

Lathraea squamaria

This 10- to 25-cm-high perennial, which has no chlorophyll and hence is not coloured green, is a parasite on the roots of deciduous, and infrequently also coniferous, trees. It occurs randomly in humus-rich woodlands, mostly at lower elevations.

The thick, branched, scaly rhizome bears a thick, fleshy, upright stem which is glabrous and coloured pink or white. The leaves, likewise white or pale pink, are scale-like, heart-shaped and alternate.

The flowers are arranged in one-sided racemes. Each flower, which is peduncled, is subtended by a rounded-ovate bract. It is composed of a bell-shaped, bluntly five-toothed calyx, coloured pink and glandular hairy, and a tubular funnel-shaped bilabiate corolla, also coloured pink except for the lower lip which is red. The four stamens are of two different lengths and the filaments are joined with the corolla tube. Pollination is by insects though instances of cleistogamy (self-pollination of un-opened flowers) have also been observed. Fertilization is followed by the development of a unilocular capsule with several large seeds.

Parasitism is not at all unusual among members of the figwort family but most are partial parasites, i.e. they are green plants that absorb only water and the minerals it contains from the host through their roots. Toothwort is a perfect parasite that must obtain even the products of photosynthesis from the host plant, because it has no chlorophyll of its own what-soever.

Type of plant
dicotyledon

Diploid no.
2n — 42

Flowering period
March — May

Fruit
capsule

longitudinal section of flower

rhizome

Ribwort

Plantago lanceolata

This perennial with narrowly-lanceolate, glabrous leaves arranged in a ground rosette, reaches a height of 10 to 40 cm. It is common in meadows, pasture-land, waste ground, sandy places and by waysides.

The grooved stem is usually longer than the leaves, which are pointed and more or less upright. They are three- to five-veined and taper at the base into a stalk. The scape is terminated by a short, cylindrical spike.

The flowers grow from the axils of brown, glabrous, membranous bracts. The calyx is composed of two joined and two separate segments. The corolla is 2 to 3 mm long and brownish. The stamens are two to three times as long as the corolla. Pollination and fertilization is followed by the development of an ovoid, lidded capsule containing two seeds.

Ribwort is a well-known medicinal herb. Formerly its leaves were applied to wounds, nowadays it is used in the preparation of cough syrups.

Plantago lanceolata is a cosmopolitan plant – which means that today it has a worldwide distribution and is found on most continents. It has been introduced to Africa and North America, Brazil, Chile and Argentina, and even to Sri Lanka, Australia and New Zealand.

The related Mountain Plantain *(Plantago atrata)* from the Alps has an entirely glabrous stem and leaves with a ciliate margin and a prominent dark primary vein.

fruit

flower

Type of plant
dicotyledon

Diploid no.
2n – 12

Flowering period
May – September

Fruit
capsule

Hoary Plantain

Plantago media

This perennial, which reaches a height of 10 to 50 cm, is found in meadows and pastures.

The scape is rounded, erect or ascending, and much longer than the leaves which are arranged in a ground rosette. These are broadly-elliptic, five- to nine-veined, and gradually narrow into a short stalk. The entire plant is more or less randomly hairy.

The scape ends in a dense, cylindrical spike. The bracts subtending the flowers are shorter than the flowers and pubescent. The calyx is glabrous and composed of four fused segments with broadly-ovate lobes. The corollas are up to 4 mm long, tubular or funnel-shaped and whitish. The four stamens have violet anthers and are approximately five times as long as the corolla. The flowers are pollinated by the wind. The calyx is persistent, remaining on the fruit, which is a lidded capsule.

Hoary Plantain is a valuable fodder plant. Practically cosmopolitan in its distribution, it occurs in a number of forms which are variously evaluated. Great Plantain *(Plantago major),* also a cosmopolitan, is equally extremely variable, e.g. in the number of seeds per capsule and in the number of leaf veins.

Type of plant
dicotyledon

Diploid no.
2n — 24

Flowering period
May — September

Fruit
capsule

diagram of flower

detail of inflorescence of *Plantago major*

inflorescence of *Plantago major*

Vervain

Verbena officinalis

This 20- to 60-cm-high plant may often be encountered in waste ground, pastureland and fields.

The erect, four-angled stem is glabrous and becomes woody at the base; it is covered with opposite leaves. The lowest leaves are small, elongate, coarsely notched or lobed, and narrow at the base into a short stalk. The middle stem leaves are larger and partially split into three leaflets, the upper leaves are sessile and longish-lanceolate. All are stiff, roughly hairy and greyish-green.

The small flowers, which grow from the axils of sessile bracts, are arranged in terminal racemes that become longer in the fruit. The calyx is composed of four to five segments that are joined into a tube which is approximately 2 mm long and glandular. The corolla, composed of five fused segments and indistinctly two-lobed, is coloured pale violet, or very occasionally white.

Vervain was formerly used in folk medicine. It is very widely distributed. The other members of this genus are found mostly only in America, particularly in the subtropical regions, and only some are grown in Europe for ornament, e.g. *Verbena peruviana* with violet-red flowers and *Verbena rigida* with violet blooms.

diagram of flower

Type of flower
dicotyledon

Diploid no.
2n — 14

Flowering period
July — September

Fruit
nutlets

Sweet Woodruff

Galium odoratum

Syn. *Asperula odorata*

This 15- to 30-cm-high perennial herb is a common plant of deciduous, chiefly beech, woods.

The erect stem is four-angled, smooth and glabrous. The deep green leaves are arranged in whorls of six to nine leaves. The lowest are longish-ovate, those at the top longish-lanceolate. They are entire, glabrous, rough on the margin and with a sharp tip. The bracts are very tiny.

The atrophied calyxes are a mere rim at the base of the funnel-shaped corollas, which are white, up to 6 mm long, and composed of four spreading lobes. The flowers are pollinated by insects. The fruit is covered with hooked bristles.

Sweet Woodruff contains high concentrations of coumarin and for this reason is a valuable culinary herb (the wilting top parts have a pronounced aroma). The tender young leaves are an essential ingredient of Germany's 'maibowle', giving it its characteristic aroma. Their pleasant fragrance is also the reason why dried plants were put in linen closets.

In most earlier textbooks the illustrated plant is listed as *Asperula,* the genus to which it was assigned by Carl Linné. Nowadays other criteria are considered to be important features of identification distinguishing the two genera *Galium* and *Asperula,* namely: the number of veins in a leaf, the number of leaves in a whorl, and the length of the corolla tube. In accordance with these the illustrated plant belongs to the genus *Galium.*

Type of plant
dicotyledon

Diploid no.
2n — 44

Flowering period
May — June

Fruit
double achene

diagram of flower

leaf

Lady's Bedstraw

Galium verum

This species is common in dry meadows, pastureland, hedgerows, on sunny slopes and in dry edges of thickets.

The creeping rhizome bears erect or ascending stems reaching a height of from 30 to 60 cm. They are glabrous or only shortly-pubescent and rounded with four raised lines. The leaves are arranged in whorls with eight to twelve in each whorl. They are narrowly-linear and pointed with a revolute margin. The upper surface is dark green, the underside is felted with a prominent median vein.

The flowers are in dense, terminal panicles and smell of honey. The corollas are 2 to 3 mm in diameter with pointed lobes and coloured deep yellow. The fruits are glabrous and smooth or warty.

Lady's Bedstraw was formerly used in cheese-making to curdle milk, for it contains a coagulant enzyme.

It is a collective species which includes two micro-species: *Galium verum* proper with prostrate, ascending or erect stems, 1-mm-wide leaves, and a very dense inflorescence, and *Galium wirtgenii* with erect stems, 2-mm-wide leaves and scanty, loose inflorescence. The latter is not fragrant and is generally found at lower elevations.

flower

longitudinal section of flower

Type of plant
dicotyledon

Diploid no.
2n — 22, 24

Flowering period
(May) June — September

Fruit
double achene

Common Valerian or **All-heal**

Valeriana officinalis

This 30- to 150-cm-high perennial grows from a cylindrical, shortly creeping, underground rhizome that has a pronounced odour. It occurs in open woodlands, high-stemmed grasslands, damp chalky meadows and damp ditches.

The upright stems are simple and grooved, with several pairs of pinnatisect leaves. The lowest are stalked, those at the top are sessile. The flowers are usually arranged in dense inflorescences. The corollas are pale pink to white.

This species is used as a medicinal herb; the rhizomes and roots contain oils which have a sedative and antispasmodic but at the same time mildly stimulating effect.

Valerian is distributed throughout most of Europe but is sparse in the south. It is a collective species embracing a number of microspecies. *Valeriana pratensis* grows in damp chalky meadows whereas *Valeriana officinalis* (syn. *Valeriana exaltata*) is found in open woodlands, grasslands and ditches. *Valeriana wallrothii* (syn. *Valeriana collina*) flowers as early as May in open woodlands, the edges of thickets and on embankments. *Valeriana repens* (syn. *Valeriana procurrens*), on the other hand, does not flower until August; it occurs in high-stemmed grasslands and beside mountain streams. Also found by water, alongside rivers, is *Valeriana sambucifolia* which flowers from as early as May.

Type of plant
dicotyledon

Diploid no.
2n — 14, 28, 56

Flowering period
June — September

Fruit
achene

rhizome and roots

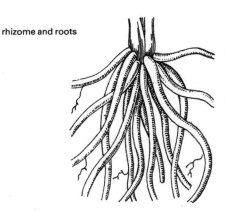

Wild or Fuller's Teasel

Dipsacus sylvestris
Syn. *Dipsacus fullonum*

Damp waste ground and watersides are where you will find this 50- to 200-cm-high biennial with its erect, angled stem which is prickly on the angles but otherwise glabrous, and branched dichasially at the top.

The stem grows from a basal rosette of short-stalked leaves that are prickly on the upper side, along the median rib on the under side, and ciliate on the margin. The stem leaves are long and lance-shaped and joined at the base into pairs. They are more or less entire, glabrous and prickly on the margin.

The flowers are in ovoid heads 5 to 8 cm long. The corollas are pale violet but may also be white. The flowers open in succession from the centre of the head outward.

Dipsacus sylvestris, distributed in central, western and southern Europe, is apparently the species that by breeding and selection gave rise to the Cultivated Teasel *(Dipsacus sativus),* grown in southwestern Europe. This plant has larger flower-heads which when dry were formerly used to raise the nap on cloth. In the opinion of other authorities, the Cultivated Teasel is derived from the Mediterranean species *Dipsacus ferox,* indigenous only in Corsica and Sardinia.

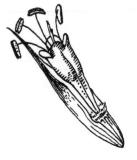

flower

Type of plant
dicotyledon

Diploid no.
2n — 16, 18

Flowering period
July — August

Fruit
achene

Field Scabious

Knautia arvensis

The flowers of this plant brighten fields, fallow land, meadows, pastureland, waysides and forest margins in almost all of Europe.

The branched rhizome bears an upright, 30- to 80-cm-high stem which may be simple or branched and is often glabrescent at the top. The basal leaves are broadly-oblanceolate to obovate and a mat greyish-green. The stem leaves are usually lyrate-pinnate.

The flowers are in heads with hairy and sometimes glandular peduncles. The heads are either herma-phroditic or only pistillate; the former measure 3 to 4 cm in diameter, the latter are only 15 to 20 mm. The calyx has eight plumose bristles. The corolla is blue-violet, less often reddish-violet or even yel-lowish-white. The marginal flowers are conspicuous-ly radiate. The mature achenes are 5 to 6 mm long and bristly-hairy.

This extremely variable species includes several microspecies. *Knautia arvensis* proper has bluish to reddish-violet flowers and pinnately divided stem leaves; it occurs in meadows, fallow land and by waysides.

Knautia kitaibelii has yellowish-white flowers and undivided or only slightly divided stem leaves; it occurs in meadows, by waysides, in forest margins and on railway embankments. *Knautia pannonica* has blue-violet flowers and grey-pubescent, conspicuous-ly pinnatipartite leaves with dainty segments.

Type of plant
dicotyledon

Diploid no.
2n — 20, 40

Flowering period
May — August

Fruit
achene

inner floret

marginal flower

Yellow Scabious

Scabiosa ochroleuca

This plant, which may be biennial or perennial and reaches a height of 20 to 80 cm, occurs on sunny slopes and in dry wasteground.

The upright stems are pubescent at the top, usually branched about midway, and carry two to five pairs of leaves. The latter are lyrate-pinnatisect.

The flowers are in a long-peduncled head 15 to 35 mm in diameter. The calyx has a membranous rim and up to 6-mm-long bristles. The corollas are pale yellow. The achenes are deeply grooved and covered with random hairs.

Found in the Balkans are several species that are very similar to this scabious: *Scabiosa balcanica* with nearly glabrous leaves, *Scabiosa webbiana* with leaves that may even be felted, *Scabiosa fumarioides* without calyx bristles, and *Scabiosa triniifolia* with calyx bristles up to five times as long as the corolla.

And do you know which one is sometimes described as having black flowers? No plant has really black flowers but one south European species is a popular ornamental, because its large flowers are often coloured dark purple. It is *Scabiosa atropurpurea* which has the darkest blooms of all European plants.

flower with calyx and epicalyx

Type of plant
dicotyledon

Diploid no.
2n – 16

Flowering period
July – October

Fruit
achene

Peach-leaved Bellflower

Campanula persicifolia

This lovely bellflower may be encountered in open woodlands, the margins of woods and thickets.

Growing from the rhizome is a simple, erect, sparsely-leaved stem 30 cm to 1 metre high. The leaves are deep green on the upper surface and a paler green on the underside. The lowest are longish-ovate to oblanceolate and shallowly crenate or nearly entire; the margins are more or less ciliate. The leaves in the middle of the stem and those at the top are narrowly-lanceolate to linear and sessile, whereas the lower ones have short stalks.

The flowers are short-peduncled and grow singly from the axils of small bracts. They are arranged in a simple, more or less one-sided raceme. The sepals are linear and extend one-third to half the length of the corolla; later they are flared. The corolla is broadly bell-shaped and split into five parts, divided about one-third of its length into rounded-ovate, pointed lobes. It is blue-violet in colour, but very occasionally may be almost white. The flowers are pollinated by insects. The inferior ovary develops into a capsule that dehisces by three openings.

This species is widespread in practically all of continental Europe but is absent in Britain and Ireland.

Type of plant
dicotyledon

Diploid no.
2n – 16

Flowering period
June – September

Fruit
capsule

longitudinal section of flower

Creeping Bellflower

Campanula rapunculoides

This perennial, which is 20 cm to 1 metre high, grows in woods, thickets, fallow land and by waysides.

The creeping rhizome bears an erect, unbranched stem that is bluntly-angled and glabrous or only shortly-pubescent. The basal leaves are long-stalked and longish-cordate, the lower stem leaves short-stalked and longish-ovate, and the remaining leaves more or less sessile and ovate to lanceolate. All are shortly-hairy and usually glabrescent on the upper surface, and all have a blunt tip and crenate margin. The basal leaves have withered and died down by the time the plant flowers.

The flowers, which have very short peduncles and are subtended by bracts, are arranged in one-sided racemes. The calyx lobes are longish-linear and re-flexed. The bell-shaped corolla is about four times longer than the calyx and divided about half-way into five spreading glabrous lobes; it is coloured blue-violet or very occasionally almost white. The capsules have three pores at the base.

diagram of flower

Type of plant
dicotyledon

Diploid no.
2n – 68, 102

Flowering period
June – September

Fruit
capsule

Spreading Bellflower

Campanula patula

This bellflower, which may be biennial or perennial, reaches a height of 15 to 60 cm. It grows in meadows and at the edges of thickets.

The stems are angled and erect or shortly ascending. The leaves are longish-elliptic or longish-ovate. Whereas the basal leaves have short stalks, the stem leaves are sessile and only few in number, gradually giving way to bracts.

The flowers are long-peduncled and arranged in a loose, spreading panicle. The calyx lobes are lanceolate to subulate and about half the length of the corolla. The latter is funnel-shaped, up to 35 mm long and divided about halfway into longish-ovate, pointed, glabrous lobes. It is coloured pale blue to dark blue or very occasionally white. The capsules open by three pores at the base.

Spreading Bellflower is found in the mountains of Europe but is absent in the northwestern and southern districts. It occurs as various subspecies in the various mountain massifs.

The related Rampion Bell *(Campanula rapunculus)* has a turnip-like root which was formerly used in salads. This species is distributed south of a boundary from the Netherlands to Poland. It was at one time widely cultivated, chiefly in the Mediterranean region.

Type of flower
dicotyledon

Diploid no.
2n − 20

Flowering period
June—July

Fruit
capsule

flower with deeply divided corolla lobes

215

Common Sheepsbit

Jasione montana

Sheepsbit, a 10- to 60-cm-high biennial, occurs in sandy pastureland, sandy rock debris and dry, sandy pine woods, but never in chalky soils.

The stems are usually erect, simple or more often with spreading branches, and variously leaved. The basal leaves are longish-lanceolate and blunt and have usually died down by the time the flowers appear. The lowest stem leaves are elongate, those in the middle and at the top lanceolate; all are sessile with an undulate, finely-toothed margin.

The flowers are clustered in globose, terminal heads up to 25 mm in diameter. The involucral bracts are ovate, the calyx lobes linear. The corolla is up to 15 mm long and divided all the way to the base into linear lobes; it is coloured pale violet or very occasionally nearly white. The mature capsule is spherical.

Jasione montana is distributed throughout practically all of Europe, north Africa and Asia Minor. It is very variable.

The related Perennial Sheepsbit *(Jasione laevis,* syn. *Jasione perennis)* differs by having leaves that are not undulate and nearly entire, non-flowering shoots (the Common Sheepsbit does not) and flower-heads up to 30 mm in diameter. This west-European species grows in sandy and grassy situations and also avoids chalky soils.

flower

Type of plant
dicotyledon

Diploid no.
2n — 12

Flowering period
June — August

Fruit
capsule

Chicory

Cichorium intybus

This perennial herb, which reaches a height of 50 to 150 cm, grows by waysides, in fallow land and in wasteland.

The stems are stiff, angled and erect with spreading branches. The leaves in the basal rosette are stalked, runcinate and more or less bristly-hairy on the underside. The lower stem leaves are similar to the basal leaves but sessile. The leaves at the top of the stem are elongate to lanceolate. The plant exudes white milk when bruised.

The flowers are clustered in heads up to 40 mm in diameter. All the flowers are ligulate and open only in the morning. The outer involucral bracts are ovate, outspread and shorter than the inner, upright bracts. The corollas are bright blue, but very occasionally may be whitish or pinkish. The cypselas are fringed with bristles.

Subspecies *sativum* is grown for its fleshy roots, used to make a coffee substitute. Wild plants belonging to the subspecies *intybus* have a hard root.

The related Endive *(Cichorium endivia)* is cultivated for its leaves which are cooked or blanched and used for salads in the Mediterranean region, mostly in southern France and Italy.

Type of plant
dicotyledon

Diploid no.
2n — 18

Flowering period
July — October

Fruit
cypsela

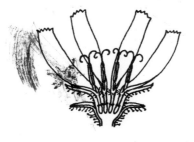

Schematic longitudinal section of anthodium of the subfamily Cichorioideae

root

Mouse-ear Hawkweed

Hieracium pilosella

Syn. *Pilosella officinarum*

Dry meadows, pastures, grasslands and fallow land is where you will find this 5- to 30-cm-high perennial.

The lanceolate to obovate leaves form a ground rosette. They are green to grey-felted above and are always white-felted underneath. Rising from the centre of the rosette is an erect, leafless stem. The plant forms long, slender stolons covered with long hairs or white felt and a small number of leaves that become smaller towards the end of the stolon.

The stem is usually terminated by a single anthodium, very occasionally two. The involucre is broadly-ovoid and felted. The corollas are yellow with rust-coloured stripes on the outside of the marginal florets.

This is an entirely independent species from the evolutionary viewpoint; it has no microspecies or even subspecies and only occasionally forms transitional species with certain other species.

Mouse-ear Hawkweed is widespread in almost all of Europe except certain islands (for example, the Azores, Crete and Iceland).

Type of plant
dicotyledon

Diploid no.
2n — 18, 27, 36, 45, 54, 63

Flowering period
May — October

Fruit
cypsela

fruit

Grim the Collier

Hieracium aurantiacum

This perennial grows in mountain meadows from a rhizome which has numerous scaly underground runners and leafy surface runners. The upright or ascending stems are 20 to 40 cm high.

The soft, deep green basal leaves, arranged in a rosette, are lanceolate or spatulate and entire or only faintly toothed. The stem leaves, usually four, are randomly hairy and sparsely glandular.

The stem carries as many as twelve flower heads (anthodiums), the one in the middle usually positioned lower than the rest. This is one of the few members of the genus with orange flowers. The peduncles supporting the heads are covered with black, spreading hairs. The involucral bracts are dark with a paler margin.

The diploid number is extremely variable for *Hieracium aurantiacum* often forms so-called transitional species with other mountain hieraciums. Though it is not one of the most variable members of the genus it is usually divided into two subspecies — the type subspecies and subspecies *carpaticola,* which has involucral bracts about half as long and differs in certain other characteristics. Both are distributed in central and northern Europe.

Type of plant
dicotyledon

Diploid no.
2n — 27, 36, 45, 54, 63

Flowering period
July — August

Fruit
cypsela

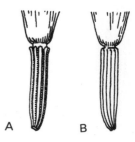

Diagram of the difference between the two subgenera of the genus *Hieracium:*
A — *Pilosella* (the ribs of the cypsela terminate in tiny teeth beneath the pappus)
B — *Hieracium* (the ribs are joined in a narrow ridge without teeth)

Common Dandelion

Taraxacum officinale

Syn. *Taraxacum vulgare*

This well-known perennial, 10 to 50 cm high, grows in meadows, pastures and fields as well as in wasteland and on dunes.

The leaves, forming a basal rosette, are obovate to narrowly lanceolate, generally narrowing abruptly into a stalk and as a rule deeply runcinate.

The scape is glabrous or slightly woolly and hollow; when broken off or otherwise bruised it oozes a white, milky sap. It ends in a yellow inflorescence (anthodium). The involucre is dark green. The corollas are yellow, very occasionally nearly orange. The mature fruits (brownish cypselas) are smooth or thickly covered with blunt-tipped tubercles in the upper half and long-beaked. The pappus is white.

This species embraces approximately 150 microspecies that are not always readily distinguished, for study of the group is extremely difficult. Identification is a very exacting task and even the distribution of these microspecies is not definitely known.

Taraxacum laevigatum has pale-yellow corollas often flushed red at the base, white-edged involucral bracts and reddish-brown cypselas. It is a plant of dry sunny slopes and turf, rocks, and sandy situations.

fruit with bristles

Type of plant
dicotyledon

Diploid no.
2n — 16—18, 20, 23—29, 32, 36, 37

Flowering period
April — September

Fruit
cypsela

Smooth Sow-thistle

Sonchus oleraceus

This tall weed with an erect, hollow, glabrous stem reaching a height of 50 cm to 1 metre, may be encountered in fields, fallow land and wasteland.

The small leaves are soft and coloured greyish-green. The bottom leaves are longish-ovate, undivided or runcinate-pinnatifid, and narrow at the base into a wide-winged stalk. The stem leaves are sessile and sagittate at the base with pointed auricles. Otherwise the leaves have prickly teeth.

The flower-heads are arranged in a simple or compound cyme. The peduncles supporting the heads are slightly thickened. The involucre is ovate-cylindrical and conspicuously narrow in the middle. The corollas are yellow, sometimes striped with violet or brown outside. Very occasionally one may encounter specimens with white flowers. The mature cypselas are 3 mm long, brown, and faintly triangular with transverse wrinkles. When broken off or bruised, the plant freely exudes a milky sap.

Very similar in appearance is the related Prickly Sow-thistle *(Sonchus asper),* which differs by having leaves with rounded auricles and a conspicuously lower diploid number of chromosomes − 2n − 18.

Both species are distributed in Europe, northwest Asia and north Africa.

Type of plant
dicotyledon

Diploid no.
2n − 32

Flowering period
June − October

Fruit
cypsela

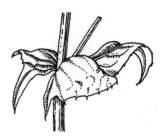

base of leaf with auricles

Goatsbeard

Tragopogon pratensis

This plant, which may be biennial or perennial and reaches a height of 30 to 60 cm, grows in meadows, pastureland and by the wayside.

It has a simple or sparsely-branched stem. The leaves embrace the stem with their broad base; those farther up are increasingly narrower and longer, finally giving way to linear-lanceolate bracts.

The stem below the flower-head is slightly thickened, but only just beneath the involucre. The involucre is up to 30 mm long and is composed of eight to ten lanceolate, white-edged bracts which are the same length as the florets. The latter are all ligulate and coloured sulphur-yellow. The anthers are bicoloured — the bottom half yellow, the upper half blackish-violet. The cypselas are up to 20 mm long and furnished with a beak of the same length. The pappus is big, upright, dingy white and composed of intertwined feathery hairs.

Goatsbeard is widespread in almost all of Europe, where it occurs as a number of subspecies. The subspecies *pratensis* is distributed throughout this range; subspecies *minor* with involucral bracts about twice as long as the ligulate florets and often with a red margin is found in western and central Europe; and subspecies *orientalis* with golden-yellow ligulate florets and fruits with beak shorter than the cypsela is often encountered in central and eastern Europe. Sometimes these subspecies are classified as separate species.

Type of plant
dicotyledon

Diploid no.
2n — 12

Flowering period
May — August

Fruit
cypsela

fruit with pappus

Smooth Hawk's-beard

Crepis mollis

This perennial, which reaches a height of 30 to 90 cm, grows in damp meadows and in mountain districts.

It has a black rhizome from which rises an erect, leafy stem that is usually glabrous, though it may be hairy as are the leaves. The latter are soft, entire or with shallow, distant teeth. The bottom leaves are elliptic to longish-ovate and stalked. Those in the middle of the stem are usually longish with a rounded or faintly heart-shaped base attached directly to the stem. The uppermost leaves are linear-lanceolate.

The stem is sparsely, corymbosely branched at the top and carries heads measuring up to 35 mm in diameter. The involucre with a double row of bracts is blackish-green and covered with stellate hairs and glands. The corollas are yellow and nearly twice as long as the involucre. The cypselas have twenty smooth ribs; the pappus is soft and flexible and pure white.

This species, found chiefly in central and south-eastern Europe, is usually differentiated into the following three subspecies: subspecies *mollis* of mountain meadows and high-stemmed grasslands, subspecies *succisifolia* of watersides, springs and damp thickets, and subspecies *velenovskyi,* which apparently grows only in the Elbe River region. The subspecies differ in the indumentum, shape of the leaves and shape of the stem beneath the flower-head.

Type of plant
dicotyledon

Diploid no.
2n — 12

Flowering period
June — August

Fruit
cypsela

leaf of the related and very similar *Crepis biennis*

Golden-rod

Solidago virgaurea

This 20-cm- to 1-metre-high perennial grows in woodland clearings, the edges of woods, heaths and other grassy places.

The erect stem is glabrous or randomly hairy and covered entirely with leaves. The bottom leaves are ovate to elliptic, narrowing at the base to a long stalk, and serrate on the margin; those at the top are lanceolate and sessile.

The anthodiums are 10 to 20 mm in diameter. The involucre is cylindrical. The elongate bracts are pointed and glabrous. The flowers are golden yellow. Those in the centre are tubular and shorter than the involucre, the outer florets are ligulate and much longer than the involucre. The cypselas are 3 to 4 mm long and hairy.

This species occurs as two subspecies. Subspecies *virgaurea* has flower-heads 10 to 15 mm in diameter clustered in dense racemes and grows prevalently in woodland situations. Subspecies *minuta* is only 5 to 25 cm high and its flower-heads, which measure 15 to 20 mm across, are arranged in simple or only sparsely-branched, spike-like inflorescences; it grows at elevations of up to 2,500 metres in mountain meadows, on rocks in the dwarf-pine belt and similar mountain situations.

The North American species *Solidago canadensis* is grown as an ornamental in practically all of Europe.

A – central disc floret   B – strap-shaped ray floret

Type of plant
dicotyledon

Diploid no.
2n — 18

Flowering period
July — October

Fruit
cypsela

Daisy

Bellis perennis

This, the most common of wild flowers, grows in meadows and pastureland.

The erect, 5- to 15-cm-high scape is pubescent and ends in a single flower-head about 15 mm across. The receptacle is conical and hollow. The hemispherical involucre is composed of a double row of bracts. The disc florets are tubular, hermaphroditic and yellow. The ligulate ray florets are white or tinted pink to purple on the underside. It is a characteristic of this plant that the flowers are not damaged by even a severe frost. The mature cypselas are about 1 mm long, smooth and without a pappus.

The Daisy is used in folk medicine as an ingredient in various herbal teas. It is distributed throughout practically all of Europe.

Found in southern Europe is the species *Bellis sylvestris* which can be distinguished from *Bellis perennis* with certainty only after determining the diploid number, which is 2n − 36 (54) in the case of *Bellis sylvestris*. Both are often grown as ornamentals. Breeding and selection has yielded a great many varieties differing in the size of the flower-heads and the size and colour of the ray florets. Also widely grown are the double forms.

Type of plant
dicotyledon

Diploid no.
2n − 18

Flowering period
March − November

Fruit
cypsela

fruit

closed flower

Alpine Aster

Aster alpinus

This perennial, up to 20 cm high, grows on high ground.

The stems are usually erect, leafy, unbranched, and each is normally topped by a single flower-head. Both stems and leaves are shortly-hairy. The lowest leaves are spatulate and short-stalked, the stem leaves are longish-lanceolate, entire, three-veined and sessile — attached directly to the stem by the narrowed base of the blade.

The big anthodium is nearly 5 cm across and the involucral bracts are herbaceous, lanceolate and ciliate on the margin. The disc florets are golden-yellow, the ligulate ray florets (as many as forty) may be more than 2 cm long and are coloured bluish or pinkish. The ovaries develop into cypselas with a pappus composed of two rows of hairs.

The Alpine Aster is distributed from middle Germany and southern Poland to the Pyrenees, Balkans and the Caucasus. It is a popular ornamental, grown in many forms in the rock garden. It often occurs as an escape and is locally naturalized even at lower elevations.

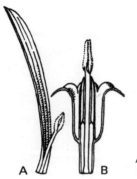

A – longitudinal section of a ligulate floret
B – longitudinal section of a tubular floret

Type of plant
dicotyledon

Diploid no.
2n – 18, 36

Flowering period
July – August

Fruit
cypsela

Cat's-foot

Antennaria dioica

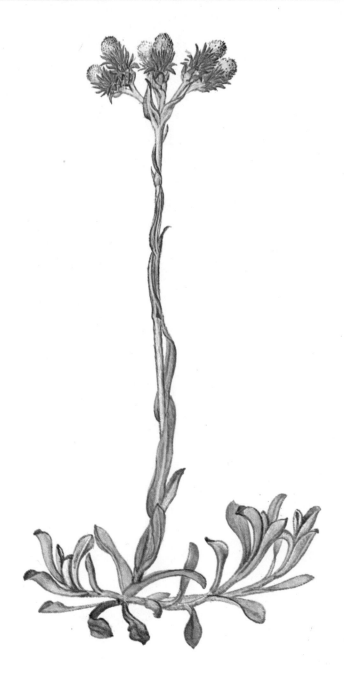

This perennial, which reaches a height of 5 to 20 cm, grows in open woods, heaths and pastureland.

The creeping rhizome, which anchors the grey-woolly plant, has creeping, leafy surface shoots. The erect stems are shortly-branched at the top where the flower-heads are located. The leaves on the surface shoots are spatulate, whereas the stem leaves are lanceolate and those at the very top are linear and pointed. They are usually green and glabrous on the upper surface and covered with silky grey wool on the underside.

The inflorescence is composed of 3 to 13 anthodiums with imbricate involucres. The bracts in the hermaphroditic anthodiums are white or pink, blunt, and shorter than the florets. The bracts of the female anthodiums are pink to reddish-violet (sometimes even white), pointed, and longer than the florets. The anthodiums differ also in the colour of the florets: hermaphroditic florets are pale yellow or reddish with a reddish pappus, female florets are pink to red with a white pappus. The cypselas that develop after fertilization are very short — only 1 mm long.

Cat's-foot was once used as a medicinal herb. It is widespread in practically all of Europe, although in the south it is found only locally in the mountains. Found in the Carpathians and Pyrenees is the related species *Antennaria carpatica*.

Type of plant
dicotyledon

Diploid no.
2n — 28

Flowering period
May — July

Fruit
cypsela

hermaphroditic flower

anthodium of female plant

Wood Cudweed

Gnaphalium sylvaticum

This plant may be seen in open woods and woodland clearings.

It is a grey-felted perennial with a short rhizome and erect, 20- to 40-cm-high, twiggy stem, covered thickly with leaves. These are faintly pubescent to glabrescent on the upper surface and grey-felted on the underside. The bottom leaves are lanceolate, entire and pointed, single-veined and short-stalked. The stem leaves, which become smaller from the ground upward, are narrowly-lanceolate to linear and are also single-veined.

The small anthodiums are in clusters of two to eight in the axils of lanceolate bracts. The involucral bracts have a broad, pale edge and a brown, horse-shoe-like spot at the tip. The outer bracts are slightly woolly. All the florets are tubular and coloured pale brown. The central florets (only threee or four) are hermaphroditic, the outer florets (up to seventy arranged in several rows) are all female. The cypselas are 1.5 mm long and hairy.

The related Highland Cudweed *(Gnaphalium norvegicum)* has stem leaves conspicuously three-veined to faintly five-veined and a white pappus, unlike that of Wood Cudweed which has a pinkish colour.

Both species may be found in practically all of Europe.

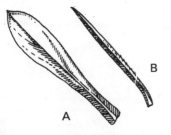

A — leaf from the middle section of the stem
B — bract subtending a single inflorescence

Type of plant
dicotyledon

Diploid no.
2n — 56

Flowering period
July — September

Fruit
cypsela

Mountain Arnica

Arnica montana

This perennial herb, reaching a height of 20 to 60 cm, grows in foothill and mountain meadows, pastures, heaths, on grassy slopes and in woodland clearings, usually avoiding chalky soils.

The oblique, underground rhizome bears a ground rosette of 2- to 4-cm-wide leaves. Rising from the centre of the rosette is an erect, simple or only sparsely-branched stem with usually one but sometimes two pairs of opposite, sessile leaves.

The stem is terminated by a large anthodium, 6 to 8 cm across, beneath which there are sometimes two more. The involucre is glandular-hairy. The tubular as well as ligulate florets are coloured yolk-yellow. The fruit is a cypsela with a pale yellow pappus.

This medicinal plant was formerly widely gathered in central Europe, which led to its complete disappearance in places and is the reason why it is now on the list of protected species in many countries.

The related *Arnica angustifolia* is found in the arctic regions of Scandinavia, arctic Siberia, Greenland and arctic North America. And even plants of Tierra del Fuego at the southernmost tip of South America are classified as *Arnica angustifolia*.

Type of plant
dicotyledon

Diploid no.
2n — 38

Flowering period
June — August

Fruit
cypsela

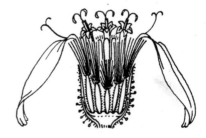

schematic longitudinal section of anthodium

Three-partite Bur-marigold

Bidens tripartita

This 20-cm- to 1-metre-high annual grows in water-logged ground, by the waterside and in ditches.

The erect stems are much-branched (the branches are opposite), glabrous or pubescent and are often coloured reddish-brown. The stem leaves are three- to five-partite and narrow into a winged stalk.

The branched stem ends in solitary, globose anthodiums which are 15 to 25 mm across and either upright or drooping. The involucre is composed of 5 to 8 enlarged, leaf-like outer bracts and small, ovate inner bracts coloured brownish-yellow.

The tubular florets are the same colour; the ligulate florets are absent. The cypselas are brownish-green, thickly covered with deflexed bristles on the edges and in this species usually furnished with three 'teeth'. Other members of the genus usually have two 'teeth' – hence the Latin name *Bidens* (*bi* meaning two and *dens* tooth).

This Bur-marigold is distributed throughout Europe except the extreme north and extreme south. It is the most variable Bur-marigold of all the approximately ten species. The many deviations in certain aspects of the leaves and anthodiums were most probably influenced by the soil factor and perhaps also by the time of germination of the cypselas. For this reason it is best to view deviations from the type species as ecotypes.

fruit with bristles

Type of plant
dicotyledon

Diploid no.
2n – 48

Flowering period
July – October

Fruit
cypsela

230

Yellow Chamomile

Anthemis tinctoria

This plant, which may be biennial or perennial and reaches a height of 20 to 60 cm, grows on sunny banks, stony slopes, overgrown rock debris, fallow land and waste ground.

It has a branched, many-headed rhizome from which rise erect or ascending woolly stems that may be simple or sparsely branched at the top. Each branch carries a single flower-head and alternate, pinnatisect leaves. The leaf rachis is narrowly-winged.

The anthodiums measure up to 4 cm in diameter. The involucre is cup-shaped, the receptacle hemispherical with lanceolate, entire, cuspidate scales. Both the tubular and ligulate florets are golden-yellow. The mature cypselas are glabrous, four-angled and edged with a narrow membrane at the top.

Yellow Chamomile appears in many varieties and its range embraces most of Europe, even though it is absent on some islands and in some parts of the northwest. The flowers, which contain xanthophyllous and carotenoid pigments, were formerly used as a yellow dye. Many other species with yellow or orange flowers are found in Europe, though white species predominate. There are approximately fifty *Anthemis* species in Europe.

Type of plant
dicotyledon

Diploid no.
2n — 18

Flowering period
July — September

Fruit
cypsela

schematic longitudinal section of anthodium

Yarrow

Achillea millefolium

This perennial, which reaches a height of 15 to 50 cm, grows in meadows, fields and pastures, by waysides, in hedgerows and in other grassy places.

The stems, rising from a creeping rhizome, are upright, branching at the top into a dense corymbose panicle. The leaves are woolly at first, later randomly-hairy to glabrescent, lanceolate in outline, and twice to thrice pinnatisect.

The anthodiums are up to 6 mm wide. The involucre is ovoid and yellow-green edged pale to dark brown. The disc florets are dingy white, the ray florets white, very occasionally pink, reddish, or yellowish. The mature cypselas are silvery-grey and narrowly-winged on either side.

Achillea millefolium is widespread in almost all of Europe, western Asia, North America and Australia. This collective species includes some eight microspecies, and *Achillea millefolium* proper occurs as two subspecies: subspecies *millefolium* of lowland districts and subspecies *sudetica* of mountain districts. The other microspecies differ primarily in general appearance and indumentum, shape and arrangement of the leaf segments, colour of the ray florets, arrangement of the anthodiums, and last but not least in the diploid number of chromosomes.

Anthodium of *Achillea ptarmica* which, unlike *Achillea millefolium*, is a moisture-loving species

leaf

Type of plant
dicotyledon

Diploid no.
2n — 54 (18, 36, 72)

Flowering period
June — October

Fruit
cypsela

Tansy

Chrysanthemum vulgare

Syn. *Tanacetum vulgare*

This 50- to 150-cm-high perennial grows in grassy places and hedgerows, by waysides and watersides, on overgrown rocky debris and on waste ground.

It has a profusely-rooting, creeping rhizome which bears stiff, erect, angled stems thickly covered with leaves. These are broadly oval in outline, pinnatisect or bipinnatisect, dark green above and spotted with glands on the underside. The rachis is winged. The entire plant has a pronounced aroma, particularly when rubbed between the fingers.

The small anthodiums are arranged in dense corymbs. The anthodium, approximately 10 mm across, is composed only of golden-yellow tubular florets with no ray florets whatever. The involucre is hemispherical and smooth. The mature cypselas are oval with a toothed border.

Tansy is distributed throughout most of Europe; it was once also often grown both for decoration and as a medicinal herb and has thus become established in many countries, such as Ireland, where it was not originally native. This species is also sometimes classed by itself in a separate genus — *Tanacetum* — because of the absence of the strap-shaped ray florets.

Type of plant
dicotyledon

Diploid no.
2n — 18

Flowering period
July — September

Fruit
cypsela

schematic longitudinal section of anthodium

Ox-eye Daisy

Chrysanthemum leucanthemum

Syn. *Leucanthemum vulgare*

The gay, yellow-white flowers of the Ox-eye Daisy brighten meadows, pastureland, heaths, waysides, hedgerows and grassy slopes from spring until autumn.

It is a perennial with a short rhizome and an erect, 30- to 60-cm-high stem, which may be simple or have several upright branches, each ending in a single flower-head. The lowest leaves are spatulate or oval with a steeply narrowing base. The upper leaves are long and narrow, and coarsely saw-toothed to pinnatifid with a rounded base attached directly to the stem. Those at the top of the stem are serrate to entire and spaced far apart.

The anthodiums are solitary and measure 3 to 6 cm in diameter in the wild. Cultivated garden forms may be up to 15 cm across. The involucre is hemispherical and green, the bracts overlap each other and have brown edges. The central disc is composed of yellow tubular florets; the outer ray florets are white and up to 2 cm longer than the involucre. The cypselas are ribbed.

Ox-eye Daisy is widespread in almost all of Europe, though in the extreme north its occurrence is sporadic.

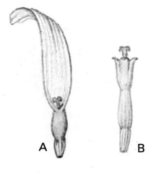

Cypselas: A — from the margin
B — from the centre of anthodium

A — strap-shaped ray floret
B — tubular disc floret

Type of plant
dicotyledon

Diploid no.
2n — 18

Flowering period
May — September

Fruit
cypsela

Mugwort

Artemisia vulgaris

Watersides, roadsides, village greens and waste ground are all places congenial to the growth of this faintly but unpleasantly odorous plant.

The upright stems, reaching a height of 40 to 120 (250) cm, often grow in clumps. They are stiff, angled, much-branched and have soft hairs. The leaves are smooth on the upper surface and greyish-white-felted beneath. The bottom leaves are short-stalked, 5 to 10 cm long, and more or less lyrate-pinnatipart-ite with a long terminal segment. The bracts in the inflorescence are simple and lanceolate.

The minute, short-peduncled anthodiums may be erect or drooping and are arranged in dense, leafy panicles. The involucres are oval and covered with greyish-white felt. The tubular florets are yellowish or reddish-brown; there are no ray florets.

This slightly poisonous plant is distributed throughout most of Europe, where it occurs as two subspecies. Subspecies *vulgaris* has a much-branched stem, 120-cm-high at the most, and grows alongside flowing water, by waysides and in thickets. Subspecies *coarctata* has a stem that is unbranched and reaches a height of more than two metres; it grows on dunes, in coastal sands and thickets, and flowers later – in October or early November.

Type of plant
dicotyledon

Diploid no.
2n — 16

Flowering period
July — September

Fruit
cypsela

diagram of a regular disc floret of the composite family

Coltsfoot

Tussilago farfara

This perennial grows from a creeping, scaly rhizome with long runners in grassy and sandy waste places, by the waterside and in fields with a high moisture content; it is one of the first spring-flowering herbs.

The erect, unbranched stem is 10 to 15 cm high during the flowering period and up to 50 cm high in the fruiting season. The leaves, which form a ground rosette, appear after flowering. They are long-stalked, round heart-shaped or oval and shallowly-toothed, the teeth distant and tipped with black. When they first appear the leaves are covered with a thick coat of white felt on both sides but this soon disappears from the upper surface.

The scales on the scape are longish-ovate and yellowish. The anthodiums, measuring 10 to 15 mm across, are borne singly at the tips of the stems and droop after the flowers are spent. The involucral bracts are green but sometimes are flushed with red. The flowers are golden-yellow. The disc florets are male, whereas the outer ligulate florets are female. The cypselas are glabrous and have a glossy white pappus.

Coltsfoot is widely used as a medicinal herb, especially the flowers which contain substances that alleviate and the common cold, coughing, influenza and asthma. It is widespread in all Europe except the Azores, Balearic Islands, Crete and most of Portugal, and is found as well in western and northern Asia and the mountains of north Africa; it has also been introduced into North America.

leaf

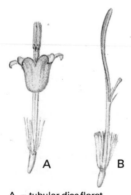

A
B

A – tubular disc floret
B – strap-shaped ray floret

fruit with pappus

Type of plant
dicotyledon

Diploid no.
2n – 60

Flowering period
March – April

Fruit
cypsela

236

Common Butterbur

Petasites hybridus

Syn. *Petasites officinalis*

In spring the flowers of this dioecious butterbur may be seen by the waterside, in damp meadows and in alder groves, and even in ditches in foothill and mountain districts.

The male plants bear racemes of dingy pinkish-violet anthodiums composed of seemingly bisexual flowers, for though stamens and pistils are both present the stigmas are sterile (only the pollen is fertile). The corollas are tubular and five-lobed.

Female plants are rare in lowland districts, growing in abundance only in the mountains. Here the anthodiums are composed primarily of pistillate flowers with tubular corolla and only a few sterile bisexual flowers in the centre.

The leaves, which appear after the flowers have faded, grow from a thick rhizome which has a pronounced odour when bruised. The leaf stalks are ribbed and conspicuously channelled with wings. The blades of mature leaves may be more than 60 cm wide. The scaly stems, often tinted violet, are 15 to 40 cm high before flowering and end in a dense raceme or panicle of anthodiums with involucral bracts also often tinted violet. After flowering the stems become longer, and fertile female plants are often more than one metre high. The cypselas are reddish-brown, ribbed and furnished with a long pappus.

Common Butterbur is distributed throughout practically all of Europe except the extreme north and south.

Type of plant
dicotyledon

Diploid no.
2n — 60

Flowering period
April — May

Fruit
cypsela

cross-section of petiole

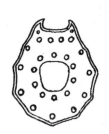

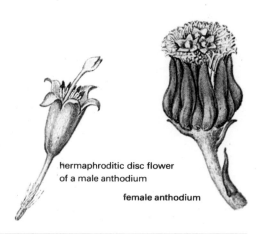

hermaphroditic disc flower
of a male anthodium

female anthodium

Alpine Ragwort

Senecio fuchsii

Woodland clearings, forest margins, humus-rich mixed woods, forest rides and ditches are the habitats of this perennial, which reaches a height of 150 cm.

The stems, which grow from rhizomes, are smooth and reddish-violet. The long lance-shaped leaves are up to five times longer than they are wide, finely-toothed on the margin and smooth between the teeth. The leaf-stalks are almost imperceptible.

The branches carrying the anthodiums are slender. The narrowly-cylindrical involucre is usually composed of eight glabrous bracts. The flower-heads are composed of approximately five yellow ligulate florets and six to fifteen tubular florets.

Senecio fuchsii is found primarily in central Europe, very occasionally also in southern Europe.

The closely related *Senecio nemorensis* has green stems. The leaves are only about three times as long as they are wide and have blunt teeth; the spaces between the teeth often have thick hairs. The underside of the leaves is covered with curly hairs and the winged stalks partly embrace the stem. The involucre is generally composed of ten hairy involucral bracts. The number of ligulate ray-florets is usually five as in *Senecio fuchsii,* but the number of tubular florets is fourteen to twenty. Unlike *Senecio fuchsii,* which grows at lower altitudes, *Senecio nemorensis* is found at higher altitudes, though it may often be encountered even in apparently unlikely localities such as certain deep river valleys.

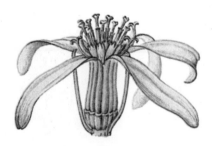

anthodium of *Senecio nemorensis*

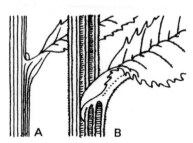

Attachment of leaves to the stem:
A – *Senecio fuchsii*
B – *Senecio nemorensis*

Type of plant
dicotyledon

Diploid no.
2n – 40

Flowering period
July – September

Fruit
cypsela

Great Burdock

Arctium lappa

This plant, which reaches a height of between one and two metres, grows in waste ground rich in humus, by the waterside, and in ditches.

It has a thick, branched, creeping rhizome and an erect, grooved, leafy stem covered with down and branching profusely. The cross-section of the stem shows that it is filled with pith. The leaves are stalked, heart-shaped or oval, green and lightly felted above and grey-felted on the underside. The basal leaves have blades up to 50 cm long, those of the stem leaves are smaller.

The anthodiums are arranged at the same level in cymose panicles at the tips of the branches. They are globe-shaped and up to 3.5 cm in diameter. The involucral bracts with hooked tips form a prickly envelope round the anthodium. They are approximately the same length as the reddish-violet florets. The cypselas are long, black and faintly warty. When they are mature the tips of the branches carrying the flower-heads become dry and the heads partially disintegrate. When a passing animal brushes against the plant these prickly 'buttons' or at least the separate cypselas with hooked bracts catch in its fur. By this means, known as zoochory, the Great Burdock is dispersed over great distances.

Great Burdock is found throughout Europe excepting the islands, its range extending through Asia Minor and all of Siberia as far as China and perhaps even Japan; it has also been introduced into North and South America.

Type of plant
dicotyledon

Diploid no.
2n — 36

Flowering period
July — September

Fruit
cypsela

Cross-section of stalk of lower leaves:
A — *Arctium lappa* B — *Arctium nemorosum*

anthodium with sharply-hooked bracts

involucral bract

Musk Thistle

Carduus nutans

The Musk Thistle, usually biennial and reaching a height of 30 cm to 1 metre, grows in hedgerows, on sunny slopes, on dry waste ground and in heaths.

The erect, spiny-winged stems branch sparsely at the top. The leaves are long and lance-shaped in outline and sinuate-pinnatifid, the segments are spiny on the margin.

The anthodiums are solitary and nodding. The spherical involucre is composed of several overlapping rows of reflexed, spine-tipped bracts. The reddish-violet corollas are tubular, five-lobed and faintly zygomorphic. The mature cypselas are up to 4 mm long, transversely wrinkled, and have a long pappus.

Musk Thistle is most common in western and central Europe.

The subspecies *nutans* has heads that measure only 4 cm across at the most, are definitely drooping and never solitary.

The subspecies *macrolepis* has heads up to 8 cm across, usually solitary, and smooth or only randomly hairy.

The subspecies *alpicola* has heads the same size as subspecies *macrolepis* that are also often solitary. However in contrast, they are thickly hairy. These thistles generally grow on higher ground.

All three subspecies have involucral bracts with long spines and a prominent mid-rib, a feature that conspicuously distinguishes them from the alpine subspecies *platylepis*.

Type of plant
dicotyledon

Diploid no.
2n − 16

Flowering period
July − September

Fruit
cypsela

Welted Thistle

Carduus acanthoides

This biennial, which reaches a height of 30 cm to 1 metre, occurs in dry and semi-dry wasteland, on sunny slopes and in grassland.

The erect stems branch from midway up. They are wavy-winged (the wings are spiny) and the branches, which are of unequal length, are curly-pubescent. The leaves are long and lance-shaped in outline and are divided into several spiny-toothed or prickly segments.

The erect anthodiums, 25 to 35 mm in diameter, are borne singly at the tips of the branches; only rarely are there several clustered together. The involucre is oval or spherical and up to 25 mm long. The involucral bracts are spiny and curve outward. The flowers are pale reddish-violet; only very occasionally are they whitish. The mature cypselas are up to 3.5 mm long and covered with fine dots.

This thistle is found in almost all of Europe with the exception of the southwestern Mediterranean region and northernmost Scandinavia.

Type of plant
dicotyledon

Diploid no.
2n — 22

Flowering period
June — September

Fruit
cypsela

leaf

Cabbage Thistle

Cirsium oleraceum

This perennial thistle reaches a height of 50 to 150 cm and grows in damp meadows and beside streams that flood their banks.

The stout, variously-thickened rhizome bears an erect, shallowly-grooved stem with a few short branches at the top. It is hollow in the centre. The leaves are soft, not prickly, edged with soft spines and coloured fresh or pale green. The bottom leaves are ovate to elliptic and undivided, but may be deeply lobed. The upper leaves are long and lance-shaped.

The anthodiums are clustered on the short, felted branches at the tip of the stem and are subtended by enlarged bracts. The involucre is ovoid-cylindrical, the outer bracts end in a soft pointed tip. The florets are pale yellow or occasionally reddish. The mature cypselas are faintly angled and up to 4 mm long.

There are few yellow-white or white-flowering species in Europe. *Cirsium spinosissimum* is a short mountain species native to the Alps and Apennines with flower-heads often in clusters of as many as ten. *Cirsium glabrum* has stems terminated by solitary heads with yellowish corollas and is native to the Pyrenees, and *Cirsium albicans,* a similar species but with whitish corollas, is indigenous to southern Spain.

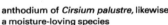

anthodium of *Cirsium palustre*, likewise a moisture-loving species

fruit

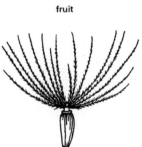

Type of plant
dicotyledon

Diploid no.
2n − 34

Flowering period
June − September

Fruit
cypsela

Cornflower

Centaurea cyanus

Syn. *Cyanus arvensis, Centaurea segetum*

This 30- to 60-cm-high annual herb is a weed of fields, fallow land and waste ground.

The erect, angled stem is usually branched. The leaves are slightly woolly but soon become glabrescent. They are lanceolate in outline. The basal leaves are stalked, the stem leaves are sessile.

The anthodiums are erect and borne singly at the tips of the branches. The involucres are ovoid-cylindrical and up to 14 mm long. The involucral bracts do not have a spine at the tip. The centre florets are hermaphroditic and violet, the outer florets are larger, pistillate, and blue. The mature cypselas are up to 3 mm long and pubescent with pappus composed of two rows of hairs.

Of the central European species the best known, apart from *Centaurea cyanus,* is the often-cultivated Mountain Cornflower or Mountain Bluet *(Centaurea montana),* a perennial herb with broad leaves and dark-edged involucral bracts found mostly only on chalky soils. Variegated Knapweed *(Centaurea triumfettii),* a decorative element among rocks and in steppes in many European countries, is a striking grey-felted plant with soft-silky-felted leaves which, like the preceding species, has heads with violet centre florets and blue outer florets.

Type of plant
dicotyledon

Diploid no.
2n — 24

Flowering period
June — October

Fruit
cypsela

fruit

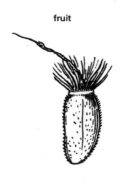

A — outer floret B — centre floret

French Hardhead

Centaurea jacea

Syn. *Jacea communis*

This perennial, which reaches a height of 30 cm to 1 metre, occurs in meadows, hedgerows, by waysides and on sunny slopes.

The stems are erect, angled and leafy. The basal leaves, arranged in a rosette, are stalked, lanceolate or ovate, undivided and edged with fine, distant teeth. The stem leaves are successively smaller from the ground upward, giving way to bracts at the top.

The anthodiums borne at the tips of the stems have ovoid involucres with three rows of bracts. The outer bracts have triangular-lanceolate appendages, those in the middle row dry, thin, rounded appendages usually coloured dark-brown (in both the appendages usually have laciniate or fringed margins); the appendages of the inner bracts are undivided. The shape, colour and appearance of these appendages are important characters of identification within the species. The flowers of this *Centaurea* are pinkish-red. The marginal florets are usually enlarged and sterile.

French Hardhead occurs in central Europe in perhaps as many as ten different subspecies. Subspecies *pratensis* has cypselas bordered with short bristles whereas those of the other subspecies are without a border. Examples are subspecies *angustifolia*, subspecies *amara*, subspecies *subjacea* and subspecies *oxylepis*. The separate subspecies differ in the shape of the leaves and the shape and coloration of the involucral appendages.

Involucral bracts: A — outer bracts B — inner bracts

Type of plant
dicotyledon

Diploid no.
2n — (22), 44

Flowering period
June — October

Fruit
cypsela

Great or Stemless Carline-thistle

Carlina acaulis

This perennial grows on warm, sunny slopes, in grassy places and in dry open woods.

The stem is usually atrophied. The leaves, forming a basal rosette, are stiff, pale green on the upper surface and edged with spiny teeth of unequal length.

The anthodiums are big (up to 15 cm across). The outer involucral bracts are leaf-like, the middle ones brownish with comb-like, spiny teeth. The inner bracts are linear, pointed, glossy white on the upper side and yellowish on the under surface. In sunny weather they expand. The florets rise from a fleshy receptacle and are white, but may occasionally be pinkish. The fleshy receptacle is sometimes eaten by children because it tastes like nuts. The mature cypselas are usually 5 mm long and the pappus is composed of palmatipartite plumose bristles.

This species occurs as two subspecies: subspecies *acaulis* with an inconspicuous stem and thickly clustered upper leaves and subspecies *simplex* with a relatively long stem (up to 50 cm high) thickly covered with leaves along its entire length. The latter prefers chalky soils.

This plant grows throughout Great Britain except northern Scotland, and in a band across Europe from France to the Caucasus.

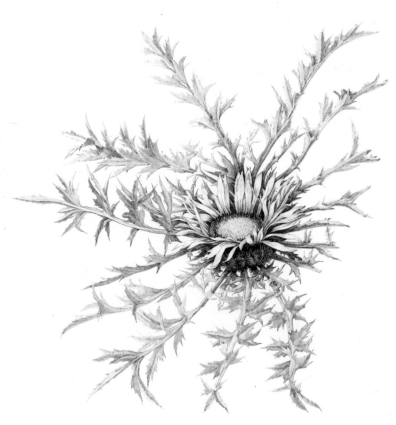

Type of plant
dicotyledon

Diploid no.
2n − 20

Flowering period
July − September

Fruit
cypsela

fruit

closed inflorescence

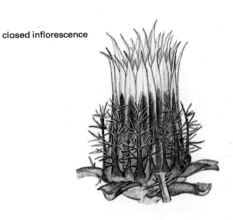

Hare's Lettuce

Prenanthes purpurea

Mountain glades, beach and coniferous woods, as well as high-stemmed grasslands are the habitats of this 50- to 150-cm-high plant.

The stems are erect, slender and glabrous. The leaves are very thin, dark green above and pale or brownish-green on the underside. The bottom leaves are stalked, longish-obovate in outline and either entire or, more often, pinnatipartite. The leaves in the middle and at the top of the stem grow directly from and encircle the stem and are long or lanceolate; the uppermost leaves give way to bracts.

The small, nodding anthodiums are arranged in loose panicles. They are peduncled and composed of three to ten florets. The involucre is narrowly cylindrical and composed of two rows of bracts; the inner bracts are linear, glabrous and flushed with violet, the outer bracts are very short. The flowers are reddish-violet, very occasionally white. They are pollinated by insects, though self-pollination is not ruled out. The cypselas are light brown and faintly grooved, with a pappus of simple white hairs.

Closely related species are found only in Asia and North America. Though *Prenanthes purpurea* has a wide distribution extending from middle France and northern Poland to northern Spain, middle Italy and Greece, no other member of this genus has been discovered in Europe.

basal stem leaf

Type of plant
dicotyledon

Diploid no.
2n – 18

Flowering period
July – September

Fruit
cypsela

Great Globe-thistle

Echinops sphaerocephalus

This robust perennial, reaching a height of 200 cm, occurs on dry waste ground, sunny slopes and sunny banks.

The stems are erect, angled, white-pubescent, glandular at the top, and simple or only sparsely branched. The bottom leaves are stalked, the others sessile or encircling the stem. They are longish-ovate in outline and sinuate-pinnatifid. The leaf segments have spiny teeth; they are glandular-pubescent and bristly on the upper surface and grey- to white-felted on the underside.

The single-flowered anthodiums are clustered in globe-shaped heads 5 to 8 cm in diameter subtended by bristly, pale yellow bracts. The anthodiums are approximately 2 cm long. The outer involucral bracts are shorter, the inner bracts twice as long, narrowing into a fine point. The flowers are steel-grey-blue, and the anthers are grey. They are followed by cypselas up to 8 mm long and covered with silky grey hairs. The pappus is composed of scales that are fringed halfway to the base.

Great Globe-thistle is found throughout central and southern Europe. In southern Greece and the Balkan Peninsula it occurs as two subspecies.

Type of plant
dicotyledon

Diploid no.
2n — 32

Flowering period
June — August

Fruit
cypsela

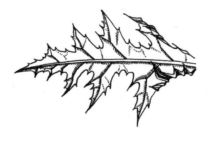

leaf

one-flowered anthodium

Flowering Rush

Butomus umbellatus

This 60- to 150-cm-high perennial is found in still water with vegetation and beside slow-flowing water throughout practically all of Europe.

It has a thick horizontal rhizome from which rises a basal rosette of leaves. These are sheath-like and three-angled at the base, gradually expanding into a flat blade approximately 10 cm long and 1 cm wide.

The erect, rounded, unbranched scape ends in a bostryx (an umbel-like inflorescence) of large flowers subtended by scale-like bracts. The flowers are regular in shape and hermaphroditic, with three greenish-pink outer perianth segments, three pink inner perianth segments, and nine stamens.

Flowering Rush is the only surviving member of the entire order Butomales — an indication of its extreme age. Fossil finds reveal that similar plants grew on lakeshores in the Mesozoic era and dating from the Cretaceous period is the fossil plant *Butomites cretaceus*. Flowering Rush is apparently the oldest remnant of a group of monocotyledons that was closest to the ancient, long extinct dicotyledons now represented only by the highly advanced water lilies. The flowering rush and water lily families apparently had common ancestors, and it is presumed that monocotyledons evolved from the ancestral dicotyledons and not the other way around.

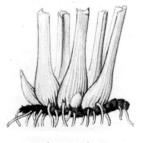

underground part

immature aggregate fruit

Type of plant
monocotyledon

Diploid no.
2n — 26, 39

Flowering period
June — August

Fruit
follicle

Common Water Plantain

Alisma plantago-aquatica

Water Plantain is a perennial that grows by lakes and ponds, in reed beds, masses of high-stemmed sedges and in damp ditches.

It is up to 1 metre high and has a tuberous, thickened rhizome. The submerged leaves are linear, while those above the water are pointed-ovate, usually with a heart-shaped base; there are many transitional forms between the two types of leaves.

The flowers are coloured white to pinkish and arranged in a pyramidal panicle. They are short-peduncled with broadly oval sepals and petals, and do not open until midday or even later. Inasmuch as they are pollinated by insects and by the wind and self-pollination occurs only rarely, only those plants with flowers above the water bear mature fruits (achenes). These are conspicuously flattened with a single furrow on the back.

Common Water Plantain, together with other species of the genus *Alisma,* is distributed throughout the whole northern hemisphere. Grass-leaved Water Plantain *(Alisma gramineum)* differs from the illustrated species by having narrowly-linear submerged as well as floating leaves and Narrow-leaved Water Plantain *(Alisma lanceolatum)* by having pinkish flowers that open already in the forenoon (they wilt in the afternoon) and leaves with a wedge-shaped base.

Type of plant
monocotyledon

Diploid no.
2n — 10, 12, 14, 16

Flowering period
June — September

Fruit
achene

diagram of flower

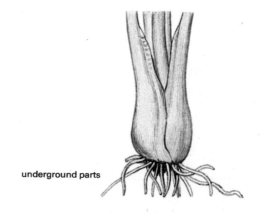

underground parts

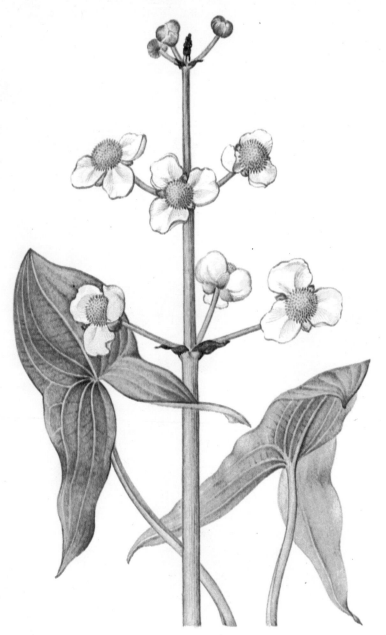

Arrowhead

Sagittaria sagittifolia

This perennial aquatic grows in still water with thick vegetation as well as in slow-flowing water and marshes.

It has a short, thick rhizome from which rises a 30- to 100-cm-high stem. The leaves are arranged in a rosette and are of diverse shape. The submerged leaves are linear to lanceolate, those that float on the water are long-stalked and elliptic to ovate, and the aerial leaves are arrow-shaped.

The flower-bearing stems are three-angled. The large peduncled flowers are arranged in a whorl forming an erect raceme. They grow from the axils of small triangular bracts and are unisexual – female flowers at the bottom and male flowers at the top of the inflorescence. The latter have much longer peduncles than the female flowers. The three sepals are broadly-ovate to orbicular, the petals, likewise three, are also orbicular and coloured white with a dark violet blotch at the base. The mature achenes have a short beak. Arrowhead multiplies by means of buds at the tips of the runners produced by the rhizome, rather than by seeds. Of interest is the fact that these buds contain even more starch than does the potato. Fortunately they do not rival it in size as well – for otherwise the leaves and flowers of this plant might by now have been lost to the peaceful shallows of most of Europe.

diagram of flower

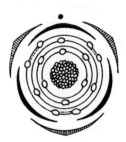

stamen

Type of plant
monocotyledon

Diploid no.
2n – 22

Flowering period
June – August

Fruit
achene

Broad-leaved Pondweed

Potamogeton natans

The floating leaves of this perennial pondweed may also be seen on the surface of still or slow-flowing waters.

It usually reaches a length of 50 to 150 cm but sometimes may even be as much as two metres long, depending on the depth of the water. In spring the stem is covered with linear phyllodes (flattened, leaf-like leaf stalks) that soon disappear. Otherwise it bears only floating leaves up to 12 cm long and 6 cm wide, the length of the stalks depending on the depth of the water. If the plant grows in dry mud the stalks are practically atrophied and the leaves are clustered in a rosette on the shortened stem.

The small flowers are arranged in spikes. They have four stamens with cup-like connectives that look like a perianth. The fruits are 4- to 5-mm-long glossy brown achenes.

Like many aquatic plants, chiefly pondweeds, the Broad-leaved Pondweed has a circumpolar distribution, which means that it occurs in the temperate regions of both hemispheres. Because of the more or less unchanging character of the aquatic habitat it shows remarkably little variability despite its extensive range. Even plants from the mountains of middle Africa, where the climate is much like that of temperate regions because of the high altitude, are considered typical representatives of this species.

Type of plant
monocotyledon

Diploid no.
2n – 52

Flowering period
June – August

Fruit
achene

fruit

flower

Common White Hellebore

Veratrum album

This 50- to 150-cm-high perennial grows in high-stemmed mountain grasslands and overgrown moors.

The stem, which is densely hairy particularly at the top, is covered with leaves that are pubescent on the underside (in young leaves the surface may be almost felted) and glabrous above. The lower leaves are broadly elliptical, the upper leaves lanceolate.

The flowers, 8 to 20 mm across, are arranged in a panicle that is up to 60 cm long and hairy. The bracts are broadly ovate. The flowers at the bottom of the panicle are hermaphroditic, those at the top are male. The perianth segments are longish-elliptic to obovate and toothed near the tip. The capsules that develop after fertilization are up to 15 mm long.

White Hellebore is poisonous.

It occurs as two subspecies: subspecies *album,* found in the Alps, with flowers green outside and white within, and subspecies *lobelianum,* relatively common in the mountain regions of Europe with perianth segments greenish on both sides.

In spring, when only the leaves appear, it is difficult to distinguish the hellebore from mountain gentians with similar large leaves, however, in the former instance they are always alternate, whereas the leaves of gentians are opposite.

flower – two different views

Type of plant
monocotyledon

Diploid no.
2n – 32

Flowering period
June – August

Fruit
capsule

Meadow Saffron

Colchicum autumnale

This perennial is a decorative element of meadows and moss-moors.

It grows from a 3- to 7-cm-long corm wrapped in a membranous skin and buried deep in the ground. In spring a bud appears on the corm, developing during the summer into a very short, thickened stem that remains hidden underground. The stem has two or three membranous sheaths at the base, several scale-like leaf-buds and flower-buds. The flowers appear above the surface and bloom in autumn.

Usually only a single flower is produced from each corm, its long tube extending up to 15 cm above the ground. The colchicum flower is thus one of the largest of all, sometimes measuring as much as half a metre, even though the greater part is concealed underground. The perianth is funnel-shaped, six-lobed and coloured violet, very occasionally whitish. The plant remains dormant until spring, which is when the stem begins to grow. The base of the stem thickens, forming a new corm beside the old one, which dies after the food reserve is exhausted. Five to six large, fleshy, lanceolate leaves appear on the stem, emerging above the surface together with the longish-ovoid capsule. The capsule bursts at maturity and the seeds, which have a fleshy appendage that becomes gelatinous in damp conditions, adhere to the feet of grazing livestock and are thus dispersed.

Meadow Saffron is widespread throughout practically all of Europe. It is poisonous and usually avoided by grazing livestock.

Type of plant
monocotyledon

Diploid no.
2n — 38

Flowering period
August — November

Fruit
capsule

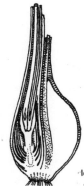

longitudinal section of corm

fruit

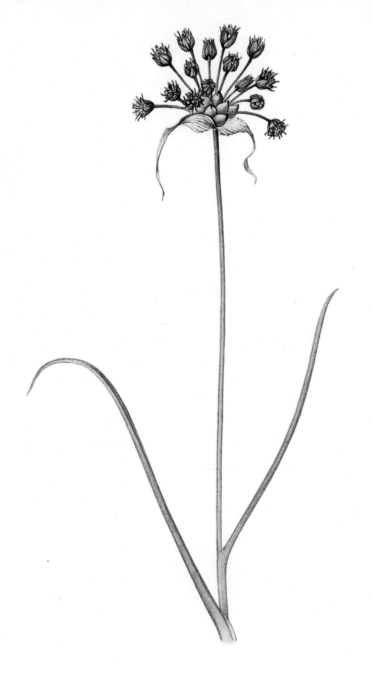

Crow Garlic

Allium vineale

This perennial, which reaches a height of 30 cm to 1 metre, grows on sunny slopes, in vineyards and by waysides, being partial to very lime-rich soils.

The herb is glabrous and grows from an ovoid underground bulb which is often encased in a single skin with several small bulblets. The leaves are greyish-green, linear, rounded and narrowly-channelled at the top.

The inflorescence is semi-globose. The spathe is composed of two long-pointed bracts the same length or longer than the umbel. Interspersed with the flowers are numerous bulbils (although sometimes the umbel may be composed only of flowers or only of bulbils). The flower peduncles are up to 25 mm long. The perianth segments are lanceolate, up to 5 mm long and tinted pale or dark purple. The stamens are the same length as the perianth segments at first, later becoming longer until they are twice as long.

Crow Garlic is distributed throughout most of Europe excepting the extreme north and east.

The related Round-headed Leek *(Allium sphaerocephalon)* differs from Crow Garlic primarily in having a spathe with short-tipped bracts, perianth segments longish-ovate, and bulb that does not break up very readily. It occurs on overgrown rock debris and rocks, on sunny slopes and in vineyards.

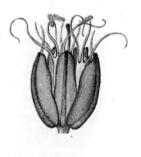

flower

seed

Type of plant
monocotyledon

Diploid no.
2n — 32 (48)

Flowering period
June — August

Fruit
capsule

St. Bernard's Lily

Anthericum liliago

This perennial, reaching a height of 30 to 80 cm, grows on stony slopes, in thickets, and on dry bushy slopes, being partial to calcareous soils.

The stem is leafless and erect. It arises from a rosette of linear basal leaves that taper to a point. The bracts are membranous.

The flowers are peduncled and form a spreading raceme at the tip of the stem. They measure up to 4 cm across and are composed of six white perianth segments, all about the same size, six stamens, and a pistil with three locules. Pollination by insects is followed by the development of the fruit — a three-sided, ovoid, pointed capsule containing numerous seeds about 4 mm long. Germination takes a relatively long time, ending only when the food reserves have been completely exhausted.

This lily, which grows in southern and central Europe, is on the list of protected species in many countries.

Likewise on the list is the related Spiderwort *(Anthericum ramosum)*, the inflorescence of which is a panicle or sometimes a raceme composed of white similar but smaller flowers, 27 mm across at the most. The capsule is also smaller, but the seeds are larger.

Type of plant
monocotyledon

Diploid no.
2n — 60

Flowering period
May — July

Fruit
capsule

fruit

Martagon
or **Turk's Cap Lily**

Lilium martagon

This perennial herb with 30-cm- to 1-metre-high stem grows in open broad-leaved woods and thickets as well as in high-stemmed mountain meadows and grasslands.

The stem, arising from the golden-yellow underground bulb, is erect with short-stalked ovate-lanceolate leaves arranged in two or three whorls at the base. The leaves at the top of the stem are alternate and sessile, giving way to smaller bracts, from the axils of which grow the flower peduncles.

The flowers are fragrant and drooping. The perianth is composed of six segments coloured brownish-pink to purplish, usually with dark spots. They are recurved and fused at the base. Protruding from the flower are six long stamens with dark yellow anthers and a long style with stigma. Because they produce a sweet nectar the flowers are visited by insects, chiefly moths.

The beauty and fragrance of its flowers have often proved fatal to this lily, for it was widely gathered in the wild and has been exterminated in places. Nowadays its distribution is sporadic and it occurs only locally in Europe.

Mountain meadows, grasslands, overgrown rocks and bushy slopes are also inhabited by the Bulb-bearing Lily *(Lilium bulbiferum)* which, as its name indicates, bears bulbils in the axils of the upper leaves. This lily has small erect orange flowers spotted brown within.

Type of plant
monocotyledon

Diploid no.
2n – 24

Flowering period
June – August

Fruit
capsule

scaly bulb

May Lily

Maianthemum bifolium

This perennial, which reaches a height of 5 to 25 cm, is lime-hating and grows in shady woods from lowland to mountain elevations.

It has a slender, creeping rhizome from which rises an erect, pubescent stem with two (very occasionally only one or three) leaves. These are short-stalked and ovate with heart-shaped base and pointed tip; they are prominently veined.

The small fragrant flowers are in four parts, stellate and clustered in two or three-flowered umbels forming a raceme. They grow on short peduncles from the axils of small, membranous bracts and are white or tinted yellow. The fruit is a berry about 5 mm across, pinkish with dark spots at first but later completely red.

The May Lily is distributed throughout practically all of Europe and is widespread also in Asia, where it extends as far as North Korea, south of which it is replaced by another species. Related species are found also in North America.

Members of the related genus *Streptopus* exhibit no resemblance to the May Lily whatsoever. For example *Streptopus amplexifolius* is a strikingly decorative element of mountain dwarf-pine spreads. It is a herbaceous plant up to one metre high with whitish bell-shaped flowers borne singly on long thin stalks. The fruit is an oval light-red berry.

Type of plant
monocotyledon

Diploid no.
2n − 36

Flowering period
May − June

Fruit
berry

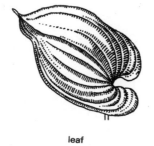

leaf

fruit

Angular Solomon's Seal

Polygonatum odoratum

Syn. *Polygonatum officinale*

This 15- to 45-cm-high perennial grows in warm woods and glades.

It has a thick creeping rhizome and arching stems, nearly two-edged at the top, otherwise angled. The leaves, coloured greyish green on the underside, are alternate, longish-ovate to elliptic-lanceolate and rough.

The fragrant white flowers are solitary, or occasionally in pairs, on peduncles in the axils of the leaves. They are regular, in three parts and club-shaped, up to 25 mm long and 7 mm wide. The filaments are united at the base with the flower tube. The mature fruit is a blue-black berry, 8 to 14 mm across and with a waxy bloom.

Angular Solomon's Seal is a poisonous plant widespread in practically all of Europe. The Whorled Solomon's Seal *(Polygonatum verticillatum)*, mostly of mountain districts, differs in having linear-lanceolate leaves arranged in whorls of 3 to 6, and Common Solomon's Seal *(Polygonatum multiflorum)* by having an oval stem and practically unscented flowers growing 3 to 5 in the leaf axils. The latter occurs in localities similar to those inhabited by *Polygonatum odoratum;* outside of Europe it also occurs locally in Asia, extending as far as Japan.

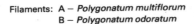

Filaments: A — *Polygonatum multiflorum*
B — *Polygonatum odoratum*

fruit

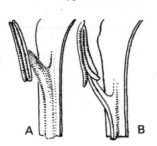

A   B

Type of plant
monocotyledon

Diploid no.
2n — 20

Flowering period
May — June

Fruit
berry

Lily-of-the-Valley

Convallaria majalis

This perennial herb reaches a height of 10 to 25 cm and is to be found in glades, open woodlands, thickets and their margins.

The branched rhizome usually bears only two, stalked, broadly-lanceolate leaves with sheath-like scales at the base. The entire plant is glabrous.

The upright scape is terminated by a loose one-sided raceme of drooping milky-white flowers with a pleasant, penetrating fragrance. They are regular and hermaphroditic. The white perianth is urn-shaped or bell-shaped and up to 9 mm long with short spreading lobes. The berry is red at maturity.

Lily-of-the-Valley is distributed throughout practically all of Europe to the Urals and Caucasus; it was also introduced in North America.

Though fragrant, it is poisonous, for it contains a large quantity of poisonous glycosides and alkaloids. It is on the list of protected species in practically all central European countries but continues to be picked in the wild. It is sold in large numbers every spring, for it is a very popular plant, even though nowadays it is grown on a large scale and supplied to the market by many nurseries.

Type of plant
monocotyledon

Diploid no.
2n — 38

Flowering period
May — June

Fruit
berry

diagram of flower

fruit

Herb Paris

Paris quadrifolia

This perennial, which reaches a height of 15 to 30 cm, grows in mixed woods, glades and thickets.

It has a long, creeping, scaly rhizome and erect glabrous stem, which usually bears a single whorl of four broadly elliptic leaves. The occasional specimen may have as few as three or in rare instances as many as seven leaves. The leaves are up to 10 cm long.

The long-peduncled flowers are erect and in four parts, regular and hermaphroditic. The perianth is composed of two whorls of four spreading segments each. The outer segments are lanceolate and coloured pale green, the inner segments are narrower, linear and yellow-green. The stamens, in two rows of four each, have short filaments and pollen-sacs joined by a connective that is conspicuously awl-shaped. The fruit is a globose blue-black berry up to 1 cm in diameter.

The flowers are pollinated by the wind although self-pollination is not ruled out. They are described as delusive in that they attract insects but provide them with neither nectar nor pollen.

This species is poisonous, particularly the berries, which contain extremely toxic substances.

Herb Paris is distributed throughout practically all of Europe, extending far into Siberia; Asia is the home of two other related species.

diagram of flower

Type of plant
monocotyledon

Diploid no.
2n — 20

Flowering period
April — May

Fruit
berry

Yellow Flag

Iris pseudacorus

The banks of still and flowing waters and shoreline thickets from lowland to foothill districts is where the lovely Yellow Flag may be encountered.

It is a perennial herb, 50 to 150 cm high, with a thick, branched rhizome and erect flattened stem branching at the top. The fresh green leaves are sword-shaped, up to 3 cm wide, and the same length as the stem.

The flowers are borne on long peduncles in the axils of bracts. The perianth segments form a tube and are coloured bright yellow. The lobes of the outer perianth segments are expanded to outspread, and coloured dark yellow with violet-brown veining in the middle. The inner perianth segments are upright, linear, and shorter than the stigma lobes. Concealed beneath the stigma lobes are three stamens. The flowers are pollinated by insects; the fruit is a three-sided capsule containing a great many flattened seeds.

This striking plant is on the list of protected species in Czechoslovakia and the German Federal Republic and deserves to be so protected in other countries as well, for it has already been exterminated in many places.

Other species of iris are likewise protected, e.g. *Iris sibirica* which has blue-violet flowers and grows in wet meadows and marshes. A noteworthy feature of this iris is that it has a rounded stem rather than the flattened two-edged stem characteristic of most irises.

Type of plant
monocotyledon

Diploid no.
2n — 34

Flowering period
May — June

Fruit
capsule

cross-section of leaf

Common Snowdrop

Galanthus nivalis

Riverside woods, valley grasslands and thickets, broad-leaved woods, mixed woods and stands of fir — those are all places where spring is heralded by the small white flowers of the Common Snowdrop.

The Snowdrop is a perennial growing 10 to 20 cm high from a bulb clothed in three brown scales. From this rise two linear, bluntly-tipped leaves, 10 cm long and 1 cm wide. They are coloured greyish-green and enclosed at the base by a sheath-like scale.

The erect scape is terminated by a nodding flower on a drooping peduncle that grows from the axil of a green, white-edged bract. The three inner perianth segments are shorter, obovate and deeply notched with a green spot at the incision. The 6 stamens have yellow anthers. The fruit is a capsule.

This plant is often grown for ornament.

It has a random distribution throughout Europe; in some places it is now extinct.

In Czechoslovakia and the German Federal Republic the underground parts are protected by law, in other words the flowers may be picked in the wild but it is forbidden to dig up the bulbs.

In southern Europe, Crimea, the Caucasus and Asia Minor there are a number of other related species but none is as popular in central Europe as the Common Snowdrop.

diagram of flower

Type of plant
monocotyledon

Diploid no.
2n — 24

Flowering period
February — April

Fruit
capsule

Spring Snowflake

Leucojum vernum

This perennial grows in shaded, damp, broad-leaved woods, mostly beechwoods, but also in spruce and fir woods as well as in damp meadows.

The globose bulb bears a flattened, two-edged scape 10 to 30 cm high, and three or four dark-green basal leaves which are linear in outline and longer than the scape.

The scape is terminated by one peduncled flower (occasionally two). This is drooping, bell-like and grows in the axil of a bract. The perianth segments are broadly elongate and white, often with a green or yellow blotch on the outside. The flowers are pollinated by insects, which besides pollen may also collect a small amount of nectar.

Spring Snowflake is native to central and southern Europe; in Great Britain and southern Sweden it occurs only as an escape that has become naturalized.

It is on the list of protected species in many European countries.

Plants with two flowers to a stem and perianth segments with a yellow blotch at the tip are classified as subspecies *carpaticum*. This subspecies occurs in the Carpathians but may occasionally be encountered elsewhere, e.g. in Bavaria. The related Summer Snowflake *(Leucojum aestivum)* has three to six flowers to a stem and a nearly spherical capsule; it grows in damp woods and flood-plain forests where it blooms from May until June. It is more common in the eastern part of central Europe.

Type of plant
monocotyledon

Diploid no.
2n – 22

Flowering period
February – March

Fruit
capsule

longitudinal section of flower

Field Woodrush

Luzula campestris

This perennial rush, reaching a height of 5 to 15 cm, grows in fields, meadows, pastures, dry hedgerows and open woods, chiefly on low ground.

The loosely tufted stem grows from a creeping rhizome. It is covered with linear leaves that are shorter than the stem. These are blunt-tipped and densely ciliate.

The flowers are in spikelets forming a compound inflorescence called an anthella. The bracts are shorter than the flowers and usually entire. The perianth segments, often ciliate, are lanceolate in outline with spiny tips, more or less the same length, and coloured brown with a wide scarious border. The capsule is blunt and ovoid and without a beak. The seeds often have a long appendage.

Sometimes the Field Woodrush is considered to be a collective species taking in approximately four different species. *Luzula campestris* proper has short runners, an inflorescence composed of two to five nearly sessile spikelets, and anthers two to six times as long as the filaments.

The microspecies *Luzula multiflora, Luzula sudetica* and *Luzula pallescens* differ in morphological characteristics of the flowers and seeds.

flower

inflorescence

Type of plant
monocotyledon

Diploid no.
2n — 12

Flowering period
March — June

Fruit
capsule

Common Cottongrass

Eriophorum angustifolium

Heather moors, moss moors and peat moors on low as well as high ground is where this 30- to 60-cm-high plant is to be found.

Common Cottongrass is a loosely tufted herb with rounded stem and channelled leaves. The basal as well as the stem leaves are encased in brown sheaths. The leaves are linear, about 6 mm wide and three-angled from the base upwards, or only at the tip. The leaf margins are rough.

The inflorescence is composed of three to five smooth-peduncled spikelets. The lanceolate bracts are brown with a white-scarious border. The perianth is composed of several smooth bristles which become longer after flowering and form a white tuft. The flowers are pollinated by the wind. The achenes are longish-obovate, wing-like and three-angled.

Common Cottongrass is distributed throughout Europe except the Mediterranean region.

The related Broad-leaved Cottongrass *(Eriophorum latifolium)* has flat leaves, a great number of spikelets and conspicuously rough peduncles. The bristles are all the same length and nearly white.

Type of plant
monocotyledon

Diploid no.
2n — 58

Flowering period
April — May

Fruit
achene

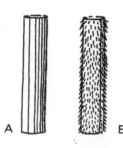

Peduncles of spikelets: A — glabrous in *Eriophorum angustifolium* B — rough in *Eriophorum latifolium*

faded flower

Wood Club-rush

Scirpus sylvaticus

This robust perennial herb, reaching a height of 60 to 100 cm, grows in marshes, damp and flooded meadows and damp ditches.

The stems are more or less erect, bluntly three-angled and hollow. The leaves are 8 to 12 mm wide, keeled and rough on the margin. The bracts beneath the inflorescence resemble leaves.

The stem is terminated by a dense peduncled inflorescence (anthella) up to 30 cm long, composed of two to five spikelets. The bracts are elongate, spiny-tipped and coloured blackish-brown. The six perianth segments resemble bristles. The flowers are wind-pollinated and develop into three-sided achenes.

Wood Club-rush is distributed throughout practically all of Europe except the Arctic and southern Mediterranean regions; it may also be encountered in the Caucasus, Siberia and North America. The related Rooting Club-rush *(Scirpus radicans)* has spikelets that are mostly solitary and more or less peduncled. It grows in the same localities as *Scirpus sylvaticus* and in the same range, but much more sparsely. Members of the related genus *Schoenoplectus* have only basal leaves. They are mostly robust herbs with a contracted anthella growing in the axil of a bract that appears to be a continuation of the stem and hence the anthella appears to be lateral. *Scirpus lacustris* is the most common species in central Europe.

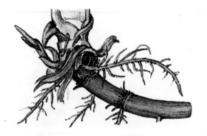

rhizome

flower

Type of plant
monocotyledon

Diploid no.
2n – 62, 64

Flowering period
May – August

Fruit
achene

Spring Sedge

Carex caryophyllea

Syn. *Carex verna*

Dry slopes, meadows and pastureland is where this 10- to 40-cm-high perennial may be found.

The creeping stoloniferous rhizome bears slender, often curving stems that are bluntly three-angled and more or less smooth. The leaves, which are shorter than the stem and 2 mm wide at the most, are flat, sometimes channelled at the base, keeled, stiff and rough-textured. The leaf sheaths are brown, slightly rough and do not break up.

The two to four flower spikelets are adjacent and sessile, sometimes the lowest is distant and short-peduncled. The terminal spikelet is male, 1.5 cm long and linear-club-shaped. Those at the bottom are female, elongated, 1 cm long and dense. The bracts resemble glumes. The glumes of the female flowers are ovate, pointed and a glossy, rusty brown; the bristle is either absent or grows from the green keel. The mature follicles are erect, obovate, and bluntly three-angled; greenish at first, later rusty, finely pubescent and imperceptibly veined.

Spring Sedge, which is distributed throughout practically all of Europe, is a member of a very large genus numbering more than 100 species in central Europe alone.

Type of plant
monocotyledon

Diploid no.
2n — 62, 64, 66, 68

Flowering period
April — May

Fruit
follicle

cross-section of stem

faded flower

fruit

Meadow Fescue

Festuca pratensis

Syn. *Festuca elatior*

Meadow Fescue, a loosely tufted perennial grass reaching a height of 30 to 120 cm, is found in meadows, grasslands, moss-moors and overgrown heaths.

The culms are smooth and curve upward from the ground. There are usually three leaves. The leaf sheaths are smooth and open. The leaf blades are likewise smooth, up to 20 cm long and 5 mm wide, more or less scratchy on the upper surface and smooth on the underside.

The spikelets, composed of five to eight flowers, are 9 to 12 mm long with usually two glumes at the base; the glumes of this species are lanceolate. The lower ones are scarious at the tip and without bristles.

Grasses are mostly wind-pollinated plants and the structure of the stamens reflects this. The filaments are slender; the anthers, which contain large quantities of pollen, are usually attached to the filament in the middle, thereby quivering and releasing pollen in the slightest breeze. The pollen grains are carried by the wind to the feathery stigmas of other flowers. The stigma matures before the stamens, thereby preventing self-pollination.

base of leaf blade with ligule and auricles

Type of plant
monocotyledon

Diploid no.
2n – 14

Flowering period
June – July

Fruit
grain

Bulbous Meadow-grass

Poa bulbosa

This tufted grey-green meadow-grass, which may be 10 to 40 cm high, is a perennial and grows on sunny grassy banks.

The culms are erect, rounded and smooth with a bulbous sheathed base, hence the Latin name *bulbosa*. The top of the culm is leafless or bears one to three leaves. The leaf sheaths are smooth and glabrous. The blades of the basal shoots are usually rolled so that they resemble bristles. The blades of the leaves at the bottom of the culm are usually flat and shorter than the sheaths. By the time the flowers appear the basal leaves are usually already dry and withered. The ligules of all the leaves are sharply pointed.

The inflorescence is an ovate to elongated panicle with rough, spreading branches. The longish-ovate spikelets are composed of four to six flowers. The grains often germinate in the spikelet while still on the parent plant. The glumes are broadly ovate-lanceolate and rough on the keel. The lemmas are longish to lanceolate and thickly hairy at the base.

This meadow grass is distributed throughout central Europe in various situations and on diverse substrates from the warmest lowland districts to high up in the mountains.

Type of plant
monocotyledon

Diploid no.
2n – 14, 21, 28, 32, 35, 39, 42, 45, 40–58

Flowering period
May – June

Fruit
grain

diagram of three-flowered spikelet of grasses

viviparity

Crested Dog's-tail

Cynosurus cristatus

This densely tufted to shortly-stoloniferous perennial grass grows in meadows and pastureland.

The short dark rhizome bears a slender culm 20 to 60 cm high and smooth like the leaf-sheaths, which are closed their entire length. The culm of grasses is usually jointed, cylindrical and hollow, as well as simple and unbranched apart from the inflorescence. The nodes between the hollow sections of the stem are supplied with tissue above the transverse partition. This tissue is responsible for the growth and elongation of the culm and likewise serves to help straighten it after it has been flattened to the ground. The leaf blades are 2 to 3 mm wide, grooved and later rolled. They are short and rough at the tip. The ligules, located at the junction of the sheath and blade in grasses, are almost 1 mm long and truncated.

The culm is terminated by a one-sided linear panicle up to 10 cm long. The spikelets are arranged in two rows on very short branches. Beside each fertile spikelet there is another, sterile spikelet resembling a comb, an impression created by the narrow lemmas numbering as many as ten. The fertile spikelet is usually composed of three to four flowers. The glumes are pointed whereas the lemmas are lanceolate, double-toothed and with a short bristle.

Dog's-tail is distributed throughout practically all of Europe excepting Scandinavia and the northern USSR.

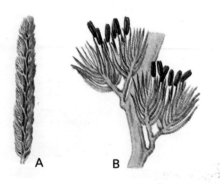

A

B

A – spike B – detail of spike

base of leaf blade with ligule

Type of plant
monocotyledon

Diploid no.
2n – 14

Flowering period
June – July

Fruit
grain

Common Quaking-grass

Briza media

This grass is a loosely tufted perennial commonly found in dry meadows, pastures and on sunny slopes both at lowland and mountain elevations.

The slender, smooth, erect culm reaches a height of 20 to 50 cm. The leaf sheaths are closed. The flat leaf blades are rough on the margin. The ligules are very short.

The inflorescence is an erect broadly-spreading panicle up to 15 cm long. The long branches are covered with numerous drooping spikelets that quake in the slightest breeze, hence the name of this grass. The spikelets are without bristles and often flushed violet. The glumes are asymmetrical, ob-ovate, keeled and expanding. The lemmas are in-flated.

Quaking-grass is found in practically all of Europe excepting the Arctic and certain parts of the Mediterranean region. It is one of the best of forage plants but is not sown in cultivated meadows because it requires rather dry conditions. The related *Briza minor,* native to the Balkans and Mediterranean region, is an annual with smaller, three-sided spikelets only about 3 mm long. *Briza maxima* has whitish spikelets more than 2 cm long; it is native to southern Europe and is sometimes grown in gardens but must be sown anew every year from imported seeds because its grains do not mature in the northern parts of Europe.

Type of plant
monocotyledon

Diploid no.
2n — 14

Flowering period
May — August

Fruit
grain

spikelet

Mountain Melick

Melica nutans

This perennial grass with slender, creeping rhizomes grows in glades, mixed woods and thickets in both lowland and foothill districts. It is often partial to calcareous substrates.

The slender, rough culms reach a height of 25 to 50 cm. The sterile stolons are up to 10 cm long. The leaf blades are flat or only slightly rolled, rough on the margin and underside and covered with random hairs on the upper surface. The ligules are short, truncate and brownish. The lower leaf sheaths are purplish.

The racemose inflorescence is one-sided, nearly 10 cm long and composed of large, two-flowered spikelets. The glumes are thin, rough, and green with purplish tip.

This grass is slightly poisonous.

It is distributed throughout Europe but is absent in northern Scandinavia, the islands, and most of the European USSR, and rare in southern Europe. The related *Melica picta* has a densely tufted rhizome without stolons and ligules up to 2 mm long. The entire plant is greyish-green, the glumes and lemmas green, the glumes with dark-violet veins. It is more heat-tolerant than the Mountain Melick and is found mostly in mixed beech woods, but usually at random.

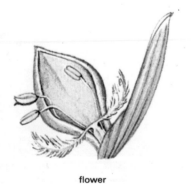

flower

Type of plant
monocotyledon

Diploid no.
2n – 18

Flowering period
May – June

Fruit
grain

Cocksfoot

Dactylis glomerata

This is a densely tufted, robust grass reaching a height of 30 to 120 cm and coloured vivid to greyish-green. It occurs in meadows, pastureland, by roadsides and in other grassy places.

The culms are erect or ascending. The leaf sheaths are more or less rough, closed and two-edged. The leaf blades are usually flat, more or less limp and drooping. The pointed ligules are up to 10 mm long.

The panicle is narrow and dense at first with the spikelets crowded at the ends of the branches, later it is one-sided and lobed. The branches are rough and divided again at the tip. The spikelets are greatly compressed, 3−4-flowered and green. The glumes are lanceolate, pointed or with a short bristle and with a ciliate keel. The lemmas also have a keel sparsely covered with spreading ciliae.

Dactylis glomerata is distributed throughout practically all of Europe and is introduced also in South America, Australia and New Zealand. It is quite variable within this extensive range.

In some places forms of this grass with leaves striped white or yellow are grown for ornament.

The closely related *Dactylis polygama* (syn. *Dactylis aschersoniana*), found in mixed woods and woodland clearings in central Europe, is a pale green grass that is always stoloniferous. The inflorescence is looser, the spikelets almost solitary and often 5−6 flowered.

Type of plant
monocotyledon

Diploid no.
2n − 28

Flowering period
May − August

Fruit
grain

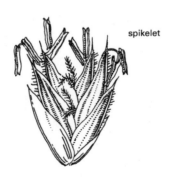

spikelet

white-striped leaf of the ornamental form

Blue Sesleria
or **Blue Moor-grass**

Sesleria varia
Syn *Sesleria calcaria, Sesleria coerulea*

This is a densely tufted, calcicolous, perennial grass which occurs in lime-rich soils on overgrown rocks, in screes, stony places and sometimes even in open woods from piedmont to subalpine elevations.

The slender erect culms reach a height of 25 to 45 cm. The leaf sheaths are glabrous. The leaf blades are flat, even in dry weather. The ligules are very short and fringed with hairs. The blades of sterile shoots have narrow whitish stripes on the margin.

The spike-like inflorescence, which is composed of separate spikelets, is cylindrical and relatively loose. The spikelets are two-flowered, sometimes three-flowered, and violet-tinted or steel blue, very occasionally whitish-yellow. The glumes, the same length as the lemmas, are ovate-lanceolate and either pointed or furnished with a bristle up to 2 mm long; they are glabrous or have random hairs along the veins. The lemmas are ovate-lanceolate and hairy on the veins, otherwise glabrous. The middle tooth has a short bristle. The palea is double-toothed, the same length as the lemma and with a random pattern of hairs on the veins.

The related *Sesleria uliginosa* is mostly found in damp calcareous meadows and forms circular spreads of turf. Unlike the preceding species it has rolled-up margins in dry weather.

lemma

Type of plant
monocotyledon

Diploid no.
2n — 28

Flowering period
March — June

Fruit
grain

Flax Darnel

Lolium remotum

This yellowish-green annual grass, reaching a height of 60 cm, is a weed of fields, chiefly of flax and serradella *(Ornithopus sativus)* − the latter is widely cultivated as a fodder plant in central and, primarily, southwestern Europe. *Lolium remotum* is a lime-hating species.

The culms are slender, more or less geniculate-ascending and rough at the top. The leaf sheaths are smooth. The leaf blades are flat, 2−3 mm wide, likewise smooth but occasionally rough on the upper side.

The four- to eight-flowered spikelets are 7 to 10 mm long, dense and coloured pale green; those at the bottom are distant. The glume is shorter than the spikelet but twice as long as the nearest lemma. The lemma is usually without a bristle.

The similar Common Darnel *(Lolium temulentum)* has longer spikelets up to 25 mm long, and glumes 15 to 30 mm long. The grains are often attacked by rust and are then very poisonous, a product of the metabolism of this rust being the poisonous alkaloid temuline, which accumulates in the grains.

Some *Lolium* species, e.g. Perennial Rye-grass *(Lolium perenne)* and Italian Rye-grass *(Lolium multiflorum)* are often sown for grazing or added to seed mixtures for lawns.

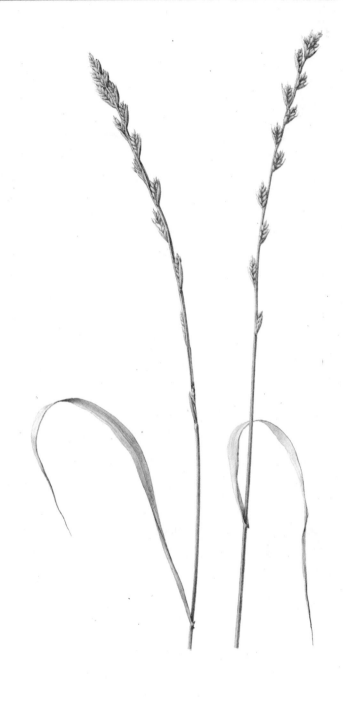

Type of plant
monocotyledon

Diploid no.
2n − 14

Flowering period
May − September

Fruit
grain

A − glume B − lemma

Tufted Hair-grass

Deschampsia cespitosa

This densely tufted perennial grass, reaching a height of 50 to 150 cm, grows in meadows and damp woods from lowland to mountain districts.

The numerous culms are erect and smooth — only towards the inflorescence do they become rough. The leaf sheaths are smooth or scratchy, the leaf blades flat and 2 to 3 mm wide. They are prominently ribbed lengthwise on the upper surface. Only in dry weather are they rolled. The ligule is 6 to 8 mm long, pointed and whitish.

The inflorescence is a spreading pyramidal panicle up to 20 cm long with rough branches that are outspread during the flowering period. The spikelets on short peduncles are purplish, very occasionally green or yellow. The glumes are elongate and blunt with a scarious border; they are purplish at the top. The lemmas are likewise purplish edged with white, blunt, toothed and with a short bristle.

This species is often divided into two subspecies: Subspecies *cespitosa* has spikelets 4—5 mm long, usually composed of two but sometimes as many as five flowers. Subspecies *parviflora* has spikelets only 1.5—2.5 mm long, and often with only a single flower.

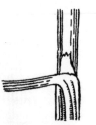

base of the blade with ligule

Type of plant
monocotyledon

Diploid no.
2n — 26

Flowering period
June—August

Fruit
grain

Sweet Vernal-grass

Anthoxanthum odoratum

This densely tufted perennial grass grows in meadows, pastures and by roadsides from low to high ground.

The many practically erect culms, 15 to 45 cm high, are smooth and sparsely leaved. The leaf sheaths are glabrous but may also be hairy, as may the leaf blades, which are flat and up to 6 mm wide. The ligules are 2 mm long, truncate and ragged-edged.

The panicle is longish-lanceolate and composed of yellow-green spikelets each with only a single flower. Both glumes are pointed. The lower glume is 3 to 5 mm long and ovate, the upper is longer and elongated. The lemmas of the two atrophied bottom florets have a hair-like bristle. There are only two stamens instead of the usual three found in most members of the grass family. In this species the lodicules (scale-like outgrowths at the base of the flower) are likewise completely absent, whereas in some grasses there are two or even three.

Sweet Vernal-grass contains large amounts of coumarin which is responsible for the plant's penetrating scent as the plant dries, and for the scent of hay in general.

Type of plant
monocotyledon

Diploid no.
2n — 20

Flowering period
June

Fruit
grain

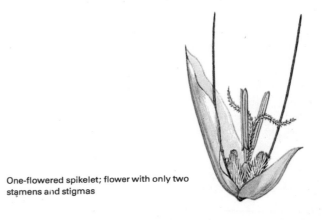

One-flowered spikelet; flower with only two stamens and stigmas

Wood Small-reed
or **Bush Grass**

Calamagrostis epigejos

This tufted perennial grass, reaching a height of 150 cm, grows in woods, woodland clearings, thickets and their margins as well as in sandy places and on coastal dunes. It dislikes lime-rich soils.

Concealed in the ground is a stout creeping rhizome with a great many long, slender stolons. From this arise stout upright culms that are rough beneath the panicle, as are the leaf sheaths. The leaf blades are up to 1 cm wide, rough and flat, but may sometimes be rolled. The ligule is up to 7 mm long, blunt and ragged-edged.

The flowers are in spikelets forming a compound inflorescence — a dense upright panicle up to 30 cm long with bristly branches. The individual spikelets are short-peduncled, crowded together and coloured greenish to purplish, becoming brown at maturity. The lanceolate glumes are up to 8 mm long with a long point and rough keel. The membranous lemma is a third as long as the glumes and has a slender bristle and tuft of hairs about midway down the back. The stamens have short filaments and yellow, orange or brownish anthers.

This grass is widespread throughout most of Europe, being absent only in northern Scandinavia and most of the European USSR.

base of leaf blade with ligule

Type of plant
monocotyledon

Diploid no.
2n — 28 (35, 42, 49, 56)

Flowering period
July — August

Fruit
grain

Timothy-grass

Phleum pratense

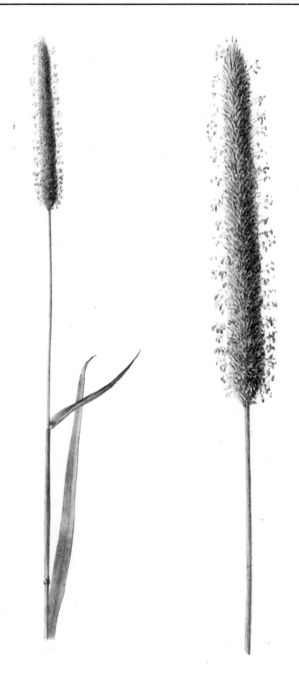

This densely tufted perennial grass, reaching a height of 10 to 100 cm, grows in meadows, hedgerows and pastureland and is also often sown in cultivated meadows.

The short, creeping rhizome bears smooth, erect or ascending culms that are sometimes thickened at the base. The leaf sheaths are smooth and glabrous. The leaf blades are flat, up to 30 cm long and rough. The ligules of the lower leaves are 2 to 3 mm long whereas those of the upper leaves are up to 5 mm long.

The inflorescence is cylindrical, up to 15 cm long and coloured greyish-green; it does not form lobes along the outer edge when bent over the finger. The spikelets are sessile. The elongated glumes are whitish-scarious with a bristle at the tip and green keel fringed with spreading ciliae. The lemmas are white-scarious and glabrous, the anthers are violet.

Timothy-grass occurs as two strains: subspecies *pratense* and subspecies *nodosum*. The first occurs in meadows in moister conditions and attains a height of one metre including the spike-like inflorescence, which is up to 20 cm long. The chief character aiding identification is that the culms are not swollen at the base. Subspecies *nodosum* occurs in dry meadows, on sunny slopes and in open woods, is relatively smaller (10 to 30 cm high with spike-like inflorescence only 1 to 4 cm long), and has culms that are swollen at the base. It prefers lime-rich soils.

Type of plant
monocotyledon

Diploid no.
2n – 14, 42

Flowering period
June – August

Fruit
grain

flower

spikelet

Mat-grass

Nardus stricta

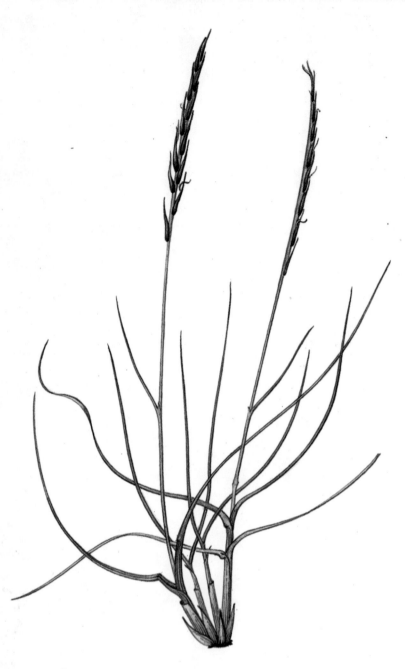

This grass grows to 10–30 cm, dislikes lime and is found chiefly on non-calcareous soils in mountain meadows, heaths and near moors.

The creeping rhizome bears tufts of closely packed rows of erect culms that are smooth at the base and usually rough at the top. The basal leaves have no blades but only glossy yellow sheaths, those farther up have green sheaths and smooth, bristle-like, expanding blades.

The linear one-sided comb-like inflorescence is only slightly thicker than the culm. It is composed of narrow, one-flowered spikelets.

Mat-grass often forms a pure grass cover, Nardeta, where dicotyledons are hard put to gain a foothold or spread amongst the dense mass of roots, and so the only occasional decorative elements found there are spring-flowering herbs with seeds that mature and germinate early, such as the Alpine Anemone *(Pulsatilla alpina)*.

Another interesting sidelight is that Mat-grass holds a unique position amongst grasses in that all related genera are extinct and only Mat-grass, a very old type, readily and almost without competition adapted to the conditions of mountain districts.

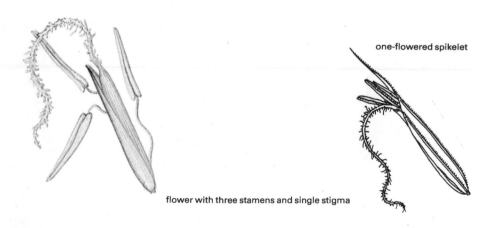

flower with three stamens and single stigma

one-flowered spikelet

Type of plant
monocotyledon

Diploid no.
2n – 26, 30

Flowering period
May – July

Fruit
grain

Common Reed

Phragmites australis

Syn. *Phragmites communis*

The Common Reed, one of the most robust of European grasses, grows at the margins of still stretches of water and in wet calcareous meadows, where it forms extensive reed beds.

The erect, stout culms are smooth and greyish-green. The leaves have long smooth sheaths. The blade is pointed, with rough undersurface covered with appressed hairs. The ligules are replaced by a fringe of long whitish hairs.

The panicles are large and dense, with a tuft of silvery hairs at the base and branches spreading only during the flowering period. The purplish spikelets are composed of three, five or as many as eight florets. The lower floret is male, the others hermaphroditic. The panicles are shimmeringly hairy in the fruit.

Common Reed occurs as three subspecies. Subspecies *australis,* common and widespread throughout most of Europe, has culms 1 cm thick and up to 4 metres high and dark-brown panicles up to 40 cm long. Subspecies *pseudodonax,* found occasionally in central Europe, mostly in the Danube delta and like places, has culms up to 2 cm thick and up to 10 cm high and light-brown panicles up to 50 cm long. The third, subspecies *humilis,* occurring in salt flats and saline soils in many countries of Europe, has narrower culms only slightly more than 1 metre high and panicles only 20 cm long.

Type of plant
monocotyledon

Diploid no.
2n — 36, 48, (72)

Flowering period
July — September

Fruit
grain

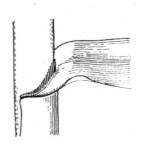

ligule in the shape of a ring of hairs

Couch-grass or Twitch

Agropyron repens

Syn. *Elytrigia repens*

This 20- to 150-cm-high perennial grass is a weed of fields, meadows, hedgerows, wasteland, gardens, railway embankments as well as coastal sands.

The erect culms are smooth and glabrous. The leaf sheaths are rough, the blades soft and translucent.

The minute spikelets form a long, dense, spike-like inflorescence. They are appressed with their broader side to the wavy axis. The glumes are practically identical and pointed, sometimes with a bristle. The spikelets do not break at the points but fall entire at maturity, thus ensuring that at least some grains will germinate even in unfavourable conditions. Its spread by the long, creeping rhizomes, however, is much more expansive, and this is the reason why Couch-grass is such a troublesome weed, occurring practically everywhere.

It occurs as three subspecies. Subspecies *caesium* includes robust blue-green plants with spike-like inflorescences more than 10 cm long found in thickets and forest margins. Subsp. *repens* includes green plants, 1 metre high at the most, with a dense spike-like inflorescence less than 10 cm long. The third, subspecies *maritimum,* includes blue-green plants, only 20 to 50 cm high with loose spike-like inflorescences less than 10 cm long, growing on the seacoast, dunes, and the like.

cross-section of leaf blade

Type of plant
monocotyledon

Diploid no.
2n — 42

Flowering period
June — September

Fruit
grain

Tall Oat-grass

Arrhenatherum elatius

Meadows, roadsides and railway embankments from lowland to subalpine regions is where this loosely tufted perennial grass is to be encountered.

The stoloniferous rhizome bears smooth glossy stems reaching a height of 60 to 120 cm. The leaf sheaths are rough and glabrous, the leaf blades flat, 4 to 8 mm wide and yellowish or greyish-green. The ligules are short and more or less truncate.

The inflorescence is a spreading panicle, usually up to 25 cm long with rough branches, occasionally tinted violet. The spikelets are two-flowered. The lower floret is male, with a bristle, and has two stamens; the upper floret is without a bristle, and hermaphroditic. The glumes are longish-lanceolate with a rough keel. The lemmas have rough veins.

Tall Oat-grass occurs as two subspecies: subspecies *elatius,* found in meadows, and subspecies *bulbosus,* found in dry meadows, roadsides and fields. The two differ in that the latter has culms with bulbous swollen base. Both are widespread throughout Europe from the mountains of the Mediterranean region to the Arctic and from the Canary Islands to western Siberia. *Arrhenatherum elatius* was also introduced into North America and Australia. Linné described this species as Tall Oat *(Avena elatior)* but it is evident at first glance that oat differs from Oat-grass by having drooping spikelets.

Type of plant
monocotyledon

Diploid no.
2n — 28

Flowering period
June — August

Fruit
grain

two-flowered spikelet

Lady's Slipper or Common Slipper Orchid

Cypripedium calceolus

Lady's Slipper grows in warm glades and open woods, usually exhibiting a preference for lime-rich soils.

The erect stem, 15 to 50 cm high, is scaly and carries three to four, sometimes five alternate clasping leaves. The leaf blade is broadly elliptic to longish-lanceolate.

There is generally only a single flower, though very occasionally there may be two to four. It is large, erect, and grows from the axil of a leaf-like bract. Of the three outer perianth segments the two lateral ones are joined to form a single, long, double-toothed segment; the upper segment is erect and ovate-lanceolate. Of the three inner segments the two lateral ones are outspread and lanceolate. All are brownish-red. The third inner segment forms a pouch-like lip 3 to 4 cm long, coloured pale yellow with red dots and purple veins inside. The gynostemium is three-angled; both stamens are appressed to the gynostemium, and the stigma is three-lobed.

Though formerly widespread in practically all of Europe it is now absent in Belgium, Holland, Saxony and Schleswig-Holstein and in Great Britain is apparently already extinct. Despite the fact that it is on the list of protected species in most of central Europe we may still encounter people returning from a weekend in the country carrying bunches of this lovely orchid, and so it is becoming increasingly rarer in the wild.

rhizome

Type of plant
monocotyledon

Diploid no.
2n − 20

Flowering period
May − June

Fruit
capsule

White Helleborine

Cephalanthera damasonium

Syn. *Cephalanthera alba, Cephalanthera grandiflora*

This perennial, reaching a height of 20 to 60 cm, is partial to lime-rich soils and is found mostly in broad-leaved and fir woods.

The creeping rhizome bears a slightly bent stem that is scaly at the base, otherwise glabrous. It is covered its entire length with longish-ovate to ovate-lanceolate leaves, up to (at most) four times longer than they are wide.

The flowers, growing from the axils of lanceolate bracts, are clustered three to eight in a scant spike at the top of the stem. The perianth segments, six in all, are elongated, yellow-white and five-veined. The outer segments are longer than the inner ones. The lip is one-third shorter than the perianth and coloured yellow inside. The gynostemium is cylindrical.

White Helleborine is still distributed throughout most of Europe, but in most central European countries it is on the list of protected species.

Rarer than this helleborine is the Long-leaved Helleborine *(Cephalanthera longifolia,* syn. *Cephalanthera ensifolia)* with flowers almost pure white and as many as twenty to a cluster, and leaves ten times as long as they are wide. Also encountered very occasionally are hybrids between *Cephalanthera damasonium* and *Cephalanthera longifolia* and also Red Helleborine *(Cephalanthera rubra)*. This extraordinary ability to interbreed is crowned by the intergeneric hybrid between the Common Helleborine *(Epipactis helleborine)* and White Helleborine *(Cephalanthera damasonium)*.

Type of plant
monocotyledon

Diploid no.
2n — 32, 36

Flowering period
May — June

Fruit
capsule

flower

flower of *Cephalanthera rubra*

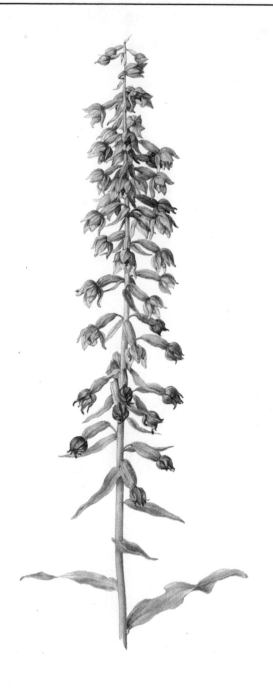

Common or **Broad Helleborine**

Epipactis helleborine
Syn. *Epipactis latifolia*

This species, reaching a height of 20 to 50 cm, grows in glades, mixed woods and thickets, both in lowland and mountain districts.

It has a short thick rhizome from which arises a tall, erect green stem, usually pubescent and sometimes also tinted violet at the top. The base is covered with brownish scales above which are longish-lanceolate to broadly-ovate leaves that are sessile and clasping and usually roughly pubescent on the underside. Farther up the leaves become narrower until they are linear-lanceolate in outline.

The flowers, arranged in a dense one-sided spike, smell like Valerian. The flower-peduncle is twisted a full 180° so that what is actually the upper perianth segment (sometimes lip-shaped) becomes the bottom segment, and vice versa. The perianth is spreading, bell-like. The three outer perianth segments are green outside and brownish-purple within. Of the three inner perianth segments the two lateral ones resemble the outer segments and the third forms a deeply divided purple lip, shorter than the other segments. The forward section of the lip is hollow, pouch-like with two humps. The flowers are pollinated by insects, although they may sometimes be self-pollinated.

As this pretty orchid is often picked in the wild and is thus in danger of disappearing it deserves to be on the list of protected species.

flower

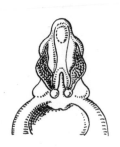

columella in the flower

Type of plant
monocotyledon

Diploid no.
2n — 38, 40

Flowering period
July — September

Fruit
capsule

Twayblade

Listera ovata

This perennial, reaching a height of 20 to 50 cm, may be encountered in damp woods and damp thickets.

The cylindrical rhizome bears a thick pale-green stem with two stiff, broadly-ovate, opposite leaves at the base. It is four-angled and glabrous below the leaves and rounded, glandular-pubescent above.

The flowers form a loose upright spike. The bracts are shorter than the peduncled part of the ovary, which is longish-ovate narrowing abruptly into a peduncle. The perianth segments are inclined towards each other and coloured yellow-green or green marked with pale violet. The lip has a green central vein.

All species of the genus *Listera*, like all members of the orchid family, are on the list of protected plants in most central European countries.

Orchids include amongst their number plants that build their own nutritive substances as well as plants that feed entirely or partly on dead or decaying organic matter. They often grow in the tropics, but three are also found in central Europe. Rarest is the Ghost Orchid *(Epipogium aphyllum)*, a non-green, waxy-yellow plant without roots and without leaves but with striking yellow flowers. Somewhat more plentiful is the Coral-root *(Corallorhiza bifida)* with striking coral-like branching rhizome and small pale-yellow flowers. The third and commonest is the Bird's-nest Orchid *(Neottia nidus-avis).*

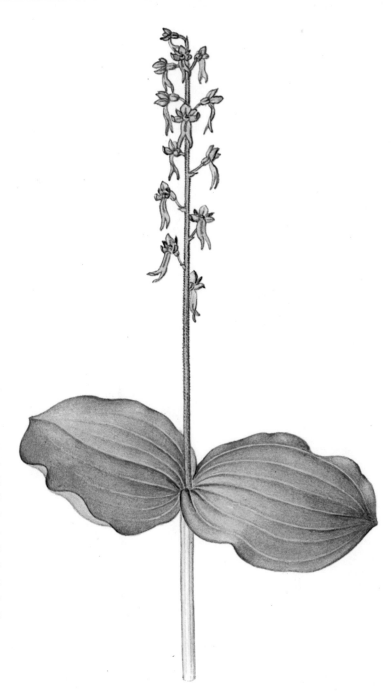

Type of plant
monocotyledon

Diploid no.
2n — 34

Flowering period
May — July

Fruit
capsule

Diagram of flower of the orchid family after resupination

flower

Lesser Butterfly Orchid

Platanthera bifolia

This perennial occurs in broad-leaved glades, mixed woods, woodland clearings and meadows.

Concealed in the ground are two ovoid undivided tubers; the wrinkled, brownish one bears the plant, the other light-yellow one is the reserve organ for the following year's plant. The stem is 20 to 50 cm high, erect, hollow, angled and grooved. At the base are two brown pointed scales and above these two opposite, broadly oval, glossy-green leaves.

The upright cylindrical inflorescence is composed of flowers with a characteristic pleasant scent, more pronounced and penetrating in the evening, at night and in cloudy weather. The perianth segments are all the same length; the outer ones are blunt and coloured white, the inner segments yellow-green. The lip is oblique. The linear, almost horizontal spur is thickened and coloured white or greenish at the tip; it is usually filled with nectar during the flowering period. The flowers are pollinated by insects which insert their feeding tube into the spur, at the same time brushing against the mature pollen sac. The pollen grains clump together and adhere to the side of the feeding tube, and when the insect visits another flower the clumps catch on its sticky stigma, thereby ensuring cross-pollination. The fruit is a capsule with a great many very light seeds.

The Lesser Butterfly Orchid is on the list of protected species in many European countries.

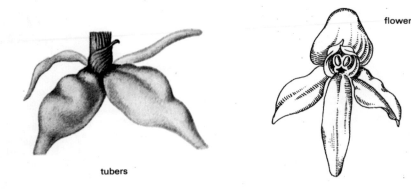

tubers

flower

Type of plant
monocotyledon

Diploid no.
2n — 42

Flowering period
May — July

Fruit
capsule

Fragrant Orchid

Gymnadenia conopsea

This perennial, reaching a height of 10 to 60 cm, grows mostly on limestone substrates, in meadows, open broad-leaved woods and thickets from lowland to mountain districts.

Concealed in the ground are two thick, digitately lobed tubers from one of which arises an erect rounded stem with one or two leathery scales at the base. Above these are alternate, linear-lanceolate leaves with a keel on the underside and an imperceptibly toothed margin.

The flowers, some fifty clustered in a spike-like inflorescence, grow from the axils of green bracts sometimes edged with violet. They are relatively small and pinkish red, very occasionally white. The lip is blunt, crenate and three-lobed. The slender spur is twice as long as the ovary. The flowers have an unusual fragrance which to some resembles that of a carnation. The similar Short-spurred Scented Orchid *(Gymnadenia odoratissima)* has a spur the same length as the ovary and more strongly scented flowers. The flowers are pollinated by insects. The fruit is a capsule containing a large number of very light seeds.

The Fragrant Orchid, like other members of the orchid family, is a protected species because its existence is threatened by indiscriminate picking as well as other external factors.

Type of plant
monocotyledon

Diploid no.
2n — 40 (80)

Flowering period
May — August

Fruit
capsule

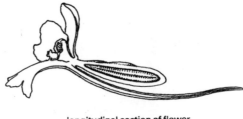

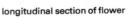

longitudinal section of flower

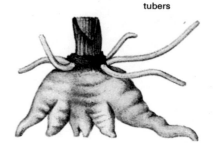

tubers

Green-winged Orchid

Orchis morio

This drought-tolerant orchid occurs in dry meadows, woodland clearings and on bushy slopes.

It has two underground tubers bearing a tall grooved stem up to 40 cm high, coloured pale green, tinged violet at the top. The leaves on the stem are bluish grey-green, 5 to 15 mm wide and lanceolate in outline, the bottom leaves almost horizontal, the ones at the top sheathed and erect.

The relatively loose spike is composed of seven to sixteen purplish flowers. The occasional specimen may have white flowers. The perianth segments are green-veined. The lip is three-lobed, violet-red with dark spots, and white at the bottom. The spur is blunt and slightly raised. The flowers of *Orchis*, as in most members of the family, have only a single stamen fused with the style into a gynostemium. The middle lobe of the stigma is modified into a beak. The pollen grains in each pollen sac stick together forming a clump. These clumps are transported by insects in the same manner as in the Lesser Butterfly Orchid. The cotyledon of the seed of the Green-winged Orchid is not supplied with sufficient food, and during germination must thus obtain its food by symbiosis from some fungus. Plants that grow from the seed do not bear flowers until after two to five years, sometimes even later.

The Green-winged Orchid is also a protected species in practically all the countries of central Europe.

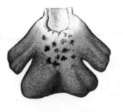

lip

underground tubers

Type of plant
monocotyledon

Diploid no.
2n — 36, 38

Flowering period
April — June

Fruit
capsule

Broad-leaved
or **Fen Orchid**

Dactylorhiza majalis

Syn. *Orchis latifolia*

This orchid grows in wet meadows, overgrown marshes, moors, heaths and damp ditches.

It has two digitately-lobed underground tubers from which grows an erect, hollow stem up to 60 cm high, grooved, and tinged with red at the top. The stem leaves are alternate, spreading and linear-lanceolate to ovate-elliptic with sheath-like stalks. The upper surface is dark green, often irregularly spotted brown.

The flowers, arranged in a dense inflorescence at the top of the stem, grow from the axils of lanceolate, red-tinged bracts. The three outer perianth segments are ovate-lanceolate and spreading to recurved. Of the three inner perianth segments the two lateral ones resemble the outer segments and the one in the middle is enlarged into a three-lobed lip prolonged at the base into a hollow, slightly drooping spur. The spur is empty, for as in *Orchis* the flowers do not provide insects with nectar. They are so-called 'delusive' flowers. Their colour is variable, ranging from pale pink to deep red. The perianth segments are conspicuously spotted. The pollen clumps are coloured green. Mature capsules contain a great many seeds.

underground tuber

lip

Type of plant
monocotyledon

Diploid no.
2n – 80

Flowering period
May – July

Fruit
capsule

Bog Arum

Calla palustris

Bogs, pond margins and flooded meadows is where the perennial Bog Arum is to be found.

The hollow, jointed, cylindrical rhizome bears an erect leafless, glabrous, 15- to 30-cm-high stem and two dense rows of long-stalked leaves with rounded-ovate, short-pointed blades.

The flowers are arranged in a spadix enclosed by a spathe coloured green outside and white within. The spadix is shortly-cylindrical with a short peduncle. The minute flowers, which are without a perianth, are mostly hermaphroditic; only those at the top of the spadix have stamens but not pistils. They are generally pollinated by molluscs. The hermaphroditic flowers have 6 to 8 stamens and a pistil, which after fertilization develops into a red berry. The seeds are violet and coated with a sticky mucilage that adheres to the bodies of birds; they may thus be dispersed often great distances.

Bog Arum is poisonous. It is found in central and parts of northern Europe and in many places is on the list of protected species. This relatively rare species is absent in Great Britain.

The related Sweet Flag *(Acorus calamus),* which grows on the banks of still stretches of water in practically all of Europe, is not indigenous to Europe at all. It is a native of eastern Asia where it also bears flowers (in Europe it does not).

fruits

single flower without perianth

Type of plant
monocotyledon

Diploid no.
2n − 72 (32)

Flowering period
May − July

Fruit
berry

Cuckoo-pint
or **Lords-and-Ladies**

Arum maculatum

This perennial, which reaches a height of 20 to 35 cm, grows in broad-leaved woods and thickets from lowland to mountain districts.

Concealed in the ground is a brown tuberous rhizome. From this arises an erect stem with scaly base and leaves with long stalks. These are expanded into a sheath at the base. The leaf is shaped like an arrow-head, longish-ovate to triangular in outline and sometimes spotted with brown on the upper surface.

The stem is terminated by a spadix enclosed by a large, deeply cup-shaped spathe, up to 15 cm long. The spathe is whitish, reddish or greenish with violet blotches inside, narrowly constricted at the base and widened at the top. The flowers in the lower part of the spadix are female, those above them are male and those still farther up are sterile. The tip of the spadix is violet-brown, club-shaped and without flowers. Following pollination and fertilization the flowers develop into red berries about 1 cm across.

Cuckoo-pint is poisonous.

The east European species *Arum orientale* has a more or less globose tuber and unspotted leaves. It is found in the Balkans, extending into central Europe as far as Czechoslovakia and perhaps also to Denmark.

Type of plant
monocotyledon

Diploid no.
2n — 56

Flowering period
June — August

Fruit
berry

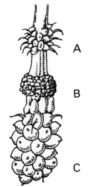

Inflorescence: A — sterile flowers B — male flowers
C — female flowers

fruits

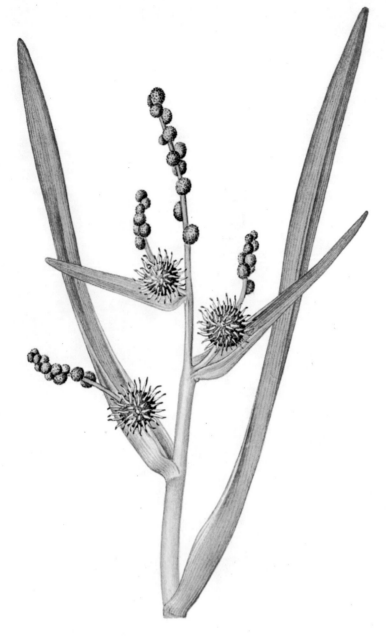

Branched Bur-reed

Sparganium erectum

Syn. *Sparganium ramosum*

This perennial is usually 30 to 60 cm high but may reach a height of 120 cm. It has a creeping stoloniferous rhizome and rigid, erect stem. The grass-like leaves are 3 to 15 mm wide, rigid, erect, three-angled at the base and keeled to the tip.

The stem is terminated by a spreading panicle-like inflorescence composed of globose heads of regular unisexual flowers. The ones at the bottom are larger, composed of female flowers, and only few in number; those farther up are smaller, far more numerous, and composed of male flowers. The perianth segments of both are membranous. After pollination by the wind the flowers develop into angular dark-brown beaked achenes.

Branched Bur-reed is divided into four subspecies according to the shape and size of the fruit: subspecies *erectum*, subspecies *microcarpum*, subspecies *neglectum* and subspecies *oocarpum*.

The related Unbranched Bur-reed *(Sparganium emersum)* has a spike-like inflorescence and the same diploid number.

Diagram of flower: A – male flower B – female flower

Type of plant
monocotyledon

Diploid no.
2n – 30

Flowering period
June – August

Fruit
achene

Lesser Reedmace or Cattail

Typha angustifolia

The Lesser Reedmace often grows on the banks of still stretches of water where it can be discerned from afar because it reaches a height of 3 metres.

It has a yellow-brown rhizome, rigid erect stems, and narrowly-linear leaves often much longer than the stems. The blades are flexible and spirally twisted into two or three coils which prevents them from being broken by the wind. The leaves have long sheaths and are partly submerged.

The stem is terminated by a striking inflorescence — a 'poker' composed of two spadices, one above the other; they are 10 to 30 cm long and spaced 3 to 5 cm apart. The upper one is composed of male flowers, the lower one at the bottom of female (pistillate) flowers. The upper flowers fall early, whereas the female flowers, coloured blackish-brown, are persistent and remain on the stem. They are pollinated by the wind. The achenes have short peduncles.

This species is distributed throughout most of Europe except Greece; also in western Asia and North America.

The similar Great Reedmace *(Typha latifolia)* has broad leaves and spadices almost touching one another.

The rhizomes of both are rich in starch, sugar and proteins and for this reason were formerly grown as food crops in some countries. The leaves, on the other hand, are used in making baskets and matting and also for roofing.

Type of plant
monocotyledon

Diploid no.
2n — 30

Flowering period
June — August

Fruit
achene

Inflorescence of *Typha latifolia* with spent upper male spadix

Common Duckweed

Lemna minor

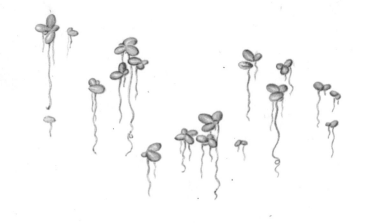

Still stretches of water and sluggish streams, not only in lowland districts but sometimes even in mountain areas, are often covered by a green film of minute floating leaves.

These belong to the Common Duckweed and are actually rounded, leaf-like thalli 1 cm across, each with a single root. They are flat both above and below, which is what distinguishes this species from the Gibbous Duckweed *(Lemna gibba)* which has thalli strongly swollen beneath.

Duckweeds flower only rarely. The flowers are minute and consist solely of a single stamen and single pistil without any perianth.

Ivy Duckweed *(Lemna trisulca)* differs markedly from both the preceding species by having longish-lanceolate, pointed thalli tapering at the base into a stalk and usually shallowly submerged instead of floating on the water. The diploid number of this species is 2n − 44.

The duckweed family, which includes some of the smallest existing plants, also includes the tiny Rootless Duckweed *(Wolffia arrhiza)* with 1 mm large, lenticular thalli that are entirely without roots. It is often introduced into central Europe from southern and southwestern Europe but flowers only rarely and only in tropical regions. A final point of interest is that it holds the record for being the smallest of all flowering plants.

longitudinal section of flowering plant of *Lemna trisulca*

Lemna trisulca

Type of plant
monocotyledon

Diploid no.
2n − 40

Flowering period
May − June

Fruit
utricle

Index of Common Names

Index of Scientific Names